CASA BLANCA

FEB 25 2002

D0403098

Riot and Remembrance

BOOKS BY JAMES S. HIRSCH

HURRICANE
The Miraculous Journey of Rubin Carter

RIOT AND REMEMBRANCE
The Tulsa Race War and Its Legacy

Riot and Remembrance

*The Tulsa Race War
and Its Legacy*

James S. Hirsch

HOUGHTON MIFFLIN COMPANY
BOSTON · NEW YORK
2002

Copyright © 2002 by James S. Hirsch
All rights reserved

For information about permission to reproduce selections
from this book, write to Permissions, Houghton Mifflin Company,
215 Park Avenue South, New York, New York 10003.

Visit our Web site: www.houghtonmifflinbooks.com.

Library of Congress Cataloging-in-Publication Data
Hirsch, James S.
Riot and remembrance : the Tulsa race war and its
legacy / James S. Hirsch.
p.   cm.
Includes bibliographical references and index.
ISBN 0-618-10813-0
1. African Americans — Oklahoma — Tulsa — History —20th
century. 2.Tulsa (Okla.) — Race Relations. 3. Racism — Oklahoma —
Tulsa — History — 20th century. 4. Riots — Oklahoma — Tulsa —
History — 20th century. 5. Violence — Oklahoma — Tulsa — History
— 20th century. 6. African American neighborhoods — Oklahoma —
Tulsa — History — 20th century. I. Title.
F704.T92 .R56 2002
976.6'8600496073—dc21   2001501615

Printed in the United States of America

Book design by Robert Overholtzer

QUM 10 9 8 7 6 5 4 3 2 1

The author is grateful to Richard K. Dozier, representing the Smitherman
family, for permission to reprint the poem by A. J. Smitherman; and to
Peermusic for permission to use lines from "Take Me Back to Tulsa" by Bob
Wills and Tommy Duncan. Copyright © 1941 by Peer International Corporation for the world except Mexico and the U.S. Peer International Corporation controls Bob Wills's share in the U.S. only. Copyright renewed. International copyright secured. All rights reserved. Used by permission.

To Gloria and Ed Hirsch,
who put their children first

Contents

Riot and Remembrance

Is the World on Fire?

ON A WARM EVENING in Tulsa, Oklahoma, a dozen black women were gathered at Mount Zion Baptist Church to discuss expanding its role in the community when Pressley Little bolted through the doors, his face glistening with sweat.

"Baby, there's a riot starting!" he yelled to his wife, Mabel. "There's shooting at the courthouse."

A black youth had been jailed for allegedly assaulting a white girl in a downtown elevator, and an incendiary front-page article about the incident had set off rumors of a lynching. About 75 armed black men marched to the courthouse to prevent a possible hanging. They were met by about 1,500 whites. A shot was fired and bedlam erupted.

It was May 31, 1921.

Eighty years later, the echoes can still be heard. They rise from a community that has struggled to reconcile and redeem one of the most tragic chapters in American race relations. They also fill a vacuum for a city that has ignored and, in some quarters, covered up the most notorious event in its proud history. Many decades after the riot, Tulsa pried open the darkest secrets of its past and did what every city — indeed, country — should do: it sought justice for a crime long since committed. It also tried to heal the wounds of neglect and hostility in a racially divided community. But it discovered, in confronting race, that justice and reconciliation are cherished but opposing virtues. To correct a historical wrong — be it for slavery or segregation, for discrimination or exclusion — is to drive a wedge even more deeply between angry blacks who demand compensation for their losses and indignant whites who disavow any responsibility. The Tulsa race riot lasted less than sixteen hours, but its search for closure overlapped America's own struggle to make peace with a painful past.

Mabel Little knew that a riot, however it played out, could not have come at a worse time. She had just realized the black version of the American dream.

Eight years earlier, she had moved from the sheltered black community of Boley, Oklahoma, to the booming oil town of Tulsa. At seventeen, she had one dollar and twenty-five cents in her pocket. Her mother predicted she would end up as a prostitute.

That was not an unreasonable idea. Tulsa's black neighborhood, Greenwood, had a flourishing red-light district of opium dens, gambling parlors, whiskey joints, and brothels. But it also had numerous merchants, entrepreneurs, and educators who turned Tulsa into "the promised land" for blacks, and into this group fell Mabel Little.

Initially, the big city disappointed her. Greenwood had only one paved street; rain turned the rest of its roads to mud. Mabel had to carry her nice shoes in a paper bag and lay down two-by-four planks just to cross an avenue. The random violence also shocked her. At a dance one night, a couple was gliding across the floor when the man's mistress approached them, pulled out a gun, and shot the man's wife dead.

But Mabel found her way. She worked as a maid in a hotel for twenty dollars a month, plus meals, and married Pressley in 1914. They had four dollars between them, but they were ambitious. They admired Greenwood's black-operated barbecue joints, grocery stores, funeral parlors, and theaters whose lights glittered in the night. They wanted to be a part of it, so they saved their money and managed to buy a three-room shotgun house; there Pressley ran a shoeshine parlor and Mabel operated a beauty salon. Her aunt Lydia in Boley had taught her how to wash, straighten, and wave hair, and as Greenwood's population soared, so too did Mabel's business. In 1918 she hired her first hairdresser, and soon after two more. She moved to the heart of the black business district and named her shop the Little Rose Beauty Salon. She was proud to be on a paved street.

There were few black hairdressers in Tulsa, and customers came from towns fifty miles away. Entertainers who appeared at the Dreamland Theatre, hookers who worked on Archer Street, and babies still in their mothers' arms — all came to Mabel Little's salon. Standing beneath a picture of Jesus with his hands folded in prayer, she worked from seven in the morning to seven in the evening to serve her more than six hundred customers. Meanwhile, Pressley opened the Little Bell Café, which prepared "smothered steak" with rice and brown gravy. After seven years of hard work — and eighteen days before the riot — they built a duplex with a new salon on the first floor and a three-room rental upstairs. They rented out a second building and also built their own home as well, with new furniture in five rooms. They drove a Model T Ford.

They were rich in property but had only fifty dollars in cash.

"They've gone to stop a lynching," Pressley told Mabel as they hurried out of the church. Panic filled Greenwood. Men and women rushed from their houses down the streets, some near hysteria. Mabel returned to their home and spent the night listening to the racing car engines, the crackling pistols, the muffled shouts. By morning, she heard airplanes buzzing overhead, and for the rest of her life she swore that those planes firebombed Greenwood.

A few blocks away, Veneice Sims heard the first bullets carom off the Santa Fe rail yard, and she knew her own dreams for the evening would be dashed

At sixteen, she was going to her first high school prom, and her date, Verby Ellison, a well-groomed youth with curly hair, had permission to keep her out until midnight. She yearned for some independence from her strict father, a well-paid mechanic for a bus company, who had recently purchased a Victrola but only allowed her to play church music. Veneice liked jazz and when her parents were out, she smuggled Mamie Smith's "Crazy Blues" onto the machine. Her father also forbade dancing in the living room. "Better not shake or shimmy," he would say.

But that night the Booker T. Washington High School band was to play in the chandeliered ballroom of the Stradford Hotel, believed to be the country's largest hotel owned by a black. By late afternoon, Veneice had carefully laid out her prom clothes on the bed she shared with her sister: a blue silk dress made by a neighborhood seamstress, silver slippers, and a dazzling pearl necklace borrowed from a family friend. But in the early evening, she heard a ruckus outside her comfortable three-bedroom home. Cars tore down the street and men shouted; Veneice tried to ignore the commotion, imagining herself gliding across the dance floor in her taffeta gown.

She heard the first gunshot. Then others. A streetlamp shattered. Her father grabbed a rifle as he bounded from the house. Veneice had no idea what was happening until he returned.

"There's a race riot," he said. "It's time to go."

Veneice rushed to her bedroom. She didn't want to abandon the gown or the pearls, but she had no choice. The oldest of six children, she followed her siblings into the family's black Ford, and as her father drove through the streets, she had no sense of what would befall her community, but she wept for all she had left behind.

George Monroe was only five years old, but he knew there was trouble. Shortly after daybreak, he heard the voices of white hoodlums on the porch of his home. Both his father, a porter who also owned a roller rink, and his mother were out of the house, leaving four children behind. As the white men reached the front door, the youngsters slid under a bed. George, the youngest, was the last child under and barely squeezed himself in. The four men, carrying torches, walked past the bed to the curtains, lighted them at the bottom, and spun back around. As they walked back past the bed, one of them stepped on George's hand. The youngster opened his mouth to scream, but his sister Lottie jammed her hand against his mouth. The men slammed the door on their way out.

With the house in flames, the crying children scrambled to their feet and made their way outside. They lived on Easton Street next to Mount Zion Baptist Church, a brick structure completed only fifty-seven days earlier. Its parishioners thought it more magnificent than any white church in Tulsa. George would later say he could stick his hand out the window and touch Mount Zion, but now the church, and indeed the entire block, was on fire. George ran down the street, but everywhere he turned the town he knew, where grocers hung fresh vegetables on a string, preachers sang "A-men," and kids barreled through the streets on bicycles, was burning. George looked at Lottie and asked, "Is the world on fire?"

Four blocks away, J. B. Stradford stood sentinel at his three-story, fifty-four-room marvel, the Stradford Hotel. Trimmed in pressed brick and set on stone slabs, it symbolized black affluence and pride in Tulsa. Stradford himself was the wealthiest man in Greenwood and one of its most outspoken. Born a Kentucky slave, he became a college-educated businessman. He was a "race man" — an ardent supporter of civil rights — who went to court to challenge the Jim Crow laws. He exhorted his fellow blacks to demand equality, which was considered subversive in the South.

Stradford often insisted that if a black man were ever lynched in Tulsa, he would personally ensure that the streets would be bathed in blood. But on the day the riot began, the county sheriff assured him that the black prisoner would not be accosted, and he urged other blacks not to go to the courthouse unless the sheriff requested their help. His pleas were ignored, and on the morning of the riot, Stradford stood at his hotel doorway to fend off the white marauders.

He was approached by a captain of the National Guard, which had been called in to restore order.

"I know you, Mr. Stradford," he said. "We came to take you to a place of safety. It's not safe for you to be here."

"If you guarantee my hotel will not be burned, I'll go with you."

"Your hotel won't be burned," the guardsman said. "It will be used as a place of refuge."

Stradford agreed to leave and was escorted to an automobile. But as he got in, he saw a "raiding squad" of white rioters break into a drugstore near the hotel and steal cigars, tobacco, and money from its register. Some of the men had already stuffed their shirts with silk handkerchiefs and fine socks stolen from other stores, and now they grabbed bottles of perfume and splashed themselves with the liquid. They moved closer to the hotel. Stradford, helpless, was whisked away in the car. When he returned, the building lay in ashes.

The Tulsa race riot looms as a singular historical event. America has experienced dozens of bloody race riots, but Tulsa's was the worst in the twentieth century and possibly in American history. Comparisons are difficult; even eighty years after the fact the death toll is in dispute. Thirty-eight were confirmed dead, including ten whites, but the true figure was well over that, perhaps even three hundred. More certain is the destruction of property: 1,256 houses were burned in a thirty-six-square-block area of Greenwood, including churches, stores, hotels, businesses, two newspapers, a school, a hospital, and a library — in short, all the institutions that perpetuated black life in Tulsa. The burned property was valued between $1.5 and $1.8 million — more than $14 million in 2000 dollars. Many homes were looted before being torched, but no white rioter was ever convicted for his or her crime (women looted as well).

While the riot was triggered by a racially charged news article, it was fueled by two headstrong forces: whites reasserting their supremacy in the South through the Jim Crow laws and disenfranchisement, and blacks demanding political equality and economic opportunity. In the years before the riot, whites imposed their will through lynchings, particularly in the South. African Americans learned that any black accused of "assaulting" — a euphemism for "raping" — a white woman violated the ultimate taboos of sex and race in America. Public hanging was deemed the appropriate punishment.

Oklahoma was particularly vulnerable to such hysteria. Spurred by free land and then by oil, it attracted whites from the Deep South. These settlers established racism as custom and wrote it as law. At the same time, southern blacks were drawn to the territory because it was not part of the Confederacy, and they believed they could create a bastion of political equality. Compounding these forces in Tulsa was a history of vigilantism and lawlessness that culminated in the total collapse of authority on that night of May 31, 1921.

For all its devastation, the riot had a quiet afterlife. Very different oral accounts were quietly passed down on front porches and in barbershops across the city, but the riot was left out of many history books, ignored in classrooms, and overlooked in newspaper retrospectives. Every city is sensitive about its image, but few cities have sold its image as brilliantly as Tulsa. Lacking oil itself, it relied on its "Magic City" boosterism to become the nation's oil capital, a vision of clean neighborhoods, thriving businesses, and happy families. It wouldn't tolerate the stories, true or not, of black corpses being thrown into incinerators, stuffed into mass graves, or dumped into the Arkansas River. A hush fell over Tulsa, and few heard the whispers of history.

Only at the end of the century did this culture of silence — or even conspiracy of silence, as some have called it — irrevocably shatter. Unlike any other race riot in American history, Tulsa's was subject to an exhaustive government inquiry that sought to determine facts, assign responsibility, and recommend reparations or other compensation to individuals or to the community at large. As the country began debating the much thornier question of reparations for descendants of slaves, Tulsa emerged as a model of how one city sought redemption. The proposition was simple enough: justice delayed does not necessarily mean justice denied; and even long after the conflict, truth can be revealed and reconciliation is possible.

But the government investigation that began in 1997 roused bitter memories, as blacks and whites fought over virtually every aspect of the riot — about who started it and who failed to stop it; about government conspiracies and aerial bombings; about the very stories that had been transmitted through generations of Tulsans. A riot that had been buried for years suddenly became a national story.

At stake were whose narrative of history would prevail and whose myths would be discredited.

For the aging survivors, however, the riot was not shrouded in myth. For Veneice Sims, it was watching Greenwood burn to ashes from a glassed-in porch above the city, where her father had taken the family to escape the mob. For George Monroe, it was a handful of melted dimes that survived the riot in his father's mailbox and were then strung together as a necklace. For the descendants of J. B. Stradford, it was trying to clear his name of any wrongdoing. And for Mabel Little, it was the knowledge that she would never have what she lost in the early morning hours of June 1, 1921. Seventy-seven years later, asked about the meaning of the event, she said: "At the time of the riot, we had ten different business places for rent. Today, I *pay* rent."

And where the Little Rose Beauty Salon once stood is still an empty lot.

I. Beginnings

The Self-Made Oil Capital

Early in the twentieth century, it was inevitable that a big city would develop somewhere in the desolate, rolling landscape that sat above North America's largest pool of oil. The Mid-Continent field, beneath parts of Kansas, Oklahoma, and Texas, helped fuel the Model T Fords that put Americans on the road, the trains that transported them across the country, and the ships and planes that prevailed in World War I. The field transformed a land of wheat, cotton, and cattle into a vital industrial resource and turned tired villages into vibrant cities. The city that best exploited this pool would be crowned the Oil Capital of the World.

That city should not have been Tulsa, Oklahoma.

For all the oil that gushed from the Oklahoma soil, not a drop was ever found in this prairie community on the edge of the Ozark Plateau. Tulsa could supply oilmen with the equipment, financing, and amenities that made their work possible and their lives pleasant, but many other towns were far better suited to serve them. Muskogee, fifty miles southeast of Tulsa, was the seat of the federal government that ruled the Indian Territory that became the eastern half of Oklahoma with statehood in 1907. In 1905 Muskogee had 12,000 citizens — more than twice as many as Tulsa — as well as paved streets, a trolley, and the seven-story Turner Hotel, the finest lodging between Kansas City and Dallas. Also bigger than Tulsa was nearby

Bartlesville, which discovered oil in 1897, as well as Vinita, Clare-more, Okmulgee, Sapulpa, and a dozen other settlements that dotted the grasslands. They viewed Tulsa as a drab cattle town with one rail-road, a dirty train depot, and a huddle of crude wooden houses. A visitor in 1905 recalled that the city lacked even its own postcard.

Located along a curl in the Arkansas River, where the oak-laden foothills of the Ozarks blend into the tawny landscape of the Great Plains, Tulsa was settled in 1836 by Creek Indians from Alabama. They called their village Lochapoka, "place of turtles." The first white settlers arrived in the early 1880s, but "Tulsey Town," as they called it, held little promise other than as a trading post for farmers. At the turn of the century, it was literally a cow town, with thousands of head of cattle routinely driven through its center, rutting streets, trampling gardens, and trailing clouds of dirt. The roads were dust storms in dry weather, swamps in rain. Residents insisted that the streets not be wider than eighty feet — anything greater was too far to walk in the mud.

Main Street was gray and pungent, with no sidewalks, streetlights, or sewers. First and Second streets, littered with watermelon rinds and horse apples, intersected Main. The smell of freshly killed ani-mals pervaded the Frisco Meat Market, which paid cash for hides and proudly hung on its storefront the pink carcasses of deer, rac-coons, rabbits, quail, and prairie chickens. Pigs and cattle roamed the streets at will, and mosquitoes bred by the millions in the rain bar-rels at each store, which offered the only water for horse-drawn fire wagons. It sometimes wasn't enough. In 1897 a blaze destroyed the city's first bank, three masonry buildings, and twelve wooden struc-tures. Schools and churches were small white frame buildings, out-houses stood behind homes, and water faucets disgorged clumps of dirt. The briny brown liquid came from the Arkansas River, which was dangerous to drink (wells provided a limited supply of potable water) and barely fit for bathing. River water gathered in tubs left a thin layer of dirt, and bathers had to towel the granules off their bodies.

The river was also an economic liability: its wide sandy bed and sudden freshets made it difficult to navigate. Steam ferries ground to a halt as cattle ambled in the river past the hapless passenger boats. The Arkansas separated Tulsa from the oil and gas fields west of the city, which gave other towns the edge in serving the petroleum companies and their suppliers.

Other handicaps, both natural and manmade, deterred growth. The long summers were inescapably hot, forcing families to sleep on mattresses outside their homes. Tulsa had telephones — three hundred in 1905 — but no phone book. The city was further crippled by its inadequate facilities; raising money for public services was almost impossible before statehood. When the Robinson Hotel, a converted livery stable, was built in 1904, there was no sewage system, so the hotel ran its waste into an open ditch a few blocks away. Protesting neighbors won an injunction against the hotel, which eventually built its own sewage lines directly to the river. Its owner then held a "sewer banquet" for thirty-two of the protesters.

Tulsa's raw frontier image was shaped by the spitfire cowboys who rode into town, filled up on illegal whiskey, and dashed through the streets shooting at lighted windows. They sometimes fired pistols over the heads of congregants leaving church, the screams of the women delighting the provocateurs. Tulsa tolerated outlaws, even offering them sanctuary. Bill Doolin, whose gang terrorized banks, trains, and post offices, was an occasional resident, and the four Dalton brothers were fixtures. Their exploits robbing and terrorizing innocents had been luridly described in the press, and they boldly walked down Tulsa's streets, ate at its cafés, attended its churches, and purchased large quantities of gunpowder and ammunition from its merchants. Rumors of Dalton raids sometimes forced shopkeepers to barricade their stores with sugar sacks and barrels, and armed men kept watch for the outlaws on rooftops. But the attacks never materialized. Years later, Tulsans would fondly remember the Daltons for their quiet, courteous manner, but the city's renown as a haven for bandits contributed to its lawless reputation.

In 1900, only two years after its incorporation, Tulsa was a grim, isolated backwater of 1,300 people, lost among the many prairie towns of the Oklahoma and Indian territories. These communities were soon dealt a devastating blow by technical advancements in agriculture. The arrival of tractors and combines eliminated most field hands. The sharecropper became expendable, and as marginal farmers moved on, many towns and villages languished or disappeared entirely. That could have been Tulsa's fate. Instead, it became one of the most remarkable boomtowns in American history, and it did so with a can-do bravado and a shameless boosterism that shaped its self-image for the rest of the century.

To survive and prosper, Tulsa's pioneers first had to overcome the physical and economic liabilities of the Arkansas River.

In 1901 the area's first major oil discovery occurred at Red Fork, a hamlet three miles southwest of Tulsa. With newspapers across the country trumpeting the "Great Oil Strike," Red Fork drew throngs of oil workers and investors, most of whom bypassed Tulsa to avoid the expense and time of crossing the treacherous water on unpredictable ferries. In response, Tulsa's leaders wanted to build a bridge across the Arkansas for pedestrians and wagons, so they submitted a bond issue; voters, suspecting the oil craze would be short-lived, defeated it. It looked like Tulsa would miss its chance. But three private citizens raised $50,000 on their own and built a toll crossing, the 11th Street Wagon Bridge. Opening on January 4, 1904, the steel bridge soon carried the tools and lumber traveling to Red Fork. Its inscription read: YOU SAID WE COULDN'T DO IT, BUT WE DID.

Near this bridge was an older crossing used by Tulsa's one railroad, the Frisco. Business leaders prodded the Frisco to send special daily trains to and from the Red Fork oil fields so that workers could escape from the grease and grime. Each morning, the oil-men from Tulsa ate a massive breakfast at the Pig's Ear, across from the train station, while the proprietor's wife packed their lunches. Then they boarded a fifteen-car train called Coal Oil Johnny, which passed through Sapulpa and dropped off workers in and around Red Fork. In the evening it brought them back to Tulsa, where a boomtown was slowly taking shape. The drillers, tool dressers, roustabouts, and investors rubbed elbows with the railroad men, cowboys, and merchants as they sat down to the best fried chicken in all the oil country.

Ultimately, the Red Fork strike produced far less petroleum than expected. Its peak of a hundred barrels a day fell short of a great gusher, and its production soon dissipated to five or six daily barrels. But Tulsa had established its name in the oil patch.

Bridging the river was one challenge, but even more important was linking Tulsa to the rail network that was now connecting destinations in the Oklahoma and Indian territories and beyond. The pioneers did not leave this matter to luck or fate. In 1901 the Katy Railroad announced plans to complete a line from Muskogee to Pawhuska; the new rails would cross the Frisco tracks about seven miles east of Tulsa, sending its traffic to competing towns. All the oil in the world wouldn't save Tulsa if the trains were taking the financiers and roughnecks to other communities, so the city's leaders hastily formed the Tulsa Commercial Club, which later became the Chamber of Commerce. Club officials approached Katy's executives with their own survey and insisted that running the line through Tulsa would create a shorter and less expensive route to their final destination. To help persuade the railroad men, the Tulsans also pledged to secure a right-of-way (valued at $3,000) and gave a "bonus" — others called it a bribe — of $12,000 (or about $239,000 in 2000 dollars) that came in a promissory note underwritten by virtually every merchant and business in the city. Tulsa got the railroad, and the businessmen who represented the city grew rich in the coming oil bonanza. Three years later, the Commercial Club used the same strategy to forge another link to the outside world when the Midland Valley Railroad announced it would place a line through Red Fork. To convince the Midland officials to direct their rail through Tulsa, this time the "bonus" was $15,000. That year the city also convinced another railroad (the Santa Fe) to redirect its tracks through Tulsa, this time with no financial sweeteners.

Coaxing the railroads to Tulsa secured the city's future as the major distribution point for the petroleum industry throughout the Southwest, and it sealed the doom of its immediate rivals, including Red Fork. What's more, it established a pattern that was reinforced many times over the years: when Tulsa had a problem, its business leaders solved it. They were self-made men building a self-made city, and their work had just begun. They had figured out how to bring people to Tulsa on rail and over water; now they devised a plan to attract those people. They needed a massive public relations campaign (before public relations had even been invented), and they got it with their barnstorming boosters.

In 1905 Tulsa's leaders decided to take the story of their city directly to the country. One hundred of the town's leading citizens donated one hundred dollars each and chartered a train to carry them 2,500 miles through scores of midwestern cities and towns. This group was dubbed the One Hundred Club, although only eighty-nine men actually went. On the eve of their departure, their wives and children worked throughout the night to decorate the train with streamers and banners touting Tulsa as oil country. Attached to the side of a coach was a huge map of the Oklahoma and Indian territories and a picture of a large derrick. Outsiders thought the venture pointless. Tulsa was not on most maps, so why would anyone move there?

But the One Hundred Club created its own frenzy. The men sent telegrams to other cities' business clubs and newspapers asking to be met at the train depot so they "could induce a few hundred men of money to locate in the greatest city in the world." The train carried a printing press borrowed from the *Tulsa Democrat;* at each stop, it cranked out pretentious news pages, one of which read in part:

> Tulsa wasn't on the map because it grew faster than maps can be printed.
>
> Tulsa was a magnificent metropolis of seven churches and not a single saloon.
>
> The clink of one dollar against the other was in Tulsa's national air.

Wearing bowler hats and dark overcoats, the Tulsans brought their trombones, tubas, and drums, heralding their arrival at each stop by blaring songs and waving American flags. But they also needed a feature act to turn out the crowds, so they asked a young cowboy named Bill Rogers, who lived in Claremore, twenty-nine miles away, to join them. Years later, as Will Rogers, his virtuoso roping skills were captured in movies, and his wit earned him fame as a writer and humorist. But on this trip he dazzled crowds with his lariat — he roped a group of men in the pit of the Chicago Board of Trade — and fashioned Tulsa's reputation as a magical place.

The booster train created a windfall of publicity for Tulsa. The prestigious *St. Louis Post-Dispatch,* for example, wrote: "Down in Tulsa, they have a theory that whatever helps the town helps the citizens. It's a pretty good theory too. It makes nations as well as cities great."

The publicity surrounding the trip was so great that three years later, the Tulsans organized a second, even more ambitious excursion. This time they promoted both their young city and their new state of Oklahoma, established the previous year. They traveled through Kansas City, St. Louis, and Chicago, then eastward to Cleveland, Pittsburgh, and New York, ending in Washington, D.C. — fifteen states and 2,972 miles in sixteen days. The band and the printing press were back, and a Creek and a Cherokee joined them as swarthy reminders of the city's Indian tradition. They learned a cheer:

> Come, everybody!
> Get off the grass!
> We're from the town of natural gas!
> From Indian Territory and don't give a rap!
> Move to Tulsa and get on the map!

The boosters captured the imagination of dignitaries and commoners alike. The governor of New York, Charles Evans Hughes, welcomed the group at Manhattan's Union Station, and state and local officials paraded them down Fifth Avenue, past cheering New Yorkers. In the capital, President Theodore Roosevelt gave them a party, and they received an ovation when they visited the House and Senate. Returning to the Chicago Board of Trade, they created such a ruckus that the telegraph wires suspended operation. From New York came a frantic query asking what was the matter. "Nothing," went the response. "Tulsa is here."

When the group returned home, 8,000 cheering supporters greeted them at the Katy Station, Oklahoma's lieutenant governor, chief justice, and speaker of the house among them. A scheduled parade was canceled because the streets were too jammed. Even before the train returned, the Commercial Club had received two sacks of letters requesting information about Tulsa, the new state, and opportunities for investment. Robert T. Daniel, a wealthy land developer in Miami, had read accounts of the 1905 expedition and moved to Tulsa, believing that it was the promised land. He built two of the city's first skyscrapers, the Daniel Building and the Hotel Tulsa.

The triumphant excursions begat endless publicity gimmicks. The Commercial Club paid $1,000 for a three-reel film about Tulsa and its oil fields. Local publishers produced booklets on expensive paper that ranged from bombastic praise for the city to vapid agricultural statistics; in 1915 the Chamber of Commerce published a booklet, "Tulsa Spirit," with stories about economic growth and cultural enrichment. Another book bore the title *Tulsa: A City with a Personality.* The careful cultivation of Tulsa's image, where the "clink of one dollar against the other" could be heard in the air, was central to its ultimate success. A name had already blossomed for Tulsa — the Magic City — and by 1908 it had a postcard called "Moonlight over Tulsa," showing electric lights strung like pearls above Main Street.

As new and larger oil fields erupted in Oklahoma, this alluring image would ensure that Tulsa attracted the financiers who bankrolled the oil digs and the roustabouts who worked in the fields — as well as the women who ran the homes, raised the children, and worked in the schools, bars, and brothels. But the publicity had one drawback: the influx of capital and manpower could just as easily cease if the town's image was somehow sullied, if Tulsa were known not as a magic city but as a city of destruction and bigotry. Those issues confronted Tulsa before long, but in the meantime it pursued its destiny as the new El Dorado, a place of fabulous wealth and boundless opportunity.

On November 22, 1905, two Tulsa wildcatters, Robert Galbreath and Frank Chesley, were drilling for oil on a farm owned by Ida Glenn about twelve miles south of the city. Their bit touched a sandbar, and the well blew into production — and was soon anointed "the biggest small field in the world." The new gusher held such riches that when a curious reporter tried to visit the site a few days later, he was barred by men with shotguns. In March the partners hit an even larger well only three hundred feet from the first. Initially, the wells gushed so profusely that the oil simply collected on the ground, without the benefit of tanks. Waterfowl often mistook these "lakes of oil" for ponds, so café owners served "roast duck," a cheap dish frequently on the menu.

Fortunately for the natural habitat, Glenn Pool rigs and tanks soon appeared across a field eight miles long. "The whole country-side," one pioneer oilman recalled, "had a bristling appearance from hundreds of wooden derricks rushing into the sky." By 1907 ninety-five oil companies were working the field, having sunk more than a thousand wells; they produced almost twenty million barrels of oil in that year alone. Glenn Pool enabled Oklahoma to lead the nation in oil production in its first year of statehood. It made a few lucky men instant millionaires, and it flushed millions of dollars into Tulsa. The money, wrote the Oklahoma historian Danney Goble, "was spent on capital with drilling companies, freight companies, and supply companies. It was spent on wages in Tulsa's stores and for Tulsa's homes. It was spent on necessities, on luxuries, on children — and on gambling, liquor, and women. It made Tulsa rich. It made Tulsa wild. And it made Tulsa big."

While Glenn Pool's output peaked in 1911, the following year saw an even bigger eruption, the Cushing field, forty-five miles west of Tulsa. It was the most spectacular pool of its size in the world. Rousing gushers blasted uncontrollably from the earth, and streams of slimy black liquid flowed down creeks and ravines as frantic producers threw up dams to stop the waste. By 1915, the Cushing field was producing 300,000 barrels a day — nearly one fifth of all the oil marketed in the United States.

Money rolled into the city. In 1914 it had only three banks with more than $1 million in deposits; two years later, all nine banks had deposits exceeding that amount. It made sense for the *Oil and Gas Journal*, the industry's bible, to move to Tulsa in 1908. The new publisher, Patrick Doyle, lived in Oil City, Pennsylvania, the site of America's first oil field, and the journal had been published in Beaumont, Texas, the home of the great field at Spindletop, which ushered in the modern oil industry. But with the best oil days over in

Ohio, Pennsylvania, and West Virginia, and with Spindletop dried out by 1911, Tulsa rightly claimed the title of Oil Capital of the World.

The arrival of the oil field workers in Tulsa was like a shot of adrenaline in an already caffeinated body. They wore khaki shirts, leather boots, fedoras, and trousers splattered with oil and mud. They were reckless, free-spending, muscular, quick-tempered, violent, hard-drinking, and eager for a gamble. But even in his Sunday attire, an oilman could usually be recognized by the wad of tobacco in his cheek (fire hazards at wells forced him to chew instead of smoke). Danger loomed in the oil fields, where men were killed when thunderstorms torched tanks and windstorms toppled derricks. Another hazard came from nitroglycerin, which was used to discharge wells by breaking up oil-bearing strata. When a wagon hauling the unstable compound hit a pothole, the resulting explosion would leave a huge crater in the ground and rattle windows for miles. Passersby could only speculate on whether the bits of flesh came from man or horse.

But these dangers were eclipsed by the lust for profits, with opportunities rippling throughout the Tulsa economy. Barbershops, restaurants, and grocery stores posted perpetual HELP WANTED signs. Contractors searched for craftsmen in the building trades. The oil producers and investors were always hunting for drillers, tool dressers, geologists, and pipeliners. Teenage boys hauled buckets of hot bathing water to oil workers living in makeshift inns with no plumbing. Bootleggers sold anything they could pour in a bottle. The "shady-ladies" ran around with stockings full of money.

Tulsa's growth was staggering. Between 1907 and 1910 its population more than doubled, to 18,182 from 7,298. From 1910 to 1920 the number almost quadrupled, to 72,075. The newcomers stood in line, waiting for others to finish, in cafés, restaurants, and hotel dining rooms. Barbershops stayed open all night, giving numbered cards to customers as they entered. Carpenters, plumbers, painters, bricklayers, and electricians also worked through the night, beneath bright floodlights, on stores, office buildings, and no-frills board-and-batten bungalows.

By 1909, there were seven jewelry stores, all near Second and Main streets, two auto dealers, and two dressmaking emporiums, including the Parisian Parlor. Watermelons were still sold from horse-drawn buggies, but the town had forty-eight grocers, thirty-three restaurants, six bakeries, and three wholesale meat markets. Main Street was paved by 1908, and two years later eighty more blocks had received the same treatment. In time, a stately four-story courthouse was built of gray stone and marble imported from Italy.

The surveyor who laid out the rest of downtown named the streets cleverly. Those west of Main were named after cities west of the Mississippi River, starting with Boulder, Cheyenne, and Denver. East of Main were cities east of the Mississippi — Boston, Cincinnati, and Detroit. These names seemed to reflect Tulsa's big-city aspirations.

The opening of the Hotel Tulsa on May 12, 1912, symbolized the town's image of glamour and wealth. The absence of a fine hotel had been a serious drawback for a city trying to become a commercial center, but this ten-story marvel filled that role. "It means another milestone in the onward march of Greater Tulsa — the biggest single advancement yet," proclaimed the *Tulsa World*. Located at Third and Cincinnati, it breathed frontier opulence, with rich chandeliers hanging over large brown leather chairs, brass spittoons at their feet. The Persian rugs, white and gray marble steps, and domed ceiling evoked the new riches, while the oilmen's other pursuits in the hotel — drinking whiskey, playing poker, consorting with prostitutes — embodied Tulsa's rowdy past.

The lobby was a blend of blue serge pants and grease-stained overalls, winners one day, losers the next. Oil producers, lease brokers, and wildcatters created their own informal stock exchange. To buy or sell a lease, someone would pull out a map, stick a pencil on the spot, and agree to a price. In the hotel's first fifteen years, a billion dollars in oil deals was transacted there; according to several accounts, the oil tycoon Josh Cosden once wrote a personal check for $12 million. The lobby's dominant figure was Harry Sinclair, who occupied a suite of offices on the fifth floor where he played poker, drank whiskey, and, according to legend, put together the Sinclair-White Oil Company one night in the hallway. Other regulars were Robert McFarlin, who made so much money in the Glenn Pool and elsewhere that his company became the world's largest independent oil producer in less than ten years, and J. Paul Getty, who around 1914 wore the first wristwatch seen in Tulsa.

The Hotel Tulsa captured the era's fizzy spirit. On one occasion, patrons thought that a national Indian convention in Tulsa would make a fine time to hold a bronco-riding contest in the lobby. Three strands of rope were strung around the great white marble columns to erect a corral, and powdered resin was sprinkled on the tile floor. Then a bare-chested Indian, wearing buckskin pants and a beaded headband with one feather, walked his horse through the lobby into the corral. Crowds of people gathered outside the ropes and along the marble rail of the mezzanine, and bets were placed on whether the Indian could stay mounted on the bucking bronco for eight seconds. The spectators roared as the rider banged his heels against the horse's side; the animal reared back, lunged forward, slipped, and crashed to the floor, spilling the rider to the ground. The Indian got back on his horse and this time held on for the prescribed eight seconds. But right before the gun sounded to end the ride, the oilmen on the mezzanine began pouring corn whiskey on the crowd below, setting off a mad scramble. As one spectator, Choc Phillips, recounted in his memoir:

> Those caught in the downpour around the corral, and the people lining the railing around the mezzanine floor yelled and laughed as if it was the funniest thing in the world . . . Why allow such a showy attractive place to be shattered and broken by those wild rough people? The answer was money, lots of it. It was that sort of town. Any damage to the property would have been paid for immediately, and usually without a whimper . . . Things of this nature were rather normal conduct in boomtowns.

An economic frenzy of a different sort had played out in the region once before. In the great land runs of 1889 and 1893, farmsteads could be obtained in the Oklahoma Territory by dashing forth at the sound of an official pistol and driving stakes into unclaimed ground. (The Oklahoma Sooners refer to those who jumped the gun.) These stampedes made the area a refuge for the poor, dispossessed whites who had foundered in other southern states and were trying once again to scrape out a livelihood. Oil attracted a completely different newcomer to Oklahoma, and to Tulsa — not the rugged farm boys from the South but the financial dandies and oil barons from the East, many from the fading petroleum fields of Pennsylvania and Ohio. They brought with them expansive styles, sophistication, and a desire to plant highbrow culture in the red clay of Oklahoma.

In 1908 the Tulsa Opera House staged *Ben Hur* and fancifully recreated the chariot race by putting two horses on adjacent treadmills. The women of Tulsa formed a musical organization named the Hyechka Club, from the Creek word for "music." Supported by the city's businessmen, it brought in the New York Symphony, the Metropolitan Opera Company, the Minneapolis Symphony, the Chicago Civic Opera Company, the Victor Herbert Orchestra, Toscanini with the La Scala Orchestra of Milan, and many other performers. When Amelita Galli-Curci, the brilliant Italian soprano, came to town, she performed her operatic repertoire, then brought down the house with an encore of "Home, Sweet Home." As a newspaper man later wrote, "Some of the oil queens clattered down the aisles looking like just-opened pirate chests . . . Gradually, even [they] began to learn the difference been an aria and an aardvark, and people didn't applaud so loudly between the movements by celebrated soloists."

As the downtown skyline took shape, the tycoons built mansions whose Italian marble mantelpieces, plush velvet handrails, and silver-plated chandeliers bespoke a Gilded Age of Oil. Their homes were south of downtown, beyond rows of bungalows, on wide boulevards shaded by oaks, redbuds, and dogwoods. Josh Cosden, who opened Tulsa's first refinery on the banks of the Arkansas and was a millionaire at thirty-two, is credited with building the city's first oil mansion in 1914. On 17th Street, it was fronted by six massive columns and featured grand amenities. Visitors could play tennis on an imported English clay court under electric lights — a Tulsa first — or they could swim laps in the indoor pool. One block south was a mansion owned by Carl Dresser, a native of Pennsylvania and the president of a company that supplied most of the world's oil pipeline couplings. At twenty-nine, he built a three-story Italian Renaissance villa, with a stucco façade and terracotta roof tiles. The interior featured high beamed ceilings, tile and hardwood floors, wrought-iron railings, and leaded and stained glass windows. It had five bedrooms, six baths, three sunporches, six fireplaces, and a three-car garage. It also included quarters for five servants and a large wall safe in the butler's pantry for the family silver. The dining room, with its gold-leaf ceiling, had a stone mantel with the immortal inscription: *Inter secundus res esto moderat* (In the future, among favorable things be moderate).

While the boosters relished the stories of Tulsa's wealth, many residents still lived in poverty. The oil business, in which wells gushed one day and ran dry the next, was inherently unstable, and even sustained oil flows were commercially perilous, causing overproduction, lower prices, and reduced profits. These boom-and-bust cycles capsized companies, wiped out fortunes, and prevented many workers from escaping their squalor.

In 1921 a Methodist church in Tulsa sponsored a survey of the working-class neighborhood of West Tulsa, on the west bank of the Arkansas River. Three thousand residents lived in bungalows, tents, boxes, or other threadbare structures. In one house, a family of seven all slept on dirt floors; on another block, twenty-seven people used the same outdoor toilet. Leaking roofs and poor sanitation were common, and the children lacked shoes, clothing, and food. There were 305 cases of contagious diseases — whooping cough, measles, mumps, chicken pox, diphtheria, and smallpox, all among preschool children. They "must have light and sunshine, as well as sanitary conditions, and in the case of contagious diseases, be isolated," the report concluded.

Vice also flourished. In the red brick hotels along First Street, parallel to the railroad tracks, gamblers set up their rooms, and prostitutes solicited patrons by rapping on the windows. To avoid the police, illegal whiskey was floated on rafts and in boats at night down the Arkansas River to replenish the city's supply. If it failed to arrive, word spread that "the fleet had sunk." Otherwise, "the fleet was in."

On Friday nights the pastor of the First Presbyterian Church, Charles Kerr, toured First Street, prayed with drunken cowboys and roughnecks, and tried to lead them to Jesus. On Saturday nights, when the oilmen had a paycheck in their pocket and time on their hands, murders, fights, and knifings became so frequent that the street was named Bloody First. On Sunday mornings, it was common for residents to wake up and ask, "Who got shot last night?" On one occasion, a boy left his home at dawn to deliver newspapers and found the body of a man in his front yard. The man had apparently been stabbed in a fight, staggered along the street, collapsed in the yard, and bled to death on the lawn.

Even in its early boom years, the city's lawlessness was virtually impossible to stop. In 1906 the Tulsa chapter of the Women's Christian Temperance Union marched on city hall and protested that vice was corrupting the town's youth. The mayor said he was powerless to suppress the traffic in liquor and gambling and, as for prostitutes, "We cannot send them to jail for we have no suitable place to incarcerate women." For years, the police department, like other government agencies in Tulsa, remained poorly financed and staffed. When vice squads tried to shut down the rooming houses where hookers met their clients, the proprietors appeared in court and swore they had thought the couple was married. After all, that was how they signed the registry. The roadhouses outside town, which were popular gambling dens, sat on mounted wheels, so when word came of an impending raid, the houses were simply rolled into the next county.

Tulsa debated whether it should be an open or closed town, typically slanting these arguments toward what was best for its commercial interests. Open-town advocates believed the city's anything-goes mores attracted free-spending businessmen; their closed-town adversaries considered tough law enforcement essential for Tulsa's long-term stability. These debates flared during campaigns for city office. Political challengers pledged to "clean up Tulsa" and crack down on reputed "vice lords" — prominent citizens who profited from illicit businesses and bribed police officers and newspapermen to ignore criminal behavior. When sometimes the political challengers won, they were then beholden to the same underworld interests as their predecessors, and the crackdowns rarely materialized.

Only an epidemic could inspire draconian measures. In 1918, when the Spanish influenza infected one in four Americans and killed forty million people around the world, Tulsans collapsed while walking down the street or sipping coffee in a restaurant. Old storage rooms, churches, and schools were turned into emergency hospitals, but many residents — at one point 3,000 — still had to fight the virus at home. City officials banned gatherings of all sorts and even advised people not to shake hands with friends. Under these conditions, the authorities raided the First Street hotels, swept up dozens of "undesirables" — pimps, gamblers, bootleggers, and prostitutes — and quarantined them in two old warehouses. When the epidemic subsided, it was business as usual, and sex, booze, and poker were good for business.

Ultimately, nothing would derail the boom years — Tulsans wouldn't allow it. The city was run by a benign plutocracy, which applied enlightened self-interest to bridge the Arkansas River, entice the railroads, sponsor the booster trains, even bail out failing businesses that were central to its commercial mission. In 1910 the Farmers National Bank was close to insolvency, and a run on the bank could have triggered other runs, forced shutdowns, and eviscerated Tulsa's claim as a business center for oil. The town's leading petroleum executives convened an emergency meeting. Fearing the collapse of Farmers National, the oil elite agreed to take it over, rename it Exchange National Bank, and personally guarantee every dollar of every deposit. Unlike other banks, which viewed the oil business as a crapshoot and were reluctant to finance wildcat wells, this institution catered to oilmen, and it flourished as the demand for energy soared from the growing auto industry and, later, World War I. Eleven years and several consolidations later, Exchange National operated out of a beautiful new twelve-story building at Third and Boston streets and had deposits of nearly $28 million. As Harry Sinclair later said, "All of us thought that the future of Tulsa and the future of oil cried out for an oil bank, and it became what we hoped it would, the biggest and best known oil bank in the country."

As the century's second decade rolled on, Tulsa's streets were paved as part of a large civic plan. A municipal building, a convention hall, a hospital, and a high school were all constructed. Office buildings that bore the names of their oil patrons — Cosden, Kennedy, Sinclair — were also built. Their thick carpeting, columns lined with brass and gold, polished marble floors, and long shining counters all looked, in the words of one New York writer, like "a corner torn away from Wall Street." Streets were named Harvard and Yale. Clothing stores now sold black-embroidered Chamoisette gloves for women, taffeta dresses for children, and Manhattan silk shirts for men. Cadillacs crowded the streets, and car shows were annual events, featuring — according to one advertisement — "hundreds of beautiful women, each superbly gowned at the steering wheel of every car." Tulsans still rode horses, but many of the riders had discarded their blue jeans, vests, and dangling spurs for a more sophisticated British look: tweed jackets, helmets, fine leather boots, and an English saddle that lacked the trademark embossed pommel of its western counterpart.

Social climbing was seen even in religious circles. Many poor Tulsans from the rural South had Pentecostal backgrounds, which emphasized a belief in divine healing, speaking in tongues, and boisterous expressions of faith such as clapping and shouting. But as the Pentecostals made money in the oil fields and moved up the social ladder, they sought admission to the more restrained, prestigious Presbyterian and Episcopalian churches as one more vindication of their enriched earthly status.

Overlooked in all the excitement was a growing black community north of the railroad tracks. Ambitious but restive, proud but relegated to the fringe of society, it could have existed in another state or even country. Whites knew that blacks were in their midst — the "coloreds" or "Negroes" worked as their cooks, chauffeurs, and servants — but they were not among the pioneers and visionaries who built the miracle that was Tulsa. As Tate Brady, who moved to Tulsa in 1890 and later opened one of its largest hotels, wrote about these groundbreaking days: "Indian and white man, Jew and Gentile, Catholic and Protestant, we worked side by side, shoulder to shoulder and under these conditions the 'Tulsa Spirit' was born and has lived and God grant that it never dies . . . Cursed be he, or they, who on any pretext try to divide our citizenship and destroy this spirit."

When racial violence finally did split the city, when long-ignored wounds were opened and the "Tulsa Spirit" lay in ruins, thousands would be cursed.

The Promised Land

BY THE TIME J. B. Stradford moved to Tulsa in 1899, he had reason to believe he could accomplish anything. He was born into slavery in Versailles, Kentucky, in 1861, and after the Civil War sat on the laps of Union soldiers. His father set an example of defiance and strength. The elder Stradford was named Julius Caesar, or J.C., while his son's name was John the Baptist. (It was not uncommon for plantation owners to give their slaves the names of religious and historical figures.) J.C. learned to read and write from a slaveowner's abolitionist daughter, even though the punishment for this education could have been the severing of his index finger. But by learning to read and write — at times studying his lessons while in the field, pretending to plow — J.C. could plot his escape. Slaves were forbidden to travel to another plantation without authorization from their master. When J.C. fled from his plantation, he forged his master's name on a pass, which helped him get all the way to Stratford, Ontario. There he took a variation of its name for his own. In Ontario he worked and earned enough money to return to Kentucky, before Emancipation, to obtain legal papers designating him free.

His son went by J.B., probably for the same reason many blacks of that era used initials. The single letters precluded whites from addressing them by their first name when such informality was a sign of disrespect. (Some black parents named their children Mister or Colonel to ensure that their offspring would always bear titles of respect.) Like his father, J. B. Stradford received an education, but this time legally and safely. He graduated from Oberlin College in Ohio and took classes at night to receive his degree, at the age of thirty-eight, from Indiana Law School in Indianapolis. At Oberlin he met his wife, Bertie, who died at a young age after bearing three sons and a daughter. He then married a woman named Augusta. Stradford and his family moved to various cities, including St. Louis and Lawrenceburg, Kentucky, determined never to work for anyone but himself. He became an entrepreneur, opening pool halls, shine parlors, bathhouses, and rooming houses. With broad shoulders and a square jaw, he had, in the words of his descendants, "the strength of a Mandingo warrior." He was quick to anger and, even in his late fifties, not afraid to fight — as a delivery man in North Tulsa discovered. Riding in an ice wagon, the man noticed Stradford standing on the street beneath an umbrella, shading himself from the sun.

"Why do you need an umbrella?" he asked. "The sun won't burn you."

Stradford took exception to the remark, an argument followed, and the delivery man swung at Stradford with ice tongs. Stradford pulled him down from the wagon and pummeled and stomped on him. Other black Tulsans quickly surrounded Stradford and pleaded with him to spare the man. "Kill him and they will mob you," they said, "mob" being the euphemism for "lynch." The iceman survived.

Although Stradford tried to confront state-sanctioned discrimination, he still had faith in the American system. He believed that blacks who worked hard and played by the rules could succeed and that African Americans who squandered these opportunities were "moral cowards." He was also a patriot. When he visited the nation's Capitol in 1918, he wrote in the black newspaper, the *Tulsa Star*:

> Had I the power of language to express the beauty, the sublimity and grandeur of that building and its arts, I could make you laugh. I could make you weep. When the spot was pointed out to me where nearly one hundred years ago John Q. Adams dropped dead in the House of Representatives, I stood on that spot and felt that I was standing on the line which divided time and eternity, the mortal from immortal-

ity. Then I turned around and viewed the statues of all the great men of our country, who have come upon the state of action, played their parts in the drama of life and have taken their places in the silent halls of death.

After a hotel he owned in Alexandria, Indiana, went under, Stradford moved to Tulsa because he had heard that economic opportunities abounded there for Negroes.

He arrived around the same time that another black entrepreneur, O. W. Gurley, reached Tulsa. At the beginning of the twentieth century, the city was not racially segregated. There were several Negro businesses downtown, including a barber, a real estate agent, and lawyers who employed a white stenographer. Both races patronized a rooming house on Archer and Cincinnati streets. But Stradford believed that blacks had the best chance for success by pooling their resources, working together, and supporting one another's businesses. So he bought large tracts of real estate north of the Frisco tracks, had it surveyed and plotted into blocks, streets, and alleys, and sold it only to blacks. Gurley did the same. Other real estate men, white and black, purchased adjoining land and, after laying out streets and alleys, also sold it only to Negroes. A black business district was born.

Its center was the intersection of Archer Street and Greenwood Avenue, where the first business, a grocery store, was established. It is believed that the blacks named Greenwood after a town in Mississippi, and that was how the district was known. It soon attracted a black real estate developer, a black dentist, a black physician, and a black Baptist minister. The community grew along Archer Street, which ran parallel to the Frisco track. Hardware supplies could be purchased just south of the track, on First Street, while the Acme Brick Company off Greenwood Avenue supplied the building material. Brick by brick, J. B. Stradford's vision of a black business district took shape. In 1905 the first school for Negro children opened in a Baptist church. By the time Oklahoma achieved statehood, in 1907, Greenwood had two physicians, a one-story rooming house, a newspaper, three grocers, and a handful of other merchants.

The discovery of oil transformed black Tulsa just as it did white

Tulsa. While blacks were excluded from working in the oil fields, the "flowing gold" indirectly benefited Greenwood through the high wages paid to black domestic workers. It also came from whites who gambled, drank, and pursued other illicit pleasures in North Tulsa. Its residents believed Greenwood represented a new freedom from the oppressive economy of the Old South, a new life where whites were too busy making money to be worried about putting blacks in their place.

And J. B. Stradford became the richest black man in Tulsa by building a rooming house, rental properties, and ultimately the largest black-owned hotel in America. Arriving in Tulsa six years before the first big oil strike, he could never have imagined the riches that would sweep his way. Ironically, he had come not because of what Tulsa might be but for what it had been — the promised land for blacks.

Oklahoma and its predecessor territories have a distinctive racial history, which played a critical role in the Tulsa riot. The state's racist policies helped shape the attitudes of the white Tulsans who destroyed Greenwood in 1921 and of the public officials who subsequently betrayed the community. In later years, advocates of reparations would argue that the hostile racial climate made the state at least partially responsible for the riot — morally if not legally — and therefore subjected it to financial claims from victims. These advocates would base their argument not only on the state's policies but also on its denial of the dream that Oklahoma could become a utopian homeland for Negroes.

Utopia, however, was not on the minds of the first blacks who came to the Indian Territory between 1830 and 1840. They arrived as slaves of the Five Civilized Tribes — the Creeks, Choctaws, Chickasaws, Cherokees, and Seminoles. The federal government, coveting the lands of the five tribes in the southeastern United States, forcibly removed the Indians and their slaves, marching them hundreds of miles west. Herded like animals in the middle of winter, without sufficient food or clothing and ravaged by epidemics, many of the Indians died along the way; the Cherokees alone lost nearly 4,000 members, about 22 percent of their tribe. But possibly the highest mortality rate befell the black slaves, who performed much of the manual labor on the march, such as loading freight wagons and clearing new trails. The survivors, Indian and slave, called their brutal slog the Trail of Tears.

After Emancipation, the treatment of the freedmen varied from tribe to tribe. At their worst, the Choctaws and Chickasaws were reluctant even to admit the end of slavery. But the Creeks and the Seminoles, who had a long history of intermarrying with their slaves, quickly adopted them into their tribes. Over the next twenty-five years, most of the freedmen were granted their citizenship, which meant they could vote, hold tribal lands, attend tribal schools, and receive equal justice. Intermarriage was also common in some tribes, blending racial identities for generations to come.

This integration was inviting to other blacks in the South, who were being disenfranchised, intimidated, segregated, and, most notoriously, lynched by white supremacists. These attacks helped create black separatist movements, their principal aim being to find a haven where blacks could live and work. In the 1870s and 1880s, blacks migrated in large numbers to Kansas, but harsh winters and racial hostilities proved disastrous. Desperate, they turned to the area immediately south, where the new Oklahoma Territory (1890) offered a warmer climate, abundant land, and a more tolerant Indian population. Under those conditions, the Twin Territories became a bastion for black nationalism, and talk spread of an all-black state. The new migrants had to convince enough of the five million oppressed blacks in the South to join them so that they would become the racial majority, and they were led in these efforts by Edwin P. McCabe, a black politician who had been state auditor of Kansas.

In 1890 McCabe founded the black town of Langston, eighty miles west of Tulsa, and started a newspaper. His representatives swept across the South on recruiting missions, appearing in black churches and public halls and writing to newspapers, preachers, and schoolteachers. The recruiters exhorted blacks to come to the Twin Territories in such numbers that whites would be compelled to turn the entire region over to them — which, not incidentally, might help McCabe's own political ambitions. Appealing to racial pride, McCabe urged the formation of other black towns on Langston's model, which would become "the Negro's refuge from lynching, burning at the stake, and other lawlessness." At least twenty-nine black towns were ultimately established, racial fortresses in a vast hinterland that attracted pioneers from Texas, Mississippi, Arkansas, Louisiana, Kentucky, South Carolina, Alabama, and Tennessee. Booker T. Washington visited the most famous black town, Boley, and believed it was "another chapter in the long struggle of the Negro for moral, industrial, and political freedom."

The region, in short, seemed to be moving toward more racial equality than any other place in America. As Murray R. Wickett wrote in *Contested Territory,* an account of Oklahoma's years before statehood: "By the 1890s, territorial freedmen enjoyed far more privileges than blacks in the United States proper, either the South or the North. They had every reason to believe they had found the 'promised land.'"

That promise was short-lived.

The influx of blacks into the territories coincided with the great land runs of 1889 and 1893, and McCabe's activities stirred the worst fears among white homesteaders, most of whom came from southern states that had already adopted Jim Crow laws. One white Oklahoman warned in 1890 that racial violence would erupt if blacks tried to assert their political rights, adding, "Dead niggers make an excellent fertilizer, and if the Negroes try to Africanize Oklahoma they will find that we will enrich our soil with them." Whites in Oklahoma launched a segregation campaign, which culminated in a 1901 law mandating separate schools. Whites outside the territory were equally alarmist. The *New York Times* wrote on March 1, 1890: "If the black population could be distributed evenly over the United States, it would not constitute a social or political danger. But an exclusively or overwhelming negro settlement in any part of the country is, to all intents and purposes, a camp of savages."

McCabe's vision of a black-dominated territory failed because most black sharecroppers could not afford the long journey west. As a result, by 1900 whites in the Oklahoma Territory outnumbered blacks by more than ten to one. The black towns also withered away; isolated rural farming communities could not survive in a country becoming more industrial, urban, and connected through transportation and communication lines.

The hope for racial tolerance was irrevocably shattered with Oklahoma's statehood. In the preceding years, "the Negro question" was the defining issue for the two political parties. While the Republicans were divided on voting rights and equal access for blacks, the Democrats vehemently opposed all civil rights, arguing that "Republican success means African domination." The Democrats' appeal to white supremacy led their party to a sweeping victory in the election of delegates to the state constitutional convention at Guthrie in 1906. Their first act was to elect William H. "Alfalfa Bill" Murray president of the convention. His huge hawk nose, drooping mustache, and tobacco-stained teeth made him look "like a cantankerous hick in a burlesque show," according to one writer.

But there was nothing funny about his racist doctrine. In his inaugural speech, he explained that blacks were "failures as lawyers, doctors and in other professions" and must be taught to remain in their place "as porters, bootblacks, and barbers and many lines of agriculture, horticulture, and mechanics . . . It is an entirely false notion that the Negro can rise to the equal of a white man in the professions or become an equal citizen." Murray longed for the days when blacks understood their subservient roles. "I appreciate the old-time exslave, the old darky, and they are the salt of their race — who comes to me talking softly in that humble spirit which should characterize their actions and dealings with white men."

Murray offered a fuller view in 1948 in *The Negro's Place in Call of Race,* depicting blacks as simian predators whose diminished "brain weights" consigned them to inferiority. He urged mothers to keep their daughters away from Negroes, who suffered from unmanageable sexual desires. "Social or any intimacy, with a Negro and white woman, is too great a risk to tolerate or condone. His 'stronger' [passion] may overwhelm her." Jews were not much better — unaffected by the death camps, Murray praised Hitler for being "right in his science." Almost fifty years later, a professor at the University of Oklahoma found an autographed copy at a used book sale and discovered these words inscribed by the author: "I hate Indians too."

It would be some consolation if Alfalfa Bill Murray had been just a racist crackpot who stumbled on the presidency of the constitutional convention. But he was the dominant political figure in Oklahoma in the first half of the twentieth century. After playing a major role in drafting the state constitution, he was the first speaker of the new state's house of representatives. In the 1910s, he served two terms in the U.S. Congress. After a bizarre effort trying to establish a cotton colony in Bolivia, he returned to Oklahoma and was elected governor from 1931 to 1935. In that job he liked to dispatch the National Guard, once sending it to the University of Oklahoma to enforce the segregation laws at a football game. Vulgarity, like bigotry, came easily to Murray. When a college president asked him for increased funding, the governor asked if he had ever had sex with a black woman (the exact language was deemed too offensive to print in a newspaper). Murray stayed in the news by writing books (including his 1,683-page autobiography) and by waging unsuccessful political campaigns, losing bids for the governorship, the Congress, the Senate, and even the White House. He died in 1956, in time to see his son, Johnston, serve as Oklahoma's fourteenth governor. His bust is in the capitol today.

Black scholars would later contend that Alfalfa Bill fostered the poisonous climate that produced racist laws and violence against blacks. But by the end of the twentieth century, he was fondly remembered in Oklahoma newspapers as a folksy, cigar-smoking rustic who railed against nefarious corporate interests, planted a vegetable garden in front of the capitol, and met visitors in the governor's mansion wearing only his long underwear.

The ascendancy of the Democratic Party at statehood, led by Murray, meant the denial of civil liberties to blacks, but Oklahoma was determined to out–Jim Crow the other southern states. Lawmakers argued that the eyes of the nation were on their new state, partly northern, partly southern, a state in which blacks had once held dangerous ideas of social equality. How Oklahoma handled such ideas, these men said, could determine the future of race relations in America.

The state constitution mandated segregated schools but otherwise included no segregation language, lest President Roosevelt, a Republican, refuse to sign it. However, when the state legislature convened for the first time on December 2, 1907, it passed emergency legislation requiring separate railroad coaches and waiting rooms for people of African descent. The first bill passed by the new state, it forced the reconfiguration of more than five hundred railway depots. Racial distinctions were spelled out by law; though Oklahoma had a large number of blacks, whites, and American Indians, as well as Mexicans, everyone was considered a member of the white race except those with "African" blood.

The lawmakers also passed a strong bill against miscegenation, making marriage between the races a felony that could be punished by up to five years in prison; ministers performing the ceremony were also subject to these charges. In 1910, the state took its boldest step against blacks, passing a constitutional amendment denying their right to vote through the "grandfather clause." It restricted suffrage to those eligible to vote on January 1, 1866, and their descendants, as well as immigrants. All others, meaning blacks, were required to take "literacy tests" administered by local registrars, who were usually determined to keep them from the polls. No black served in the Oklahoma legislature between 1910 and 1964.

The U.S. Supreme Court declared the grandfather clause unconstitutional in 1915, so Oklahoma set up a brief registration period for voters not already eligible. That year also saw Oklahoma respond to fears that blacks carried communicable diseases by requiring separate phone booths for blacks and whites. It was the first state to adopt such a law.

Many black pioneers fled from the new state, moving to Canada or Liberia (the destination of a "back to Africa" movement) or to northern American cities, particularly Chicago, which now promoted itself as "the promised land for blacks." Edwin McCabe, who once hoped to govern Oklahoma, now fought just to occupy the train coach of his choice. In 1908, he filed an injunction to prevent the railroads from implementing the law requiring separate coaches, but it was denied by a judge. McCabe left Oklahoma for Chicago shortly thereafter, his only consolation being that the town he founded, Langston, survived as the home of historically black Langston University.

Also devastated were the Oklahoma freedmen, the descendants of Indian slaves who had never experienced the racial oppression of the other southern states. Oklahoma "had unmanned the freedmen, destroyed their dignity and self-respect by making them much less than second-class citizens," wrote B. C. Franklin, a black lawyer who began practicing in Oklahoma in 1908. "They stood humiliated without legal recourse. They had never experienced such before and did not know how to cope with it."

Blacks in Oklahoma held angry rallies and published bitter editorials, but these protests had little effect amid increased racial violence. Lynchings were not new to the area; in 1896, the territories had ten, making it fifth in the country for most lynchings. But their number in Oklahoma escalated after statehood, and 1911 marked the first year that more blacks than whites were hanged.

As communal events, lynchings were designed to intimidate and, when applied to blacks, to reinforce the racial hierarchy that had now been codified into law. The macabre rituals were featured on postcards, showing the victim's well-dressed audience holding umbrellas to shade them from the sun, that delivered the message of fear. A card from Durant, in 1911, captured a flume of black smoke and carried the phrase "Coon Cooking." A mob of five hundred had lynched a bullet-ridden black man, carried his corpse to a vacant lot, and torched it on a pyre of lumber. The city's remaining blacks, warned "not to let the sun go down on them," got the message. They all left by sunset.

Lynchings were not simply the random acts of white mobs. They were also inexorably linked to Oklahoma's denial of basic rights to blacks. If African Americans could not vote or enter the white schools, railway coaches, or telephone booths, why should they be given due process in the courts? This rhetorical question was answered by a district judge in June 1911 when he convened a grand jury to investigate the lynching of a black woman and her son in Okemah.

Their bodies were found hanging from a bridge by a black boy taking his cow to the water. In his instructions to the jury, Judge Caruthers said:

> The people of the state have said by recently adopted Constitutional provision that the race to which the unfortunate victims belonged should in large measure be divorced from participation in our political contests, because of their known racial inferiority and their dependent credulity, which very characteristic[ally] made them the mere tool of the designing and the cunning. It is well known that I heartily concur with this Constitutional provision.

In the years following statehood, even as Greenwood's population boomed, black pioneers saw the racial atmosphere in Tulsa deteriorate as much as it had anywhere else in Oklahoma. After Tulsa annexed the Greenwood area in 1909, the district fanned out northward from the Frisco tracks to Pine Street, bounded by the Midland Valley tracks on the east and Detroit Avenue on the west. The community covered about four square miles in a small valley, with Standpipe Hill on its western edge. The boundaries changed little as blacks from the surrounding states and elsewhere in Oklahoma poured in. Between 1910 and 1920, Tulsa's black population surged from 1,959 to 8,873. This growth, however, was only slightly greater than that of the white population. The black percentage of the city's total population increased from 10.2 to 12.3 percent.

The growth of Greenwood frightened Tulsa's whites. The district was now larger than all but a few towns in Oklahoma. On April 12, 1912, the lead story in the *Tulsa Democrat* was headlined SHALL TULSA BE MUSKOGEEIZED? (Muskogee had a high concentration of black residents.) The story reported that Negroes were moving to Tulsa because of the lax enforcement of the grandfather clause and that black gamblers and bootleggers had already arrived. "Tulsa appears now to be in danger of losing its prestige as the whitest town in Oklahoma," the paper concluded.

Later that month, a Democratic victory in a local election allowed Tulsa, according to the *Democrat,* to "continue to advertise to the world that it is a white man's town, where white men rule and predominate. The effort at Negro colonization in Tulsa was put to an effective end."

White racists depicted blacks as slothful, dirty creatures whose very presence was a contagion in the community. As the Reverend James E. McConnell of the Tigert Memorial Church sermonized in July of 1914:

> The Negro has no conception of purity or chastity. They have little regard for sanitation or anything that is clean, and as a result of this impure and filthy and intemperate life, the race is going to be extinct in a few decades, unless they can be rescued from the life they live. He has no appreciation for honor or honesty. The Negro that will not steal or lie is the exception and such exceptions are rare.

The pastor also claimed that blacks were far better off as slaves, where "as a rule they were treated humanely, and in many instances kindly . . . They had more to eat and better clothes than they have today and slept in warmer beds."

In this climate of bigotry and fear, it would take courage for any black to challenge the laws of Oklahoma openly. But it did not take long for J. B. Stradford to act.

On January 2, 1909, only a few months after the state's separate-coach law went into effect, Stradford paid $3.26 for a first-class train ticket from Arkansas City, Kansas, to Tulsa. When he boarded Midland Valley Railroad train No. 8, a porter said he'd better sit in the Jim Crow car because they were not far from Oklahoma.

"I am now in Kansas," Stradford said, "and I know enough to get on the train."

A half hour into the ride, the train approached the Oklahoma border, and the conductor, Larry O'Hara, instructed the porter to enforce the law: "Tell that nigger he has to ride in the Jim Crow car."

The porter approached Stradford and said he had to move. "The Jim Crow car's ahead," he said. But Stradford didn't budge.

Next came the conductor. "This train is in Oklahoma now," he told Stradford. "You have to ride in the nigger car."

"I'll go," Stradford responded, "but I want to make a statement first."

O'Hara was in no mood for a statement. Cursing, he grabbed Stradford's arm sharply and tried to yank him out of his seat, but Stradford wrested his arm free and remained seated. The conductor then pulled the bell cord to signal the engineer to stop the train, intending to throw his recalcitrant passenger out of the car. But O'Hara reconsidered — he would have Stradford arrested at the next stop instead. The train continued on, and Stradford stood up and walked to the Jim Crow car. He noticed it was not at all equal to the other cars: it had no smoking compartment, and the seats were not as comfortable.

By the time the train pulled into the town of Pawhuska, the sheriff's office had been alerted to the ruckus, and the deputy sheriff walked on board. "I have a nigger on the train that's violated the Jim Crow law," the conductor told him. Stradford had already made his way to a nearby lunch counter and was eating a hamburger when the deputy sheriff arrested him. With another officer behind them, he took Stradford by the arm, led him through a large crowd, and walked the four blocks to the sheriff's office. Stradford was arrested for violating the separate-coach law of Oklahoma and brought before a county judge, then released on a cash bond of twenty-five dollars. When he returned to the train tracks, the Midland Valley had already left and he had to find another means home.

Three weeks later, he was tried in Osage County court. O'Hara conceded that Stradford had ultimately moved to the Jim Crow car, and the defendant was found not guilty. For many blacks, that might have been vindication enough — but not for Stradford, who sued the Midland Valley Railroad for false imprisonment and malicious prosecution. Losing in district court, he appealed to the Oklahoma supreme court. He argued, among other things, that the separate-coach laws of Oklahoma did not apply to trains that originated in other states. But the court decided against Stradford, ruling that the railroad company was simply enforcing the law of the land. More important, the court defended Jim Crow, saying it was "demanded by all the people of the state." That was false, of course, but blacks did not count. It would take Oklahoma more than fifty years to remove the law from its books.

Losing his first battle against Jim Crow did not deter Stradford from continuing the fight.

On August 4, 1916, the city of Tulsa passed an ordinance that forbade people of either race from residing on any block where three quarters or more of the residents were of the other race. (Exemptions were granted for black domestics.) The law simply codified the status quo, but it made segregation mandatory instead of voluntary. Two days later, on a Sunday afternoon, six hundred blacks gathered at the Dreamland Theatre in Greenwood to protest the law, and J. B. Stradford was among the first to speak. He was outraged as well as embarrassed because the law had been passed by a Republican administration, and Stradford had been the Republican "boss" in Greenwood. Now his own party had flung another dagger at his people.

"I tell you, gentlemen," he thundered to the crowd, "it is time that we took some formal notice of the calumnies that are being heaped upon us in unbearable quantities . . . Without any ordinance whatever we have segregated ourselves. We have our own little city and we have never tried to infringe upon the rights and privileges of the white property owners." It was a common refrain in Greenwood — we are playing by the rules, we are not bothering white Tulsans, so why are we being deprived of our rights?

A committee that included Stradford and his son, Cornelius, a recent graduate of Columbia University Law School, drafted a petition to the mayor, claiming that the segregation ordinance would "cast a stigma on the colored race in the eyes of the world." The committee then marched into a city commission meeting. Two blacks gave speeches, which the mayor and commissioners ignored, "but when J. B. Stradford asked to be heard," the *Democrat* reported, "the mayor sat up and took notice."

"I have always been a Republican and have worked hard for the ticket in every campaign, city, county, and state," Stradford said. "The boys [in Greenwood] do about what I tell them. You white Republicans asked my help in the last city campaign . . . Now that we helped elect you, we are insulted by your attempt to segregate us."

When Stradford finished, the mayor said, "Let's approve these bills." The discussion was over, the law remained; Stradford stormed out of the room.

Stradford was not the only one to believe the segregation ordinance unconstitutional. The U.S. Supreme Court invalidated it the next year, although it stayed on Tulsa's books. Whether by law or custom, Tulsa was and would be one of America's most segregated cities for the rest of the century. In *The Negro in American Civilization*, Charles S. Johnson wrote in 1930: "Although there are areas in most cities in which the Negro population is concentrated to the point of being regarded the 'black belt,' there is in no large city, with the possible exception of Tulsa, Oklahoma, a concentration approaching absolute segregation."

While it was both unconstitutional and unequal, segregation had one benefit. It gave black merchants a captive audience for their goods and services, so once dollars came into the district, many stayed in "Deep Greenwood."

This was the heart of the business district, which had expanded north from the corner of Greenwood Avenue and Archer Street to include the first two blocks of Greenwood. At the beginning, at 102 North Greenwood, was the three-story Williams Building, including a confectionary with a twelve-foot fountain and a table seating nearly fifty people. The building was owned by John Williams and his wife, Loula, who began their enterprises with an auto repair business, then built a movie house, the Dreamland Theatre. A few doors down was B. C. Franklin, the attorney who later thwarted efforts by the city administration to move black residents farther north. At 112 North Greenwood lived Emma and O. W. Gurley, the pioneer who built much of the black district. The *Tulsa Star* stood at 126 North Greenwood; its owner and publisher, A. J. Smitherman, once splashed these words across the top of his paper: THE MOTTO OF EVERY NEGRO SHOULD BE: YOU PUSH ME AND I PUSH YOU. Farther along in a less prestigious block, at 503 North Greenwood, was the office of A. C. Jackson, who was described by the Mayo brothers, the physicians who founded the Mayo Clinic, as "the most able Negro surgeon in America."

Deep Greenwood also had undertakers, cafés, pool halls, grocers, and beauty parlors, and it was the place to be on Thursday nights and Sunday afternoons, when black domestics working in South Tulsa were off. They returned home to participate in an elaborate communal dance. The men wore dark suits and off-white silk shirts, some with a twenty-dollar gold piece hanging from their watch chains. The women wore satin dresses, fur-trimmed coats, Gage hats, diamonds and other pricey jewelry. The gray streets were brightened by displays of peaches, watermelons, and candy. At times the men and women had to walk sideways because the streets were so crowded. There was no music or dancing or street performers. The parade was the performance, and conversation filled the air.

"I would sit in my father's office and just watch these people," recalled B. C. Franklin's son, the historian John Hope Franklin, who moved to Greenwood as a boy in the 1920s. "It was like a pantomime, people just moving up and down. They were going in and out of restaurants and they were just seen to be seen. They were dressed in their finest, and they looked beautiful to me."

Greenwood held a special mystique. For whites, it was always a hidden world, but one that held a naughty fascination. In 1941 Bob Wills and his Texas Playboys, a white western swing band, sang "Take Me Back to Tulsa," the most famous song about the city, which included these lyrics:

> Would I like to go to Tulsa?
> You bet your boots I would
> Let me off at Archer,
> I'll walk down to Greenwood.

The band never said what happened in Greenwood, thus preserving the secrets of black Tulsa.

For African Americans, Greenwood became synonymous with independence, pride, and resilience. By the end of the century, Greenwood in its formative years would be glorified as "the Black Wall Street." The moniker is more ironic than apt — it is unlikely that any black Tulsans traded stocks or bonds in the first quarter of the twentieth century, and compared to other black districts in America, Greenwood was modest. In 1920, for example, midsize cities like Louisville, Cincinnati, and Pittsburgh had far more African Americans, while Chicago had ten times the black population of Tulsa.

Moreover, "the Black Wall Street" hardly suggests the poverty, squalor, and neglect that were common outside Greenwood's vibrant business district and a block or two of prime housing. While it was slow to pave streets, lay sewage lines, and provide other basic services in white neighborhoods, Tulsa all but ignored the black district. By 1920, only six blocks in Greenwood were paved; the rest were uneven dirt roads with ditches that drained the rainfall. Sewage connections were rare; bathrooms and indoor toilets were luxuries few could afford. The Colored Public Health Nurse of Tulsa reported in that year that a single outdoor toilet was used by one eleven-room house and seven adjoining houses. While the elite streets had brick homes and bungalows, many people lived in weather-beaten shacks with planks, sheds, two-room cottages, the remains of old barns, and even tents. Wood from packing crates was often used to build homes. Mangy cows roamed around the outhouses, chickens ran across scattered sand, and refuse fires burned in corner lots.

After describing some of these scenes in a 1920 report, the American Association of Social Workers concluded: "While the above is a rather dismal picture, the colored community has very outstanding assets — its people."

Though Greenwood was bleak (particularly to white outsiders), it was still a magnet for impoverished blacks in rural towns and sharecropping communities across Oklahoma and the South. Blacks went to Tulsa for the same reason whites did — to make money.

It was said: "Tulsa is the oil capital of the world, but the Negro had neither oil nor capital." That was true, but oil money did flow into Greenwood through the wages that the rich whites paid their black domestic workers, wages previously unheard of in the South. Maids received $20 to $25 a week (about $331 to $414 today); chauffeurs and gardeners, $15 to $20. Porters and janitors also made good money; black shoeshine boys could pocket $10 a day.

The black servants either lived in quarters above garages or arrived at seven in the morning and left at eight in the evening. They washed linens, ironed clothes, scrubbed floors, dusted furniture, and prepared food. At a time when cooking was both an art form and heavy labor, the domestic who could whip up hog jowl with black-eyed peas, orange nut bread, and coconut tortes was greatly valued. White households had good reason to seek out black servants; their very segregation increased their appeal. Black domestics, physically and socially isolated, could not gossip about a white household to the whites' friends and neighbors. The servants and their employers were mutually dependent: the servants needed the money, and the employers needed someone black to tend the house. "When we had a white maid," one woman said, "I was always helping her. I felt kind of sorry for her and didn't want to see her work so hard. But when we have a colored girl, I don't mind letting her do all the work herself."

According to an employment survey of Greenwood in 1930, domestic service accounted for 38.7 percent of all black male employees and 93.2 percent of all black female employees — an astonishing 62.3 percent of all black workers. What's more, the domestic and personal service workers generated income for one of Greenwood's biggest industries — gambling. The betting was similar to the numbers game but known as the "policy wheel." It involved three drawings a day, and the operators of the wheel hired the porters, janitors, and domestic servants to sell "chances" to their white patrons. For a five-cent chance, a winner could pocket nine dollars. The "salesmen" would earn two or three dollars a day, and the operators would clear twenty to thirty dollars.

These "white" dollars were critical in helping support many black merchants; while Greenwood may have been socially and physically segregated, it was closely bound economically to white Tulsa.

Gambling was not Greenwood's only vice.

Prostitution, bootlegging, and narcotics were scattered throughout the district, and gunplay was all too common. These crimes, of course, made black Tulsa no different from white Tulsa, but Greenwood became associated with illicit or reckless behavior. When train porters announced the stop in Tulsa, they would bellow: "Tulsa, the tusk-hog town! Greenwood, the battlin' ground!" With Greenwood's many churches, it was said that on some streets "you could get the Holy Ghost on one corner and heroin on the other."

Archer Street was particularly notorious. Small hotels, with names like Carlton, DeVern, Imperial, and Midway, hung ROOMS signs on their doors. Some women solicited on street corners, but porters and bellhops also flagged down passersby and pimped for their "keen women" upstairs. Some motels had pianos in the lobby. A madam would greet a visitor, collect the fee (two or three dollars), and send him to a room. High-priced white hookers worked south of the railroad tracks at the Hotel Tulsa — ten dollars a visit.

Bootleggers sold corn whiskey or rye "moonshine" for thirty-five to fifty cents a pint, or up to two and a half dollars a gallon, and incurred no stigma. It was not unusual for bootleggers to date female teachers or for white politicians to solicit their support. There were also opium dens, speakeasies, and "choc" joints. "Choc" was Choctaw beer, a grapefruit juice–colored intoxicant made from a tree root.

Greenwood's dance halls also began playing a new form of music called jazz, which, to whites, was a uniquely African vice. Its syncopated rhythms and improvisational style bespoke a freedom of expression that alarmed that white elite, which preferred its "darkies" docile and quiet. Denunciations of jazz were loaded with racial code words, as seen in an article, "Jazz, the Evil Spirit of Music," from the *Tulsa World* on May 13, 1921: "Jazz expresses hysteria . . . It accords with a devastating volcanic spirit . . . Rhythm and musical vibrations for the half savage — voodooists like a powerful intoxicant. It shows the extreme to which human vibrations can control human nerves when improperly employed."

Greenwood did have more genuine dangers. Some black pioneers later said there were shootouts almost every night. An exaggeration, perhaps, but no one denies that disputes were often settled with guns. John Hope Franklin recalled sitting in his father's law office above a dry cleaning store when a bus stopped in front. A woman got off, unwrapped a pistol, pointed it straight into the store, and squeezed the trigger. "She was shooting at her husband," Franklin said. "I had my feet up, looking out the window, wondering if she's going to misfire and shoot upstairs." The woman missed both young John and her husband, leaving only a shattered store window in her wake.

White leaders occasionally railed against "Little Africa" or "Niggertown" as a criminal cesspool, even though many whites crossed the railroad tracks to visit its "hothouses." But the perception of Greenwood as a whore-chasing, card-dealing, moonshine-drinking, opium-smoking, jazz-playing, gun-toting district would later help rationalize assaults against it.

While vice and violence shook the community, they could not break its pillars of strength. Education, religion, and business were its cornerstones, and each had a singular institution that embodied the success and aspirations of black Tulsa.

Education was always important in Greenwood. As early as 1910, Tulsa County had the second lowest black illiteracy rate of any county in the state, and more than three fourths of black Tulsa's school-age children attended school. As its population grew, Greenwood built a high school but needed a principal. That task fell to a man who had grown up in the cotton fields of Mississippi.

Born in 1885, E. W. Woods fled the worn-out soil of Louisville, Mississippi, for Rust College in Holy Springs, where his mother sent him one dollar each Christmas for spending money. He later received a master's degree in government, then moved to Memphis to find a job. There he saw a flyer proclaiming an urgent need for "colored" teachers in a place called Oklahoma. He arrived in Greenwood in 1913, when a four-story school building had just been erected at the corner of Elgin Avenue and Easton Street. Named Booker T. Washington High School, it had fourteen students.

Woods, who wore wire-rim glasses and had a serious mien, was its principal for thirty-five years, and he commanded discipline, respect, and formality. He called each student by his or her surname, and the students called all the male teachers "professor." He insisted that youngsters use grammatical language in the halls and that they recite one hundred fifty words of poetry or passages of Shakespeare every day. He appointed "student governors" to promote leadership and responsibility, and at lunchtime, when students left the building to eat at home or in a café, he stood at his office window, arms folded, and silently watched their coming and going. Excessive socializing was not encouraged.

Woods lived in the elite section of Greenwood, in a six-room house on Detroit Avenue, near many other teachers. Educators were not only the most respected members of the community but also among the highest paid. Greenwood's doctors, lawyers, and other professionals received scant compensation because most of their clients were poor. Teachers lived in brick homes furnished with Louis XIV dining room sets, fine china, and Steinway pianos. Woods did not live lavishly — his $200 book collection was among his prized possessions — but directed his energies toward helping youngsters: he once offered $2,000 to a young woman who had just graduated to help her start a new business and to ride out a family emergency. His authority was such that young men interested in courting female students would ask his permission.

In 1919 the high school moved to a new two-story building on Haskell Street; it was bigger but still woefully underfunded. It had no cafeteria, auditorium, gym, or library; the teachers brought their own books to class. The school could not afford uniforms for the girls' basketball team, so the students bought their own material and made their outfits. To evoke their hornet mascot, one leg of their bloomers was black and the other was orange.

Despite the school's material shortcomings, two generations of students would testify that they never felt inferior because they took to heart the command of E. W. Woods: "You're as good as ninety-nine percent of the people," he would say, "and better than the rest."

As in most black communities, the churches loomed large in Greenwood, and most famous was Mount Zion Baptist Church.

Mount Zion was founded in 1909 by fifteen blacks who had left the First Baptist Church. They considered naming their new house of worship "Second Baptist Church," but chose "Mount Zion" because they did not want to be second in anything. They moved into a one-room frame school building, then proudly watched their membership grow. Like all black churches, Mount Zion operated in complete isolation from the white community, which allowed its congregants to be "more African" in their speech and manner than in any other sphere of their life. Praising the Lord was usually an intense and unhurried affair. The spirited singing, the "a-mens," and the "yes Lords" were part of the grammar of salvation, and the hymns and spirituals provided an emotional outlet, a catharsis, for the tensions produced by living in a hostile and racist world.

Mount Zion provided refuge, but it also battled injustice. The Reverend F. K. White, its pastor in 1913 and 1914, castigated white churches from the pulpit, charging, "Not one in a thousand will speak out in our defense." He noted that white ministers had cried out against imperialism and the mistreatment of immigrants but had ignored the sins of America against blacks. In time, he predicted, God would intervene and "make our defense sure."

But white abuse was not Mount Zion's biggest problem. In 1914, it was forced to vacate its building on three days' notice (church records do not say why; they simply describe this period as "the first series of dark days"). Moving into a former dance hall on North Greenwood, it soon built a white frame structure generously called a "tabernacle"; eventually it broke ground for a permanent church on the adjacent plot on Elgin Street. This new structure required years of planning and saving. The congregation began with $750.15 but ultimately managed to accumulate $42,000; the building, however, cost $92,000. Just when all hope seemed lost, a white contractor stepped forward with an unsecured loan of $50,000.

Five years after construction began, on April 4, 1921, the doors opened to "the church that faith built," as its congregants called it. The stately three-story brick structure was a symbol of Greenwood's affluence, a house of worship that blacks believed was superior to any white church in the city.

Black Tulsa's crown jewel stood at 301 North Greenwood, the Stradford Hotel.

By the time it opened on June 1, 1918, J. B. Stradford was already rich, owning fifteen rental houses, including one sixteen-room brick apartment building. He was earning more than $500 a month from rental income and other sources (more than $7,600 in 2000 dollars) — about five times what a white police officer earned and more than ten times what most blacks made. "I had amassed quite a fortune for a member of our group," he wrote in his memoirs. "I had a splendid bank account and was living on the sunny side of the street. I decided to realize my fondest hope and that was to erect a large hotel in Tulsa exclusively for blacks."

He wanted to create a property as dazzling as the Hotel Tulsa, which he described as "the finest building in the Southwest, an ornament, a marvel, a wonder, and a thing of beauty." If he could match that, it would mean that black travelers would not have to settle for inferior accommodations in Tulsa, that separate — in this case — would not mean unequal. Just as the Hotel Tulsa symbolized the new affluence and sophistication of a prairie city, the Stradford would be a "monument to the thrift, energy, and business tact of the race in Tulsa [and] to the race in the state of Oklahoma."

Financing it was not easy. Stradford ran out of money and had to secure a $20,000 loan to complete it. When it was finished, he had no money for furniture. The beds, rugs, and other items he had ordered languished in a railroad boxcar because he could not pay the $5,000 bill. After several days of negotiation, he rescued the furniture by paying one fourth on delivery and the rest in monthly installments.

The final cost of the hotel was $50,000, and it fulfilled Stradford's dream. The three-story structure, perhaps the largest of its kind owned and operated by a Negro anywhere in America, was trimmed in pressed brick above the windows and stone slabs below. It had fifty-four modern "living rooms" for overnight guests, as well as a gambling hall, a dining hall, and a saloon. To maintain its image, couples had to show proof of marriage to secure a room. Chandeliers hung from the ceilings in the lobby and banquet room, and on its opening night Stradford wrote: "The bright lights were flashing and the guests were tripping the fantastic toe."

The hotel *was* the "promised land" for Stradford, and its destruction would turn his exuberance into heartbreak.

3

Race, Rape, and the Rope

Tulsa's racial tensions mirrored the strife that had roiled the South for decades. By the 1890s the Reconstruction Era, which tried to erase all racial barriers to voting and holding office, had ended. Disenfranchisement and segregation prevailed, and the next forty years saw brutal battles between the blacks who resisted the new social order and the whites who used escalating violence to enforce it. Lynchings were the preferred instrument to crack down on "uppity" Negroes, particularly those accused of raping white women. This unholy trinity of race, rape, and the rope set off many confrontations in the South, defined an era of oppression — and, in the end, shaped the actions of Tulsa's black population on its own night of reckoning.

Between 1890 and 1930, 2,771 people were lynched, most of whom lived in the South and were black, according to the Tuskegee Institute in Alabama. Lynchings had been used for decades in the West, but what distinguished these hangings was their blending of torture and public theater. If the victim was executed by fire, the ritual included the application of a red-hot poker to his eyes and genitals, the smell of burning flesh as the body roasted over flames, the sizzling of blood. If killed by hanging, the spectacle promised convulsive movements of the limbs. Thousands of whites would watch these scenes, and the body might hang for days as a warning to other "impudent" blacks.

In 1904 the *Vicksburg Evening Post* described the lynching of a black man, accused of killing his white employer, and his wife before a thousand people in Doddsville, Mississippi:

> When the two Negroes were captured, they were tied to trees and while the funeral pyres were being prepared they were forced to suffer the most fiendish tortures. The blacks were forced to hold out their hands while one finger at a time was chopped off. The fingers were distributed as souvenirs. The ears of the murderers were cut off. Holbert was beaten severely, his skull was fractured and one of his eyes knocked out with a stick, hung by a shred from the socket . . . The most excruciating form of punishment consisted in the use of a large corkscrew in the hands of some of the mob. This instrument was bored into the flesh of the man and woman, in the arms, legs and body, and then pulled out, the spirals tearing out big pieces of raw, quivering flesh.

The newspapers in Oklahoma also reported the lynchings graphically and without judgment, sometimes noting the sale of the hangman's rope (cut into pieces) or the victim's fingers or knuckles. On June 13, 1913, in Anadarko, a black man was soaked in coal oil before being set on fire. "The Negro prayed and shrieked in agony as the flames reached his flesh," reported one paper, "but his cries were drowned out by yells and jeers of the mob." The charred body, its hands tied behind its back, was hanged from a cottonwood tree by a stream. "The mobsters made no attempt to conceal their identity . . . but there were no prosecutions," noted the *Eufaula Democrat*.

Indeed, perpetrators had little reason to fear the law. In 1921 *Harlow's Weekly*, an Oklahoma publication, wrote: "In Oklahoma among thousands of people it is not considered a crime for a mob to kill a negro . . . If the past is to be made a criterion for the future, it is perfectly safe at any time and at any place for any considerable number of men to gather, to take a [black] prisoner from the hands of an officer and inflict the penalty of death."

This mix of sadism and exhibitionism not only satisfied the blood lust of white spectators — it also sent a grisly message to the "new

Negro," whose defiance would be blamed for violence across the South, including Tulsa. The "new Negro" was the malevolent counterpart of the "old Negro," or "Sambo," whom whites invented during slavery and later romanticized in merchandise as a simple, carefree "darky" who lived in an antebellum racial utopia. The "new Negro," according to this view, lacked the civilizing restraints of slavery and was therefore regressing to a state of barbarism. Physical force was the only way to restrain him.

This alarming evolution was captured by Ben "Pitchfork" Tillman, a stem-winding senator from South Carolina, in a speech to his colleagues in 1907. Alternating racist condemnations with effusive praise for blacks, he said of his own servant, "A more loyal friend, no man ever had. Every child I had would share his last crust with that Negro tomorrow." But while the former slaves had benefited from the rigors of slavery, he thundered, their sons and daughters were "inoculated by the virus of equality" and were responsible for "all the devilment of which we read today."

He invoked the image that would haunt and obsess his region: white women in the rural South virtually besieged by black brutes who roamed without restraint. "I have three daughters," he said, "but so help me God, I had rather find either one of them killed by a tiger or a bear and gather up her bones and bury them, conscious that she had died in the purity of her maidenhood, than to have her crawl to me and tell me the horrid story that she had been robbed of the jewel of her womanhood by a black fiend."

"Rape" was rarely used by newspapers or in academic settings. "Assault" was the word used, so when a white psychologist told a symposium in 1904, "The crime of assault is the crime of the new Negro," everyone knew what he meant.

Whites homed in on rape as the ultimate expression of the blacks' supposed incapacity for self-control. Fear of such attacks conflated sexual and racial insecurities among whites and led to a pseudoscience of Negro sexual predation. As Philip A. Bruce, an influential Virginia aristocrat, wrote in *Plantation Negro as a Freeman* in 1889: "There is something strangely alluring and seductive to [Negroes] in the appearance of a white woman; they are aroused and stimulated by the foreignness to their experience of sexual pleasures, and it moves them to gratify their lust at any cost and in spite of every obstacle." The Negro rape of a white woman, Bruce wrote, was marked by "a diabolical persistence and a malignant atrocity of detail" unique even in "the natural history of the most bestial and ferocious animals . . . He is not content merely with the consummation of his purpose, but takes that fiendish delight in the degradation of his victim which he always shows when he can reek his vengeance upon one whom he has hitherto been compelled to fear."

Lynchings were a logical response to such perceived bestiality, and some whites openly advocated their use. One southern editor justified lynching a rapist, who "forever crushes the peace and joy" out of a woman, on the grounds that the sexual attack "starts the pulse of indignant manhood at fever heat, transforms the quiet citizen into the stern avenger, and sets the whole community in arms to rid the earth of the wretch who encumbers it — the fiend whose life is an offense against God and humanity." Rebecca Felton, a polemicist in Georgia who made fear of the "new Negro" a one-woman crusade, said: "The brutal lust of these half-civilized gorillas seems to be inflamed madness." In a famous speech at the Georgia State Agricultural Society in 1897, she said: "When there is not enough religion in the pulpit to organize a crusade against sin; nor justice in the courthouse to promptly punish crime, nor manhood enough in the nation to put a sheltering arm about innocence and virtue — if it needs lynching to protect woman's dearest possession from the ravening human beasts — then I say lynch, a thousand times a week, if necessary."

The final phrase — "a thousand times a week, if necessary" — was repeated endlessly in press reports. So great was the fear of black men menacing white women that the mere proximity of the two was considered unacceptable. In 1921 an Oklahoma congressman named Charles Carter sent a letter to President Harding protesting the suggested appointment of a black to be the registrar of the Treasury Department, which had long been a patronage job for Negroes. That had to change, the *Tulsa Tribune* reported, "because Carter pointed out that there are now 500 young white women employed in the office [while earlier] it had only seven or eight employees."

In November 1898 the tinderbox of white sexual fears, black empowerment, and politics was lit in Wilmington, North Carolina.

For some years, Wilmington's blacks had used their numerical superiority to exercise genuine political power and occupied a number of city offices. In the months leading up to the November election, racial tensions were inflamed by Alexander Manly, the outspoken black publisher of a crusading newspaper. Manly wrote an editorial questioning the moral character of white women and charging that some used the "rape allegation" to mask private affairs. Many white women, he wrote, "are not any more particular in the matter of clandestine meetings with colored men than are the white men with colored women . . . You cry aloud for the virtue of your women, when you seek to destroy the morality of us. Don't think ever that your women will remain pure while you are debauching ours. You sow the seed — the harvest will come in due time."

In fact, the harvest did come, but not as the black firebrand anticipated. On election day, November 8, Wilmington's Democratic Party captured the elections through fraud and by openly threatening blacks with violence. "Go to the polls tomorrow," Colonel Alfred Moore Waddell, a Confederate veteran, yelled to a crowd the evening before the vote, "and if you find a Negro out voting, tell him to leave the polls, and if he refuses, kill him."

The Democrats, however, were not satisfied by their victory. Two days later, white vigilantes burned Manly's printing press, then marched into a black neighborhood called Brooklyn. Armed with repeating rifles and rapid-fire guns, they outgunned the black men who tried to defend their homes with antique revolvers and shotguns, and that night, hundreds of black women and children huddled in the swamps outside Wilmington. An estimated 1,400 blacks fled in the next thirty days, including Manly. Nobody knows how many died — fourteen were readily confirmed, while some whites boasted of ninety dead and some blacks said more than three hundred.

As the first major race riot after Reconstruction, the Wilmington massacre foreshadowed similar battles over the next twenty-five years. Clearly, rape fever was not the only catalyst for these outbursts.

Class warfare also played a role, as upper-class whites found common cause with frenzied rednecks who competed with blacks for jobs and housing. Race riots occurred not only in southern cities like New Orleans (1900) and Atlanta (1906) but also in the North, where Springfield, Ohio (1904), Chicago (1905 and 1919), and Springfield, Illinois (1907), all saw battles. A full-fledged pogrom erupted in July of 1917 in East St. Louis, Illinois, where two square blocks of shanties went up in flames, whites roamed downtown in search of more victims, and mangled black corpses bobbed in the Mississippi River. An estimated thirty-nine blacks and eight whites were killed. Four weeks later, between 8,000 and 10,000 well-dressed blacks marched in protest down Fifth Avenue in New York to the steady roll of muffled drums carried by several men in the lead. A child's sign read: MOTHER, DO LYNCHERS GO TO HEAVEN?

Each riot was unique, but they followed a similar pattern. As blacks asserted their rights, restive whites grew alarmed. Then some catalyst, often a newspaper article tapping into sexual fears, would trigger a furious response by whites. A battle would ensue, the black district would be invaded, the state militia would restore the peace, and the final casualty count would be disputed.

The most significant riot during this period happened on September 22, 1906, in Atlanta, the de facto capital of the New South. During a heated gubernatorial race, four local newspapers used incendiary language in discussing race and politics, and daily headlines blared rumors of black men "assaulting" white women. Seeking economic opportunities, blacks had been moving to the city from the countryside, but the migration stirred fears among whites about an imagined "Negro uprising." Fighting soon broke out. White crowds stopped cars and dragged out and beat black passengers. Black-owned businesses were gutted, proprietors pummeled. Much of the black district was laid waste by burning and looting. An estimated twenty-six people were killed, including one white, and two hundred were seriously injured.

Rushing to the city by train to protect his wife and daughter was W.E.B. Du Bois, the brilliant activist for civil rights (and the first black man to earn a Ph.D. from Harvard). His family was not hurt in the riot, but in one article, "Litany of Atlanta," Du Bois wrote: "A city lay in travail, God our Lord, and from her loins sprang twin Murder and Black Hate . . . And all this was to sate the greed of greedy men who hide behind the veil of vengeance!"

As the riot's devastation became widely known, blacks began to reject the accommodationist doctrine of Booker T. Washington, whose acquiescence to segregation and disenfranchisement was captured in his famous "Atlanta Compromise" speech of 1895. "In all things that are purely social, we can be as separate as the fingers," he said, "yet one as a hand in all things essential to mutual progress." Washington believed political conciliation would lead to economic progress and educational opportunities, but the Atlanta riot shattered that myth for many blacks and directed support to Du Bois's alternate vision that African Americans resist abuse and discrimination. The ascendance of Du Bois as America's leading black voice — Washington would die in 1915 — struck fear in whites, who rightfully anticipated spectacular acts of black resistance against white domination.

As Du Bois's biographer David Levering Lewis wrote: "There was bitter justice in the fact that the Atlanta Compromise of 1895 would end in the Atlanta riot of 1906. In the Gresham's law of New South race relations, the 'good nigger,' loyal and understanding, would cease to exist almost overnight, supplanted by the 'bad nigger,' criminal and sexually barbarous."

The ethos of white supremacy was found throughout American life. D. W. Griffith's 1915 film, *The Birth of a Nation*, glorified the long-defunct Ku Klux Klan and depicted the supine South as ruled by corrupt black legislators, its women menaced by rape. The movie caused a sensation. After seeing it in Lafayette, Indiana, a white patron shot a black teenage boy to death. In Houston, audiences shrieked, "Lynch him!" during one climactic chase scene. President Wilson saw it at the White House and said it was "like writing history with lighting [and] all so terribly true."

Racist polemics and literature were also on the rise. In 1916 Madison Grant, a lawyer and eugenics enthusiast in New York, captured the fancy of middlebrow America with his book *The Passing of the*

Great Race. He breathlessly warned that the teeming masses from Asia and Africa as well as the mixing of races, or "mongrelization," had created "the supreme crisis of the ages." He also disclosed that "negroes have demonstrated throughout recorded time that they do not possess the potentiality of progress or the initiative from within." Another work referred to black Americans as "ten million malignant cancers [which] gnaw the vitals of our body politic."

This period also saw the return of the Ku Klux Klan, which was reconstituted in 1915, partly in response to *The Birth of a Nation.* Unlike its Reconstruction forerunner, created to intimidate carpetbaggers and Negroes, the new Klan fused white supremacy with a hellfire nativism and the defense of Protestant Christianity, turning a purely racist organization into an anti-immigrant, anti-Semitic, and anti-Catholic one as well. While the original Klan was a regional order, its successor was national, with "klaverns" established from Maine to California. While tapping into the fear of "uppity Negroes," the Secret Order was now a moneymaking scheme as well, with membership dues and services, such as insurance benefits, enriching the founders.

World War I brought some calm to race relations as Du Bois urged blacks to "close ranks" behind the American war effort. Blacks hoped that members of their race who fought for democracy in Europe would receive equal treatment at home; indeed, many Negro veterans who were treated with dignity in France demanded that same respect in their own country. But those very demands, in conjunction with a rash of nationwide labor strikes and panic roused by the Bolshevik revolution, turned the years immediately after the war into the worst period of racial strife in the nation's history. In the "red summer" of 1919, a wave of homicides, arson, mayhem, and organized racial conflict swept up from Charleston, South Carolina, to Washington, D.C., across the country to Chicago, dipping down into Knoxville, Tennessee, and then rolling over to Omaha, Nebraska. Dozens of communities were convulsed by blood-soaked riots, none worse than Elaine, Arkansas, where on September 30 a black sharecroppers' meeting in a church was broken up by police gunfire. The sharecroppers, organizing to join a progressive farmers' alliance, fired back. After a deputy sheriff was killed and several whites were injured, enraged white planters chased down black men and women in the high cotton of Phillips County; at least twenty-five blacks were killed and a thousand or more black men were packed into a stockade. After a rapid-fire grand jury indictment, twelve men were sentenced to hang (although their executions were stayed); the rest received prison sentences, their alleged crime conspiring to seize control of the county by armed force.

In 1919 seventy-six black men and women were lynched — eighteen more than in the previous year — most of them from the rural South.

Whites blamed the onslaught on ill-mannered Negroes. As the *Shreveport* (Louisiana) *Times* wrote in 1919: "We venture to say that fully ninety percent of all race troubles in the South are the result of the Negro forgetting his place. If the black man will stay where he belongs, act like a Negro should act, work like a Negro should work, talk like a Negro should talk, study like a Negro should study, there will be very few riots, fights, or clashes."

As the devastation mounted, black newspapers responded with escalating rhetoric. The *Chicago Defender*, for example, was widely distributed in the South, including Oklahoma, to encourage blacks to move to the newspaper's home, and it mixed sensationalism and fact. When Chicago itself rioted for a week in 1919, the paper published what appeared to be a box score of the dead and injured, tabulating whites in one column and Negroes in another. The display was viewed as encouraging the blacks to even the score. The riot's final death tally was at least fifteen whites and twenty-three blacks, with many more injured.

Blacks viewed their resistance, even when crushed, as a sign of pride and strength. "The Negro is breaking his shell and beginning to bask in the sunlight of real manhood," exulted the *Whip*, a black weekly in Chicago. Added *Challenge Magazine* in October of 1919: "America hates, lynches, enslaves us not because we are black, but because we are weak . . . When the mob comes, whether with torch or with gun, let us stand at Armageddon and battle for the Lord."

No one wrote more passionately than Du Bois in *Crisis*, a monthly publication. In 1918, referring to a Houston riot that saw thirteen black soldiers from the Twenty-fourth Infantry Regiment summarily executed, he wrote: "We raise our clenched hands against the thousands of white murderers, rapists, and scoundrels who have oppressed, killed, ruined, robbed and debased their black fellow men and fellow women, and yet, today, walk scot-free, unwhipped of justice, uncondemned by millions of their white fellow citizens, and unrebuked by the president of the United States."

On the heels of the "red summer" of 1919, he openly advocated armed confrontation: "To-day we raise the terrible weapon of Self-Defense. When the murderer comes, he shall no longer strike us in the back. When the armed lyncher gathers, we too must gather armed. When the mob moves, we propose to meet it with bricks and clubs and guns."

4

Mob Justice

IN THE EARLY HOURS of October 29, 1917, a bomb exploded at the home of a wealthy oilman in Tulsa, demolishing the front porch and a front wall. In the screaming headlines of the extra editions of local newspapers, the city's chief of police declared that the blast was the beginning of a campaign by the Industrial Workers of the World, a radical labor group, to dynamite the homes of the city's leading oilmen. This dire prediction never came true, but the explosion led to an act of mob vigilantism that signaled a dangerous new turn in Tulsa's brand of frontier justice.

The years during and immediately after World War I saw a confluence of events that brought tensions in Tulsa to a boil. Labor troubles, Bolshevism, recession, black empowerment, crime, corruption — all fueled civic unrest and contributed to fears that white Tulsans were losing control of their city. The response was dramatic displays of punishment against alleged wrongdoers, a crackdown delivered not by the police or other agents of the law but by ruthless vigilantes. Mob justice, swift, illegal, and at times lethal, confirmed that the city's officials no longer maintained law and order.

J. Edgar Pew, the vice president of the Carter Oil Company, a subsidiary of Standard Oil, was a fitting target for a left-wing organization. Fortunately, he, his wife, and their son escaped the blast unharmed, and suspicions immediately centered on the IWW. An official with the group who worked in the oil fields was promptly arrested but later released, pending an investigation.

The "Wobblies" represented not a racial but an economic threat. Suspected of fomenting labor strife, they were already subject to a nationwide hunt by the federal government. One month before the bombing of Pew's home, one hundred sixty IWW leaders had been indicted in Chicago for interfering with the war effort.

The Wobblies had recently established a new district headquarters in Tulsa, and the city feared that the socialist organization was taking its first steps to organize the oil workers in the Mid-Continent field. Strikes had already shackled the Louisiana and Texas fields and, in theory, could paralyze Oklahoma oil, which was Tulsa's lifeblood and essential for the war effort. A month before the bombing, the Tulsa police had raided the IWW's new offices, so it was easy for people to believe that the organization had now exacted revenge by striking an oil executive's home. The *Tulsa World*, an unabashed advocate of capitalism and the war, was particularly strident in attacking the Wobblies. Claiming to have received four letters from them that promised "the destruction of capitalist newspapers," the *World* urged vigilante solutions, editorializing two days after the bombing: "Right here is a good place to disagree with the statement, frequently expressed by Oklahoma editors, that the IWW's and other pro-Hun individuals should 'leave the country.' As a matter of fact, there is no place for them to go. The only relief is a wholesale application of concentration camps. Or, what is hemp worth now, the long foot?"

Such rabble-rousing agitated a community already on edge. The previous day, two hundred "home guards," members of a local militia, were sworn in as police officers at the Chamber of Commerce and offered an armed truck by the Ford Motor Company. The mayor warned all children to stay off the streets after 9 P.M. The newly deputized force fanned out into the hills in search of Wobblies but returned empty-handed.

One week after the bombing and with their leads fading, the police returned to the one place they knew they could find Wobblies — their district office, in the New Fox Building on Brady Street. Eleven men were arrested and charged with vagrancy, and some antiwar literature was seized. The police gathered several more suspects and vowed to arrest anyone they found near the building. A trial was held for several days in the packed municipal courtroom. One defendant, the local secretary of the IWW, was asked about his views on the government. "We are not interested in that," he said. "We are interested in raising wages." Another defendant, a pipeline worker, said that eighteen years earlier he had earned three dollars a day, and he still earned the same amount.

The *World*, outraged at the legal proprieties of the courtroom, once again advocated lynching in an editorial, "Get Out the Hemp": "A knowledge of how to tie a knot that will stick will come in handy in a few days . . . Kill 'em as you would kill any kind of snake. Don't scotch 'em; kill 'em. And kill 'em dead."

Judge T. D. Evans found all eleven defendants guilty, fined them $100 apiece, and sentenced them to jail. He also had six defense witnesses tried on the spot, declared guilty, and sentenced. But the judge struck a deal with the defendants: he withdrew their penalties in exchange for their promise to leave the city the following morning. At 11 P.M., the prisoners were taken from the jail, placed in police cars with an officer at each wheel, and driven toward IWW headquarters. They never got there.

Just after passing the Frisco tracks on Boulder Avenue, a group of men wearing black cowls and black masks jumped from behind a pile of bricks with leveled rifles and revolvers and ordered the drivers to stop. Accounts vary on whether the police stayed in the cars or left, but either way they offered no resistance. The robed men tied the prisoners' hands and feet, stood on the running boards, and trained their weapons on their captives as the cars drove on. After traveling two blocks, they were met by six more cars carrying black-clad confederates. They called themselves the Knights of Liberty, although the *World* described them as the "modern Ku Klux Klan."

They drove to a lonely ravine northwest of Tulsa, which was illuminated by a fire and the headlights of automobiles drawn in a circle. One by one, the ropes were taken from the prisoners' wrists, which were then tied to a big tree. A "knight" stepped forward and lashed the victim's back until blood ran. Then another "knight" stepped up with a whitewash brush and a pot of boiling tar and applied it to the lacerated back. Brown and white feathers followed.

One prisoner, an older man, pleaded: "I have lived here for eighteen years and have raised a large family. I am not an IWW. I am as patriotic as any man here." He too was whipped. But several prisoners defiantly proclaimed their allegiance to the Wobblies, including one man, J. F. Ryan, who had testified at length about the group's political philosophy. He was whipped twice, the second time forcing the hot tar into his open wounds.

After the last man was whipped, the leading "knight" said, "Let this be a warning to all IWW's to never come through Tulsa again. Now, get!"

The half-naked men scurried through barbed wire and undergrowth as pistol and rifle shots whizzed over their heads. Three hours later, they found refuge in a cabin where a sympathizer helped clean their wounds. Later that evening, printed signs appeared throughout Tulsa, including the train station, telephone poles, and the door of the lawyer who defended the men. They read: NOTICE TO IWW'S: DON'T LET THE SUN SET ON YOU IN TULSA. — VIGILANCE COMMITTEE.

The assault won broad public support. If anything, it fell short of the *World*'s desired lynching, although the paper was satisfied with the result. Describing the Knights of Liberty as a "patriotic body," it wrote: "As regrettable as the deportation of some very persistent and incorrigible agitators may seem, it may yet prove a deterrent to any ambitious souls anxious to follow their example." The *Democrat* offered this endorsement: "The peace officers can do almost nothing to prevent these depredations on the oil industry, and the men of the oil fields — the loyal Americans — must take the matter into their own hands."

But the view that the police officers were helpless was clearly wrong. They could have defended the prisoners — that was their job — and the accompanying officers were surely armed. It is even more likely that they were in league with the "knights," who knew precisely when and where to hijack the motorcade. One victim later said he saw extra black gowns and masks in the jail and that the chief of police was not only at the scene of the beating but was the one counting off the blows.

In any case, the authorities took no action against the vigilantes. The police made no arrests, and the city attorney concluded that he was powerless to proceed with the case because "it was not covered by any city ordinance."

The flaying did succeed in closing the IWW hall on Brady Street, although no one was ever convicted for bombing the Pew home. And the Knights of Liberty never appeared in public again except toward the end of a bond drive to help finance the war effort, when they silently marched down the street one evening with banners that warned "slackers" to "get busy." The campaign surpassed its goal in twenty-four hours.

Three years later, a carjacking led to another act of mob violence, and while it was not a racial incident, it did shake Tulsa's black community.

On the evening of August 21, 1920, a Saturday, a white taxi driver named Homer Nida picked up two men and a woman outside the Hotel Tulsa and began driving to Red Fork, where the passengers said they would be attending a dance. As he drove on the Tulsa–Sapulpa Highway, Nida became suspicious of his passengers and pulled his large Hudson into a Sinclair gas station, where he hid some money he was carrying. Back on the highway, just as the lights of Red Fork became visible, one of the men clubbed Nida on the head with the barrel of a revolver. Nida keeled over, the car swerved, and the woman in the back seat covered her face. A crash was averted, however, when another passenger grabbed the wheel. Nida was then yanked into the back seat. The new driver sped past the Red Fork dance hall at such a clip that Nida begged him to slow down or else they would be "pinched" by a police car. He also pleaded for his life, telling his captors to take his car and his money. But about a mile and a half past Red Fork, near an oil company's tank farm, the man with the gun pointed it at Nida and fired into his stomach. His body straightened like a knife, then bent over. Nida was shoved out the door and left to die on a dark road.

It could have been just another carjacking and murder in the midst of a crime wave. The city's economic boom created opportunities for everyone, including bootleggers, robbers, and other law-breakers, who used whatever means, including violence, to cash in, and neither the police nor the courts could do anything about them.* But this case proved different because, remarkably, Nida was found alive by a garage owner in Red Fork, who rushed him to a hospital in Tulsa. There he related his living nightmare to the police.

The crime mesmerized Tulsa. In front-page stories, the two white newspapers recounted the harrowing incident and described the brave victim's struggle to survive. Homer Nida was a recently married everyman, twenty-five years old, who symbolized the helplessness of a city under siege. Notwithstanding the clumsy execution of the crime, the police called it "the arch murder plot of this city." It was also covered by a black weekly, the *Tulsa Star.*

The day after the shooting, a slender white eighteen-year-old named Roy Belton caught a ride from Tulsa to Nowata, about fifty miles away. When one of the passengers read aloud the *Tulsa Tribune*'s account of the hijacking, Belton boasted that he knew the woman involved and had even overheard her discuss the crime. The passengers noticed a revolver in his pocket and grew suspicious. When they reached Nowata, they alerted the police, who arrested Belton and returned him to Tulsa.

Belton was taken to Nida's hospital bed, where the driver identified him as the shooter. Belton insisted he had spent Saturday evening with Marie Harmon, a white woman in her twenties. The police found Harmon, who confessed she had been in Nida's cab with Belton and a second man, and said Belton had pulled the trigger. The following day Belton reportedly confessed, but claimed the shooting was an accident.

As these sensational developments were splashed across the front page, Belton knew he was in jeopardy. Locked in the jail on the top floor of the county courthouse, he asked for assurances that he would not be subjected to mob violence. But by Thursday, five days after the shooting, Sheriff James Woolley had heard rumors that the courthouse might be overrun if Nida died, so he posted two extra

* In May 1921, the state legislature assigned two additional judges to Tulsa County, but the effort made little impact. There were more than 6,000 cases awaiting adjudication.

armed guards to protect Belton. On the following day, the *Tribune* ran a rare front-page photograph of Belton, whose smooth face and dark pompadour suggested teenage rebellion. The headline declared that Belton "plans to escape on plea of insanity" and that his "wealthy sister" was coming to help him at his trial.

By Friday night, Homer Nida began to weaken. He asked his wife for ice cream and ice water and pleaded to be taken home, where he was confident he would recover. But the next morning he died. Later that day, Belton was arraigned in court and pleaded not guilty to first-degree murder charges. Nida's widow told the *Tribune:* "I hope that justice will be done, for they have taken an innocent life and ruined my happiness. They deserve to be mobbed but the other way is better."

That evening, with thunder rumbling across the sky and the ground damp from recent rain, a small group of armed men quietly gathered south of downtown. A half hour later the men, some with handkerchiefs over their face, drove to the courthouse. Word quickly spread, and the crowd swelled to a thousand people. Some of the masked men entered the courthouse, confronted Sheriff Woolley at gunpoint, and demanded that he turn Belton over to them. The sheriff tried to resist.

"Let the law take its place, boys," he said. "The electric chair will get him before long."

But the intruders disarmed Woolley, pushed him upstairs, and commanded that he instruct the guards to release Belton. Ignoring the other two prisoners, they hustled Belton out of the courthouse, shouting, "We got him, boys! We got him!"

The prisoner's hands were tied, and he was placed in Nida's cab, which had been stolen from the authorities. About a dozen cars drove through the streets, and a line of hundreds of vehicles soon formed. The procession headed out of town, its headlights dotting the road for nearly a mile. When police cars reached the scene, all they could do was follow the mob.

After twenty minutes, the cars reached a desolate road in Jenks, about nine miles south of Tulsa. Beneath faint moonlight, the spectators left their vehicles and moved slowly forward, some chanting "Rope, rope." Belton was escorted to a large sign as several gunshots were fired into the air "to add glamour to the procession," the *World* noted. A long piece of quarter-inch rope was brought forward. With the prisoner standing motionless, the noose was tied.

"Does that aggravate you any?" one man asked as he slipped the rope over Belton's head.

There was no reply.

As the crowd surged forward, men with rifles and guns tried to keep them back, receiving help from an improbable source. At least two uniformed police officers were also trying to keep the mob under control, creating the bizarre scene of cops trying to maintain law and order at an illegal lynching. One report said the police directed traffic. And the *Tribune* noted, "For perhaps the first time in history [a city] was presented with the spectacle of the written law's guardians acting tacitly in co-operation with a lynch law mob."

The rope was thrown over the top of the sign.

"What are the last words you want to say?"

"I'm innocent," Belton said calmly. The rope was pulled taut. The victim's legs drew up quickly to his chest, then dropped. The crowd stood in silence as the body hung motionless. The noose was cut eleven minutes after it had been tightened, and Roy Belton was pronounced dead.

The mob approached, yelling and rushing for the body. Belton's shoes and trousers were ripped off as hundreds tried to snare bits of clothing for souvenirs. Late arrivals grabbed at the almost-nude form. The rope was sold for fifty cents an inch.

Governor James A. Robertson condemned the lynching, apparently Tulsa's first, and sought to oust Sheriff Woolley for failing to protect the prisoner. A grand jury investigation ensued, but no indictments were issued and no public officials were reprimanded. The *World* attacked the governor for contributing to the general lawlessness by his "pardoning orgy" of various defendants. It then called the lynching "a righteous protest" by "a citizenship outraged by government inefficiency, and a too tender regard for the professional criminal." The *Tribune* noted that "lynch law is never justified" but assailed the courts and "our high officials" instead of the executioners. Sheriff Woolley called the hanging "a black eye on Tulsa" but felt the noose had a silver lining. "I believe that Belton's lynching will prove more beneficial than a death sentence pronounced by the courts," he said. "It shows to the criminal that Tulsa men mean business."

The most telling remark came from the new police chief, John A. Gustafson, who believed the hanging was inevitable. "I do not condone mob law," he said, "but Tulsa has a peculiar situation and the sentiment here is not so prejudiced against this kind of lynching."

There was, however, at least one public dissenter — A. J. Smitherman, editor of the *Star,* who understood what the lynching meant for the black community. If a frenzied mob could kidnap a white prisoner, hang him, and win plaudits for the effort, then no African American in custody would ever be safe, particularly if charged with a brutal offense. "There is no crime, however atrocious, that justifies mob violence," Smitherman wrote. "The lynching of Roy Belton explodes the theory that a prisoner is safe on top of the Court House from mob violence." In an editorial later that year, he made it clear that blacks should not be idle if one of their own faced mob justice: "It is quite evident that the proper time to afford protection to any prisoner is *before* and not during the time he is being lynched."

Even before Belton's lynching, blacks had realized that Negro prisoners were not safe in police custody. In March 1919, three black men were arrested and incarcerated for shooting a white ironworker. As rumors of a race riot spread, a group of armed blacks, reported between fifteen and seventy-five, went to the city jail to investigate the status of the prisoners. A tense conversation ensued, but a deal was brokered that allowed a delegation of blacks to visit the prisoners and confirm their safety. There were no lynchings and no riots, but the encounter was extraordinary for the taboos it broke — armed blacks crossing the invisible race line of the city, entering white Tulsa, and making a demand. The *Tribune* would later describe the event as "an armed invasion."

In 1920 the new police chief, Gustafson, was charged with reorganizing the department, cracking down on vice rings, and driving out violent criminals. "If I fail, I'll resign," he boldly pledged. But Gustafson, a Swedish American with thinning dark hair and a high forehead, was a peculiar choice to run the department. He had been on the Tulsa police force in 1916 but was discharged for "unwarranted actions." Otherwise, he worked in the shadowy business of private security, running his own agency at the same time he was the police chief. Tulsa County's new sheriff, Willard McCullough, complained to the city commissioners about Gustafson, saying that he had been connected with the underworld for his entire career and had only worked with "snitches and crooks." The sheriff predicted he would have only those kind of men on his force, "which would be a menace to the city of Tulsa."

Gustafson, at forty-six, inherited an undisciplined, demoralized force of fifty-five, which included two blacks who patrolled Greenwood. In 1919 half the force went on strike, demanding higher wages. After three weeks, the city raised officers' salaries to $125 a month from $110, and the walkout ended. "Not to be outdone, the prisoners in the city jail also went on strike," wrote Ronald Trekell in a friendly history of the department. "One by one, each of the fifteen prisoners went out of the back window and escaped into the night leaving the city bastille empty." Indeed, prisoners often escaped by chipping mortar away from the steel bars.

In March 1921 Gustafson fired more than a dozen officers for various offenses, including unnecessary violence against a prisoner, intoxication, sleeping on the job, and insubordination. Two officers were discharged for "holding up" a couple of boys, and a clerk was dismissed for inaccurate reports. The corruption, dissolution, and racism of the department, including the new chief, came to light in a subsequent state investigation, which included the testimony of W. H. Clark, the "police matron" of the department beginning in May 1920.

When she went to the jail on New Year's Day of 1921, she saw the chief of detectives, James Patton, having sex with a female prisoner. This was not unusual. Another female prisoner told Clark she was pregnant with an officer's child. A third woman, detained for the immigration authorities in Canada, was allowed to come and go as she pleased, by orders of Chief Gustafson, because she went out with a different officer each night.

Clark reported that confiscated liquor was never destroyed but placed in a vault and carried away by the officers. A woman who was arrested on charges of drunkenness and disorderly conduct said she bought her whiskey from a police captain. Prisoners who made long-distance calls gave their money to the chief's secretary, who pocketed the coins and charged the calls to the department.

The women inmates had no place to bathe, had no clean mattresses, and were subject to harassment; the black maids who worked in the jail were physically abused. Clark recounted Detective Patton's tirade at the female prisoner from Canada who was arguing with a black woman. "Shut up!" he screamed. "You are not as good as a nigger; all these sons-of-bitching foreigners ought to be killed." Cursing the prisoner further, he told her not to run or he'd shoot her. The inmate was so badly shaken that Clark had to call a physician to calm her, but the police matron figured she got off lightly.

"I know of an occasion," she testified, "where [Patton] whipped a Negro woman with rubber tubing."

Clark's repeated complaints to Gustafson and the police commissioner, an elected official, were ignored, and she left in February 1921, after nine months on the job. Three months later, the mayor called a "court of inquiry" to investigate charges that the police overlooked gambling, prostitution, and bootlegging, but the inquiry concluded that "open vice" did not take place in Tulsa. IMPEACHMENT OF POLICE FALLS FLAT, said a *World* headline.

The police department, inept, corrupt, racist, and misogynist, was redeemed, but it would not survive its next test.

No one railed against crime and corruption more than Richard Lloyd Jones, a swashbuckling journalist who in 1919 moved from Wisconsin to Tulsa and purchased the *Democrat*. He renamed it the *Tribune* and turned it into a sensational, scandalmongering publication of corny gimmicks, moral rectitude, and arrogant provocation.

The six-foot-tall Jones cut a striking figure. At forty-six, he had wavy brown hair, a ruggedly handsome face, and a well-groomed bearing; he changed his white dress shirts in the middle of hot days to ensure he always looked his best. He was the son of an eminent Unitarian minister in Chicago, and each Saturday he wrote a "sermonette" in the *Tribune* along the lines of "Greatness," "Peace," "Compassion," and "Love." He had never learned how to type, so he dictated his editorials with his stentorian voice, pacing the floor, angrily jutting his jaw, and pounding a table to make a point. In daily homage to Western civilization, his editorials quoted from the likes of Plato, Cato, Cicero, Emerson, Jefferson, Lincoln, Daniel Webster, and Henry Ward Beecher.

But Jones's news coverage more closely resembled that of a tabloid. Page 1 consisted of banner headlines about murders, lynchings, carjackings, and vice, as well as chronicles of Jones's own battles with the high and mighty. He wrote editorials castigating Governor Robertson, calling him a "pious and self-righteous public-minded man who has played intimately with and for the [unscrupulous] politicians." The governor dashed off a short letter from the capitol in Oklahoma City, saying that the editorial was a "great injustice" and urging Jones to see him personally and make a correction. Jones printed his response on the *Tribune's* front page. It began: "Your imperious telegram received."

In his first two months, Jones accused theater owners of running "crime-breeding reels" that produced lawless behavior and called on them to melt the wax dummies of desperadoes set up outside each theater to attract customers. The owners, stung by the attack, withdrew their advertising. Jones was also a strident critic of Mayor T. D. Evans, who served from 1920 to 1922. Jones's friend and patron, Charles Page, opposed Evans on a major water project for Tulsa, and Jones appeared to be criticizing the mayor on behalf of Page. He hired an investigative reporter to write stories on corruption in city hall under the mysterious byline "Investigator X," and he assailed the police for its "long record of being conspicuously incompetent." When the 1921 "court of inquiry" exonerated the police department, the publisher wrote an editorial, "Whitewashed." He also received a number of bomb threats; after one, he signed a front-page editorial: "We have edited this paper behind the typewriter. We can, and if need be WE WILL, edit this paper behind the typewriter AND THE GUN."

Jones liked publicity stunts as well. To boost early circulation, he sponsored a beauty pageant and paid a hundred dollars in gold to the winner. Three hundred women entered; the *Tribune* slowly whittled down the field, and many photographs were published. RACE NARROWS, HOUSEWIVES, TYPISTS LEAD, said a headline. The winner, Irene Moise, was a raven-haired stenographer. "She hardly ever hits the wrong key," her employer told the *Tribune.*

This rollicking style increased paid circulation, which in the twelve-month period ending in March 1921 rose by 45 percent, to 27,149. The gain was front-page news.

If Jones embodied the cosmopolitan aspirations of the city's elite, he also reflected its deplorable attitude on race. He did not write much about racial issues, but his editorials revealed his xenophobic and white supremacist attitudes. He opposed the admission of Hawaii to the Union because it had too many "Orientals." America, he once wrote, had "always helped the world's incompetent people," specifically those in India, China, and Japan. Locally, Jones defended the Ku Klux Klan; on Christmas of 1921, when the Secret Order was making inroads into Tulsa, he wrote: "There are many noble-minded men working in the KKK, believing that the failure of public officials warrants drastic action . . . In this they are right . . . The KKK of Tulsa has promised to do the American thing in the American way." This support came in handy several months later when the Klan threw a force of men around Jones's home to guard it against a bomb scare.

In the early years of the *Tribune,* the news pages mostly ignored the city's Negroes and wrote of them only in terms of their incompetence, inferiority, or criminality. Brief articles appeared about blacks, often from other parts of the state or country, who were lynched, arrested, drunk, or divorced. But when word spread of a possible crime involving a black man and a white woman in Tulsa itself, a great story beckoned.

II. The Riot

When Hell Broke Loose

O N MAY 30, 1921, Memorial Day, the heavy morning rains in Tulsa reflected the holiday's sobriety. Hundreds gathered in cars or in the entrances of buildings along Main Street, and at 10 A.M. policemen on motorcycles led a procession of cars draped with American flags and bunting, followed by doughboys who still fit into their uniforms and schoolchildren bearing flowers. A band played martial music, and a tractor pulled a flag-draped casket. The spectators cheered, and after the parade, a cortege drove to a memorial service at Rose Hill Memorial Park Cemetery, where a bugle played taps, gunshots were fired to salute the dead, and a male quartet sang old army songs.

A collapse in the city's chief industry had made these days difficult. A year before, oil had sold at three dollars a barrel, but, owing to Mexican imports and a production glut, the price had now sunk to one dollar. Unemployment was high, and according to one estimate, 60 percent of the Oklahoma oil industry had been shut down. Tulsa had risen from the prairie to serve the oilmen, so a downturn affected even the affluent neighborhoods. "Every third house in Maple Ridge and Sunset had a For Sale sign on it," the *Tulsa World* later wrote.

The holiday festivities gave Tulsans a respite on the last weekend before the wealthier families departed for cooler climates. When the rain finally cleared, the temperature spiked to a humid ninety degrees, but downtown remained busy. A new motion picture, *The Passion Flower,* was showing at the Strand, and the Lyric had a matinee.

Though the streets were crowded with office workers and shoppers, it is unlikely that anyone gave Dick Rowland a second thought when he walked into the Drexel Building at 319 South Main, a nondescript four-story structure wedged between two other office buildings. Rowland headed for the elevator and stumbled into history.

At nineteen, Rowland was a light brown, well-built African American who had dropped out of high school and shined shoes at a downtown pool hall on Third and Main. His outgoing personality was well suited for a job that prized hustle and personal service. Shines cost only a dime, but the tips were good for bootblacks like Rowland, who would deliver the finished shoes to businessmen. On his own, Rowland often turned heads in Greenwood. He wore handmade suits, flashed wads of cash, and sported a diamond ring, earning him the nickname "Diamond Dick." Notwithstanding his pretensions, he was a minor figure in the community.

The largest tenant in the Drexel Building was Renberg's, a stylish men's clothing store stocked with silk suits and gabardine trousers; the building also held business offices, although some of them, and probably even Renberg's, were closed on Memorial Day. The building had one other important feature — one of the few bathrooms downtown available to blacks, a dirty cubicle designated Colored Restroom on the top floor, accessible by an elevator in the rear. On this day, the elevator operator was Sarah Page, a white seventeen-year-old who, after a divorce, had recently moved to Tulsa from Kansas City. Rowland entered the elevator, either to deliver a pair of shoes or simply to use the bathroom.

At some point thereafter, Page screamed. A white clerk inside the building raced to the elevator as Rowland fled, and the clerk summoned the police. Exactly what happened between Page and Rowland, two teens from different worlds on the same rickety elevator, has been a source of endless speculation. Some have said the two were lovers who had a fight. Others have said she was a prostitute and he was her pimp. Or, in the most widely accepted version of events, the two were simply strangers who had an honest mishap:

when the poorly built elevator did not stop on the same level as the floor, Rowland tripped against Page, and when he grabbed her arm to apologize, she screamed.

What is known is that the police were notified that Dick Rowland had tried to sexually assault Sarah Page. The police, however, were skeptical. If they believed that a black man had tried to rape a white woman, they would have launched a sweeping manhunt. But no such dragnet took place, no urgent commands were issued, and by day's end no arrests had been made.

In his 1946 master's thesis on the riot, Loren Gill interviewed the police commissioner at the time of the incident, James M. Adkison, and the police captain, George Blaine. Gill wrote of the allegation that the police "were quietly conducting an investigation," but they "did not attach sufficient importance to the event to file the name of the girl." Indeed, common sense alone should have cast doubt on the rape claim. Only a black man with a death wish would try to rape a white girl in broad daylight inside a downtown office building on a major thoroughfare of a bustling city.

But it was Tulsa, and the mere hint of black-on-white rape, however flimsy the evidence, could trigger a deadly reaction. By the following morning, another warm day, when the Rotary Club was scheduled to meet at 12:10 P.M. at the Hotel Tulsa and hundreds were going back to work, the city was buzzing about the incident. Fearing trouble, the police dispatched two officers, Henry Pack, who was black, and Henry Carmichael, who was white, to arrest Rowland either to show the authorities' serious intent to investigate the charge or to protect him from reprisals.

Word of the arrest made its way to the newsroom of the *Tulsa Tribune*, whose first editions hit the streets about 3 P.M. The shrill voice of a newsboy pierced the spring air: "Negro assaults a white girl!" The story appeared in the bottom right corner of the front page:

NAB NEGRO FOR ATTACKING GIRL IN ELEVATOR

A Negro delivery boy who gave his name to the public as "Diamond Dick" but who has been identified as Dick Rowland, was arrested on South Greenwood avenue this morning by Officers Carmichael and

Pack, charged with attempting to assault the 17-year-old white elevator girl in the Drexel Building early yesterday.

He will be tried in municipal court this afternoon on a state charge.

The girl said she noticed the negro a few minutes before the attempted assault looking up and down the hallway on the third floor
of the Drexel Building as if to see if there was anyone in sight but
thought nothing of it at the time.

A few minutes later, he entered the elevator she claimed, and attacked her, scratching her hands and face and tearing her clothes. Her
screams brought a clerk from Renberg's store to her assistance and the
negro fled. He was captured and identified this morning both by the
girl and the clerk, police say.

Rowland denied that he tried to harm the girl, but admitted he put
his hand on her arm when she was alone.

Tenants of the Drexel Building said the girl is an orphan who works
as an elevator operator to pay her way through business college.

The *Tribune* thus transformed a dubious elevator encounter into a
blend of menacing images and racist buzzwords: the Negro with a
gaudy name lurking in the shadows . . . the clawing of her flesh and
ripping of her clothes . . . the helpless orphan who wants only to
work her way through business school . . . the fearful cry . . . the
fleeing predator who is captured and taken into custody. Rowland's
denial was beside the point. He admitted touching her. The headline
assumed guilt.

The story sent an electric charge through Tulsa. The talk of lynching raged "like a prairie fire," according to one white witness. Commissioner Adkison, an elected official, called his appointed police
chief, John Gustafson, about the rumors, and Rowland was promptly
moved from the city jail on Second Street to the county jail on Sixth
Street and Boulder, which was more securely protected on the top
floor of the county courthouse. At 3:30 P.M. Gustafson received another phone call and was told, as he later testified, that "there was a
report out that this Negro was to be lynched."

The *Tribune's* article did not mention a lynching, but the newspaper may have published an editorial by Richard Lloyd Jones even
more inflammatory than its news story. In the coming years, blacks
in Tulsa (and some sympathetic whites) would claim that they either

saw or heard of an editorial headlined TO LYNCH A NEGRO TO-NIGHT. But Jones's editorial on May 31 has been excised from the record. The original bound volumes of the defunct publication apparently do not exist. The newspapers, instead, were preserved on microfilm, but before the May 31 edition was converted, the entire editorial page was cut out. The front-page story was also sliced out, leaving a literal hole in history — but other copies of page 1 survived the *Tribune*'s effort to conceal its role.

Riot scholars have spent decades searching for the editorial, but its greater significance lies in the perception of a cover-up orchestrated by the city's elite. The *Tribune*'s story was inflammatory enough to light a short fuse. The newspaper's motive in publishing such a reckless article could simply have been mercenary, for lurid crime stories had been part of Jones's effort to boost circulation. Politics may also have been involved. Jones had launched an angry crusade against the city administration, using high crime rates as his cudgel, and a racial assault might have been seen as a pointed reminder of the town's lax law enforcement.

Even at 4 P.M., only an hour after the *Tribune* appeared, police officials feared the explosive combination of forces: a black man held in jail, a newspaper making irresponsible claims, a city with a recent history of mob justice, and defiant blacks in Greenwood who had previously marched into white Tulsa to assert their rights. Down at city hall, the police commissioner received a call from an unidentified man, who said, "We're going to lynch that Negro tonight, that black devil who assaulted that girl." Adkison went to the courthouse and advised the sheriff, Willard McCullough, to take the prisoner out of town, but he refused.

"It would be impossible for anyone to take the Negro out," he said.

Over the next two hours, as Tulsans made their way home from work and read the *Tribune,* a white crowd began to gather around the courthouse. As tensions mounted, three white men walked up the steps, entered the building, and demanded to see Dick Rowland. There they met the sheriff.

At fifty-four, McCullough was an experienced lawman who sported a whiskbroom mustache and carried a pearl-handled .45-caliber pistol. Nicknamed "Uncle Bill," he was known for defusing trouble with negotiation, firing his pistol no more than five times in his entire career. He was first elected sheriff in 1910, and one of his first assignments was to execute a convicted black man by hanging. He called it "about the worst job I ever had to do." He was not the sheriff when Roy Belton was lynched nine months earlier but had since won reelection, and now, with Rowland in jail, he stood in the same spot as his predecessor, a mob knocking on his door.

"There's been talk of lynching," McCullough told the three men, "but you might as well go because no one is going to get the Negro."

The men left the courthouse and returned to their car on Boulder Street, where the sheriff saw them talking loudly and waving their arms.

Unknown to the crowd on the street, Sarah Page had been questioned at the police station. She had hedged in her accusation of Rowland and suggested she would not press charges. Whatever legitimate case may have existed against the black youth was crumbling, but by nightfall, the authorities had few concerns about his innocence or guilt. The issue was whether the white "mob" — the term used by McCullough — would be kept at bay. The sheriff instructed a half-dozen deputies to disable the building's sole elevator on the top floor and to station themselves behind a steel door at the top of a narrow winding staircase. It was the only way to get to Rowland.

Gustafson continued to get phone calls about lynching rumors, and he and his chief of detectives made two quick trips to the courthouse between 7:30 and 9 P.M. The whites outside the building had diminished to a gathering of curiosity-seekers — men, women, children, "the picture show crowd," according to a photographer. The group was large — by nine o'clock an estimated four hundred — but it appeared that the authorities had succeeded in thwarting the angry whites.

They did not anticipate the angry blacks.

After the *Tribune* came out, someone called one of the black theaters in Greenwood to warn of trouble, and the news galvanized the community. A consensus emerged around one idea: no black man would be lynched that night, not on their watch. It was a matter of pride and principle, of blacks in Greenwood refusing to submit to the ultimate violation of body and spirit, of the "race men" taking a stand. As I. H. Spears, a black lawyer, later said, "Every time I heard of a lynching, it made me want to purchase more ammunition." In an interview more than fifty years later, Neddie Caver, whose family owned a dry cleaner's in Greenwood, said, "Those men [in Greenwood] had to be men. That's the way they were, and they just couldn't let them lynch that young man."

But while everyone agreed a lynching should be stopped, disputes arose over what should be done and how much the authorities should be trusted. The younger, more militant blacks were rounding up guns and ammunition in preparation for battle. Older, more established African Americans, while equally opposed to lynching, sought to avert a destructive confrontation that would cost them — the wealthiest in Greenwood — the most.

O. W. Gurley, the real estate mogul who was one of Greenwood's founders, learned of the possible lynching by 4 P.M. He walked to the courthouse and spoke to the sheriff.

"Gurley, there won't be any lynching as long as I'm sheriff," McCullough told him. "If you keep your folks away from here, there won't be any trouble."

Gurley accepted this assurance, and in a meeting in front of his two-story brick hotel at 112 North Greenwood, he tried to persuade combative African Americans that the authorities would protect Rowland. But his effort failed.

"You're a damn liar!" one of them said. "They took a white man out of that jail a few months ago and they're going to take this nigger out."

"Fellow, you ought to be put in jail right now," Gurley responded. The younger man then drew a Winchester on Gurley, but Spears, the lawyer, intervened before anyone was harmed.

Down the block, B. C. Franklin, the lawyer who had recently moved to Tulsa, rushed down the stairs of his rooming house when he was told about a large group of young Negroes gathering on a nearby corner. He saw two world war veterans, one black and one white, firing up the crowd by telling combat stories, describing life in

the trenches, and emphasizing that strategy and surprise can overcome numerical weakness. The white veteran, assessing their current
predicament, suggested that someone set fire to houses in different
parts of the city to relieve the pressure on Greenwood and to prod
the governor to dispatch the National Guard. "If you don't do this,"
he said, "they're going to burn you out before this thing is started."

At that point, Franklin moved in and warned against such a tactic,
knowing an overt act of aggression would ensure the destruction of
the black district. His appeal worked; the crowd soon dispersed, but
as it did the white soldier, who was probably part of a radical political organization, said to his black counterpart: "A great mob is form-
ing, and you are at a disadvantage you can never overcome in an
open fight."

Another meeting convened at the *Tulsa Star* about 6:30 P.M., attended by J. B. Stradford and A. J. Smitherman, the two strongest
leaders in the community. They would use any means necessary to
prevent a lynching, but they were also prosperous and would suffer
extraordinary losses in a riot. They knew that black Tulsans, about 12
percent of the population, could not possibly win a fight against the
more numerous and better armed whites.

By the time the meeting began, McCullough had already spoken
to Stradford, reiterating his pledge that Rowland would be safe.
When called to address the crowd, Stradford spoke hesitantly at first.
He said he was not surprised that whites might try to lynch a member of their race because of "the bitter feeling against our group."
And he said that night as he had said often before: "The day a member of our group was 'mobbed' in Tulsa, the streets would be bathed
in blood."

He continued: "If I can't get anyone to go with me, I will go single-
handed and empty my automatic into the mob and then resign myself to that fate."

But Stradford instructed the men to go to the courthouse only if
they knew Rowland's life was in jeopardy or the sheriff called them
for help. "I advised the boys to be sober and to wait until the sheriff
called for us," he wrote in his memoir. Smitherman took the same
position, exhorting the men to retaliate against aggression but not to
start trouble. The two leaders wanted to show strength in the face of

a possible lynching, but they didn't want the hostilities to spiral out of control. It was a high-wire act with no margin for error.

At 7:30 P.M. about thirty blacks, some carrying weapons, walked in the gloaming to the courthouse. McCullough, told of their arrival, instructed his black deputy sheriff, Barney Cleaver, to handle the matter.

"Boys, where are you going?" Cleaver asked.

"We're coming to see about the lynching," one said.

"Now, this boy is upstairs and the cage is locked upstairs, and there is no way anyone can get to him. Go back."

The group left without incident, walking north on Boulder Avenue, but the whites remained on the courthouse lawn. Some of the men wore their Palm Beach suits and ties; others had short-sleeve shirts. But as night fell across the city, the crowd got younger, tougher, and larger. On most nights, downtown Tulsa attracted hard-drinking, swaggering white men, a transient population of machinists and tool dressers who went to Tulsa to work in the oil fields and then returned home to some other city. Tonight the swirl of excitement and danger at the courthouse was irresistible. At one point, the sheriff urged the crowd to disperse, but he was met with hoots. "You must be a nigger lover!" one man yelled. "If you come up here, I'll show you," the sheriff shouted back.

In black Tulsa, the rumors of a lynching persisted. Men gathered in billiard halls and gambling parlors along Greenwood Avenue to discuss matters. At 9 P.M. a black girl entered the Dixie Theatre in Greenwood, walked down the aisles, and whispered something to each person. The theater's owner, a white man named William Redfearn, looked into the street and saw a cluster of men talking excitedly. He heard that a lynching was to take place, so he promptly shut down the theater.

A false report circulated that whites had stormed the courthouse, and blacks on foot and in cars began to stream across the tracks toward downtown. Gustafson, in his office, saw the movement, got into a police car with another officer, and drove toward the courthouse. Before arriving, they stopped and disarmed two blacks.

At 9:15 P.M. about twenty-five armed black men arrived at the courthouse in two cars, some of them standing on running boards or sitting on the fenders. Parking on Sixth Street, they walked beneath the streetlights to the courthouse steps. Unlike the courthouse visit two hours earlier, this one occurred at night with cars and guns, a brazen move that stunned the growing crowd of whites. Oddly, policemen were scarce; area beats that were normally patrolled at this hour went untended. As later revealed in notes from police, there were apparently only "5 policemen on duty between court house & Brady hotel notwithstanding lynching imminent," an area of eight blocks.

The black men approached the courthouse steps. This time, McCullough stood at the top.

"I'm the sheriff of Tulsa County," he said. "Now you men in the street listen to me. Go home before a lot of people get hurt. You have no business coming up here and parading around with guns like that. If you are law-abiding people, you will go home before real trouble starts."

A black man shouted: "We'll go home when we get that Negro boy you want to lynch." Another echoed: "That's right. We ain't going nowhere without him." Others mumbled in agreement.

"No one is going to be lynched here," McCullough said. "There is not going to be a charge against the young man. The white girl has admitted that he did not harm her. She said she was nervous and scared, and so she screamed when he grabbed her. That is all there is to the case. She is a very nervous person, but she is not going to press charges because no harm was done. So go home now. I give you my word the Negro will be released in the morning."

But some of the blacks were not satisfied. "If there is no charge, why don't you turn him over to us now?"

"I can't release him tonight. It isn't possible."

"Why not? If there ain't no charge, why can't you let us take him?"

"Because he's telling a damn lie!" another black man yelled. "If we leave him here, he's a goner. They'll hang him high as Judgment Day."

"Listen to me," McCullough said. By now he was winded from all the yelling. "No one is going to hang anybody from this jail, but I can't turn him over to you tonight. Only a judge can release a person once he's been charged with a crime." A judge, he said, could do that in the morning but not before. As hundreds of whites watched this standoff, McCullough told the blacks he could not release Rowland for a second reason: the town was not run by angry mobs or armed citizens. "We can't give in to lawlessness, so go home before trouble starts."

The blacks discussed the matter among themselves, then turned and left.

Once again, a confrontation had been averted, but by then the authorities were beginning to lose control.

For the whites at the courthouse, the night was no longer about the chance to watch or participate in a lynching but about defending themselves against a potential black onslaught. Armed blacks had already come into their part of town, and if they came back, the whites would be prepared. Some went from the courthouse to their homes or cars to get guns, while others headed nine blocks west to the National Guard Armory, on Sixth Street and Norfolk Avenue, where a cache of arms was under lock and key: eighty Springfield rifles, six .45 Colts, six Browning automatic rifles, automatic pistols, and 16,000 rounds of ammunition.

Major James A. Bell, of the 180th Infantry, went to the armory at 9 P.M. when he heard that a Negro might be lynched and that blacks in "Little Africa" were arming to prevent it. He called both the sheriff and the police chief, who told him that the "Negroes were driving around town in a threatening mood." But both men assured Bell that they would handle any disturbance. Nonetheless, he notified the commanding officers of Tulsa's three National Guard units, who were in the armory, preparing to leave for camp at Fort Sill the next day, to put on their uniforms, gather their arms, and prepare for action. He also told them to notify all the Guard members in Tulsa to report to the armory quickly but quietly.

Minutes later, a mob of white men reached the armory and began pulling at the window grating on the west side of the building. Bell, who had gone across the street to his house to get his uniform, saw the attempted siege. He grabbed his pistol, returned to the armory, and commanded the whites to cease. He then circled to the front of the building and saw between three hundred and four hundred more whites.

"What do you want?" he called out.

"Rifles and ammunition," one replied.

Bell said they couldn't find them there.

"We don't know about that. We guess we can," one said.

Bell said the armory's weapons were only for guardsmen and ordered them to disperse. But the mob pressed forward against the door. Then Bell drew his pistol.

"The men inside are armed with rifles loaded with ball ammunition and they will shoot promptly to prevent any person from entering," he said. Finally, the mob withdrew, and Bell immediately ordered a ring of guardsmen around the armory and a man on the roof as well.

Word of the unrest in Tulsa reached state officials in Oklahoma City. Charles Barrett, the Oklahoma National Guard's commanding general (also known as adjutant general), called Bell, who told him of the white mob's efforts to break into the armory. Moments later, Barrett received a call from another Tulsa guardsman, Major Byron Kirkpatrick, who had just seen a group of armed blacks gather five blocks east of the courthouse, on Elgin Avenue and Fifth Street. A number of trucks and cars "heavily laden with armed men" were driving rapidly toward the courthouse, firing bullets into the air. Kirkpatrick described the blacks as a "mob."

Barrett had received consecutive reports that two mobs, one white, one black, were rampaging through the city. He called Bell at the armory again and told him to mobilize Company B at once and to render any assistance necessary to maintain law and order.

At 10 P.M. the Dreamland Theatre, the largest in Greenwood, shut down when the projectionist saw a growing commotion on the street. Across town, about 1,500 whites, including armed men, convened at the intersection of Sixth and Boulder, next to the courthouse. While blacks were making scattered forays into white Tulsa, they had not reappeared at the courthouse since the sheriff turned them away almost an hour earlier. But about 10:10 P.M. another contingent of about seventy-five armed blacks walked en masse through the crowd to the building. They may have returned because they had heard further reports about whites storming the courthouse, or perhaps they were simply determined to get what they wanted — Dick Rowland. They may have been emboldened by their earlier incursions that night into the forbidden land of white Tulsa. At least some were drinking. The black officer Henry Pack later said that these men "soaked themselves in 'choc' beer and whiskey until they became crazed with the drink and cared nothing for their lives or the lives of anyone else."

Reaching the courthouse, they once again confronted Sheriff McCullough, as well as Deputy Sheriff Cleaver, who assured them that Rowland was safe.

"Parading around with these guns is against the law," McCullough said. "Violence is easy to start but hard to stop." He then pointed to the top floor of the courthouse. "Look up at those windows. See those gun barrels pointed at you? They will cut down the first person that makes a move to take this courthouse over. Now go home before a lot of people get shot."

The blacks backed off again, but they did not make a clean break. According to a black witness, a white man approached a tall African American carrying an army revolver.

"Nigger, what are you doing with that pistol?"

"I'm going to use it if I need to."

"No, you give it to me."

"Like hell I will."

They struggled and then, with the gun pointed high, a shot was fired. The blast stunned the crowd into momentary silence.

Then, as the sheriff later said, "all hell broke loose."

A hail of bullets erupted in a ten-second fusillade, and the outnumbered blacks scattered down the street and into nearby alleys. But some were left dead or dying on the ground, while whites also lay moaning on the grass. The first black killed, according to a 1931

Scribner's story, "lay writhing on the sidewalk, under a billboard from which smiled winsomely the face of Mary Pickford, America's sweetheart."

The blacks needed to reach Greenwood, seven blocks north, where they had reinforcements and could use the familiar ground to their advantage. But with armed whites in hot pursuit — and with additional whites from cars and movie theaters soon joining them — the flight to Greenwood bogged down in a ground war.

Along Fourth Street, two blocks north of the courthouse, a black man with a gun burst from an alley and ran east toward Main Street; several whites rushed out of the alley behind him. One of them raised a rifle to shoot, but the others pushed down the barrel for fear that an errant bullet would fly into the crowds on Main Street, less than a block away. Suddenly, a Cadillac came speeding down the street, horn blasting and tires squealing. It swerved toward the black man, and a young woman poked a shotgun out of the window and fired a blast at him from less than twenty feet away. He dropped and rolled toward the curb, twisting in pain as the car peeled away. Other gunmen fired at him as well. In seconds a large crowd had gathered around the man. "He was bleeding so badly," a witness later wrote, "that if it had not been for his hands, it would have been impossible to tell if he was black or white."

An ambulance rolled up and the attendants asked the crowd to step aside, but a large white man picked up the victim's rifle. "Hold it," he said. "Don't touch him. There are a lot of people who've been hurt who need you. Go help them."

"Why not this one? He needs us too, doesn't he?"

"Because he's a nigger and he was up here hunting trouble. Maybe he shot some of the white men."

The attendant hesitated.

"Get going in a hurry," the man with the rifle said, "or you'll join him with a bullet in the guts. Which is it?"

The ambulance left.

Watching the encounter was George H. Miller, a white physician who was working late that evening at the Unity Building on West Fourth Street. Dr. Miller later said that the attackers did not stop with gunshots: "I went over to see if I could help him as a doctor, but the crowd was gathering around him and wouldn't even let the driver of the ambulance, which just arrived, pick him up. I saw it was an impossible situation to control, that I could be of no help. The crowd was getting more and more belligerent. The Negro had been shot so many times in his chest, and men from the onlookers were slashing him with knives."

The white rioters, denied guns at the armory, broke into sporting goods stores, pawnshops, and hardware stores in a loud, frenzied scramble for automatic pistols, shotguns, rifles, and ammunition. They also stole jewelry, leather goods, and clothes in a sweep that amounted to $43,000 in stolen property. Hardest hit were Bardon's Sporting Goods on First Street and J. W. McGee's Sporting Goods on West Second Street, right across the street from police headquarters.

Skirmishes continued to break out downtown as the blacks tried to fight their way back to Greenwood. The ones who had earlier displayed bravado and defiance were now in desperate retreat. As A. C. Krupnick, a photographer whose pictures of the riot appeared in the *New York Times*, said: "The Negroes became the hunted game."

In one instance, a black man who was being chased by whites opened the stage door of the Royal Theater on Main Street, where *One Man in a Million* was playing. Racing inside, the black man found himself before the picture screen, blinded by the flickering light from the projector's booth. Shielding his eyes, he found the steps leading from the stage past the orchestra pit. Then one of his pursuers saw him and yelled, "There he is, heading for the aisle." As he finished the sentence, a shotgun blast dropped the black man dead. The stunned crowd screamed and clawed to get out of the theater.

At the nearby Rialto Theater, someone ran inside and shouted: "Nigger fight! Nigger fight!" One patron, William R. Holway, a white engineer, walked across the street and stood behind two big pillars at Younkman's Red Cross Pharmacy, where he saw a black man running across the street get shot. "We stood there for about half an hour watching, which I shall never forget," Holway recalled. "He wasn't quite dead, but he was about to die. He was the first man that I saw shot in that riot."

Around midnight, a small crowd of whites gathered around the courthouse, yelling "Bring the rope!" and "Get the nigger!" But the lynch party was long gone. Dick Rowland remained safe in jail.

Major Charles W. Daley, of the Inspector General's Department of the National Guard in Tulsa, was out of the city when the shooting began. When he reached the West Tulsa Bridge at 11:45 P.M., several men stopped him with the news: *the Negroes were trying to take over the city.* For the hours and days — indeed years — to come, that belief guided the actions and thoughts of many white Tulsans. It was not a riot. It was a black *insurrection,* an *uprising,* an *invasion* of downtown Tulsa by gun-toting, whiskey-drinking heathens bent on conquering its inhabitants. A rumor circulated that when a white messenger boy had gone to Greenwood to deliver a telegram, he was grabbed by thirty Negroes, beaten, kicked, tied to a post, whipped with a piece of wire, then set free and given these orders: "Tell them this is what happens to white people who come to our town." The Magic City was under siege from the violent instincts of a lower race, and from that misguided assumption flowed a tragic course of events.

Tulsa's history of vigilantism took a disturbing twist when two white men walked down Main Street with urgent news. "We are deputizing groups of men with automobiles to patrol the streets that separate the white and Negro sections of town," one said. "We want to be certain that a lot of black men don't sneak over and rape and kill a lot of white women during the night."

Unlike past vigilante efforts, in which private citizens worked outside the law, the police department itself legitimized self-styled lawmen with police badges, ribbons, and even guns. Others received commissions as "special deputy sheriffs." Laurel Buck, a twenty-six-year-old bricklayer, arrived at the police station and, as he later testified, "was told to get busy and try to get a nigger." The same instruction was apparently given to Walter White, the light-skinned, blue-eyed assistant secretary for the National Association for the Advancement of Colored People, who traveled throughout the South to write exposés about lynchings. Alerted to the maelstrom in Tulsa, he said he arrived in time to be deputized with fifty other whites at city hall. "I had to answer only three questions — name, age, and address," he later wrote. "I might have been a thug, a murderer, an escaped convict, a member of the mob itself . . . none of these mattered; my skin was apparently white, and that was enough." After White was sworn in, a fellow "deputy" casually remarked: "Now you can go out and shoot any nigger you see and the law'll be behind you."

In his report on the riot, Captain Bell of the National Guard said that five hundred men had been deputized. The police chief "did not realize that in a race war a large part, if not the majority, of these special deputies were imbued with the same spirit of destruction that animated the mob. They became as deputies the most dangerous part of the mob."

Shortly before the riot began, Governor Robertson was told about the unrest in Tulsa. He called General Barrett and ordered him to call the chief of police or sheriff to see if the National Guard was needed. Barrett placed the call, but Chief Gustafson, who did not want to seem helpless in his first crisis, assured him that the civil authorities could control the situation.

When the shooting began, Gustafson sat in his office on the second floor of police headquarters, four blocks from the courthouse. As men raced past him and shots rang out in the air, he concluded that his department could not control the city. He called Captain Bell at the armory and asked him to dispatch the local units of the National Guard "to clear the streets of Negroes."

These Guard units consisted of about two hundred twenty white men, and its commanding officer, Lieutenant L.J.F. Rooney, sent small detachments to protect the waterworks, power plants, and other points likely to be attacked in a riot. He also took fifteen to eighteen men from the armory to the police station, where he found between one hundred twenty-five and one hundred fifty men with guns drawn in military formation. Many were with the American Legion. "I took control of them," Rooney said.

The first phase of the riot, for whites, was effectively a numbers game: the authorities sought to amass a large enough force to deter an assault from blacks in Greenwood or in other parts of the state. But just as the police were reckless in granting special commissions, so too was the National Guard. When Major Daley reached the police station at 12:05 A.M. (he was also the police inspector), white men with pistols and rifles had gathered around, and a white "mob" — Daley's word — of one hundred fifty had assembled on the corner of Second and Main. After consulting with Rooney, Daley selected a half-dozen former servicemen to be his "assistants," then instructed the mob that it could help maintain order if it followed his instructions — thus creating a police force by fiat.

He formed patrols of twelve to twenty men, each led by a former military service man, and told them to "gather up all the Negroes" but not to fire a shot unless to protect life. These roving sentries, fanning out on foot and by car, were also ordered to bring in blacks from servants' quarters, as Daley feared the "bad Negroes" might set fire to whites' homes. In addition, Major Kirkpatrick took charge of "a body of armed volunteers," perhaps members of the American Legion, to patrol downtown. The police had only sixteen patrol cars; to equip this ad hoc force, vehicles were either volunteered or commandeered, and one hundred were soon on the streets. By midnight about two hundred fifty blacks had been brought to the police station.

Conferring such legal authority — apprehending suspects — on untrained, loosely supervised "deputies" wearing overalls, their pockets bulging with stolen guns whose price tags still clung to the end, defied every protocol, but it reflected the feverish attitudes of white Tulsans: the riot was a Negro rebellion that had to be quashed with extraordinary measures. The phrase "Negro uprising" is used often in the National Guard's reports; one guardsman even referred to blacks as the "enemy."

Even if the Guard had been evenhanded, it would not have had the manpower to restore order amid thousands of white rioters. Daley estimated that at least 5,000 armed white men were on the streets that night. The only chance the city had to quell the disturbance was for the Oklahoma militia to send large numbers of troops from other parts of the state. But proud Tulsa resisted. Neither the sheriff nor the police chief nor the mayor ever placed a call for help to Oklahoma City. It took Major Kirkpatrick, at 12:35 A.M., to prepare a telegram for the governor, a request that required the signatures of the police chief, the sheriff, and a judge. Getting them from Gustafson and District Judge V. W. Biddison was easy, but McCullough was still barricaded on the top floor of the courthouse with Dick Rowland. He thought the telegram messenger was a member of the lynch mob and would not open the door. A *Tulsa World* reporter who knew McCullough finally got the telegram to him, and he reluctantly signed it. "While I do not feel the situation warrants help from the outside," the sheriff said, "it is always best to play safety first."

Finally, at 1:46 A.M., Governor Robertson received the duly signed telegram: RACE RIOT DEVELOPED HERE. SEVERAL KILLED. UNABLE TO HANDLE SITUATION. REQUEST THAT NATIONAL GUARD FORCES BE SENT BY SPECIAL TRAIN. SITUATION SERIOUS. By two-fifteen the governor had called the Guard. A special train with Commander Barrett and about one hundred men left Oklahoma City at 5 A.M.

In Greenwood, news of the fighting spread slowly. Many blacks, such as B. C. Franklin, simply went to bed. Shootings were common enough in Tulsa, and they assumed that the blacks who ventured south of the railroad tracks would bear the brunt of the trouble. J. B. Stradford, by then sixty years old, had little interest in the fray. He was at the initial courthouse confrontation, but he later said he was there as a peacemaker. After the first African American had been shot, C. F. Gabe, a black man, sought Stradford out at his hotel and pleaded with him to help restore calm. "Let's go and get the boys back from over there," he said.

But Stradford had made his position clear: he would do whatever it took to stop a lynching, but he would not participate in a street brawl. "Gabe, I ain't going up," he said.

There was no Negro invasion. The blacks who appeared at the courthouse and survived the gun battle escaped across the railroad tracks to Archer and Cincinnati, where they made their stand. The riot would no longer be fought in white Tulsa but in Greenwood, two square miles of flatlands with railroad tracks on its southern and eastern borders. The fashionable brick homes of Detroit Avenue lined the western boundary, while gnarled shacks on Pine Avenue marked the northern fringe. Its thriving commercial hub, the intersection of Greenwood and Archer, had paved streets, and buildings were fortified by steel beams and girders. Elsewhere, jagged dirt roads, rutted from burros pulling vegetable wagons, curved around homes made from packing crates.

It was all foreign terrain to white Tulsa, which seemed to favor the blacks.

Shortly after midnight, fierce gunfire erupted along the Frisco railroad tracks, an important line separating Tulsa's white and black commercial districts. When an inbound train arrived, its passengers were forced to dive to the floor. One group of blacks fired from behind the Frisco depot, while other blacks began shooting from a higher perch in frame buildings. Tales of heroic fighting would be passed down for generations in black Tulsa. One army veteran, "Peg Leg" Taylor (he lost a leg in the war), became a legend for defending Greenwood by gunning down whites. While such tales are prone to exaggeration, even Lieutenant Rooney of the local Guard said that the blacks "fought like tigers."

But ferocity could not neutralize the one great vulnerability blacks had by fighting from Greenwood — fire. In the battle along the Frisco tracks, several white men, trained in warfare, crawled up to buildings filled with snipers on Archer and threw lighted oil rags inside. The buildings burst into flames, and the wind blew the fire to other buildings, streaking the southern boundary of Greenwood with a hot orange blaze.

The night was just beginning in white Tulsa.

The anticipation of a bloody showdown created a festive, blustering atmosphere, where a dangerous blend of whiskey, guns, and racism roiled. "We saw drunks staggering along the streets hanging on to half empty bottles," Choc Phillips wrote in his memoirs, "and now and then one would face skyward and scream and whoop as loud as possible. Instead of the crowds on the streets diminishing as the hours passed, they grew larger. A great many of those persons lining the sidewalks were holding a rifle or shotgun in one hand and grasping the neck of a liquor bottle with the other. Some had pistols stuck in their belts."

But without the enemy in their midst, the mob lacked a mission.

Around 2 A.M., a huge crowd gathered at the corner of Second Street and Lewis Avenue, where a man stood on top of a car. "Men, we are going in at daylight," he announced. "Meetings like this are taking place all over town and across the river in West Tulsa. Be ready to go at daybreak."

Another man stood up. "If you have more ammunition than you need, or if what you have doesn't fit your gun, sing out. There will be somebody here that has the right caliber. Get busy and exchange shells until everybody has the right size. Then have every gun loaded and ready to shoot at daylight."

Others in the crowd chimed in: "They came looking for trouble by coming into town with guns and trying to take over . . . they started the trouble and we will write the finish so they will never forget this night . . ."

Another man stood up. "Be ready to go to Niggertown," he said. "We're going over there and burn it at daybreak, and we'll teach the trouble hunters a lesson they won't forget."

Everyone was to meet at the freight depot, but someone came forward with new information: a train of Negroes from Muskogee was coming to Tulsa. The crowd began running to the Midland Valley Railroad passenger station off Third Street. "Let's hurry, men. The Muskogee niggers want a shootout — we'll give it to them!" someone called out

The National Guard had already received reports that blacks were driving to Tulsa from Muskogee, Sand Springs, and Mohawk, so patrol cars had been dispatched to form a blockade. Now, responding to the train rumor, the Guard sent patrols to the station. Once again a large crowd formed along either side of the railroad tracks, behind boxcars, and on the station platform. Some climbed telephone poles and took up posts on the roof of the station.

"Now everyone get ready," someone yelled, "and when that train arrives, don't let a black man get off it alive."

Trigger fingers ready, they waited, but no train arrived.

In Greenwood, the fires along Archer Street still simmered, but they had been contained. White marauders had set several other buildings on fire, including a hotel, but the damage had not spread. Occasionally, a car full of whites roared into Greenwood, guns blazing, but they were met with defensive gunfire from blacks. Seymour Williams, a high school teacher and army veteran who had been wounded in France, used his army revolver to defend an intersection all night. Amid the chaos, numerous blacks began streaming out of Tulsa, hoping to find safety in the surrounding countryside or with friends. But by 2 A.M. the shooting and the incursions had all but stopped, and some blacks began to think that the riot was over *and that they had won.* They had stood up to the invaders on their southern boundary and repelled their advance. They had suffered casualties, but so too had the whites, maybe even more.

And Diamond Dick Rowland was still alive.

In the early hours of June 1, thousands of armed whites gathered in three main clusters along the northern fringes of downtown, opposite Greenwood. One group assembled behind the Frisco freight depot, a long line of men outlined by glowing dots of tobacco. As dawn began to sweep away the darkness, a young man in a white shirt stepped from behind the building and looked north into the Negro district. Then a shot was heard, and he went down in a gasp. Two men jumped out, grabbed his feet, and dragged him back to safety. Someone tore open his shirt: in the center of his chest was a spot the size of a cigarette butt, turning reddish blue. His eyes rolled to the top of his head, and blood gushed out of his mouth with each gasp. A man ran his hand beneath the victim's body; when he freed it, it dripped profusely with blood. Someone yelled for an ambulance, but the man interrupted him. "It's too late," he said, wiping his hand on a handkerchief. "He's dead." The bullet, from a high-powered rifle, had passed completely through his body.

Minutes later a siren wailed, and the invasion of Greenwood began.

The Invasion

FIVE WHITE MEN in a green Franklin led the charge across the Frisco tracks, but the car had gone no more than a block before it was halted by a cascade of bullets that shattered the windows, chipped the paint, and killed the occupants. Thousands of screaming men, guns in hand, began pouring out from behind the depot, from behind long strings of boxcars and piles of oil well casings. Hundreds more came from behind the nearby Frisco and Santa Fe passenger stations, and they came from behind the Katy depot four blocks north. Rebel yells and "Indian gobblings" were heard above the din of gunshot fire. A machine gun placed on top of a grain elevator opened fired on black Tulsa as cars speeding east on Brady and Cameron provided additional support.

Crowds of people — some just watching, some taking pictures — converged on the southwestern edge of Greenwood. They moved not in one mass but in small groups of four or five, dividing their labor along the way. Reaching an unoccupied home or business, one rioter would put his gun against the lock and blow it off. Once inside, the group would confiscate valuables, like jewelry or silver, smash everything breakable, open trunks and bureau drawers, wrench telephones from the walls, and trample it all. Then they piled up all the bedding, furniture, and other inflammables, scattered kerosene, and applied matches.

In one last indignity, the rioters piled the furniture, bedsprings, and other objects in front of the house, literally exposing the inner life of a family. Dr. R. T. Bridgewater, a black assistant county physician, returned to his home at 507 North Detroit to find his piano as well as his elegant furniture on the street. As he described it:

> My safe had been broken open, all of the money stolen, also my silverware, cut glass, all of the family clothing, and everything of value had been removed, even my family Bible. My electric light fixtures were broken, all the window lights and glass in the doors were broken, the dishes that were not stolen were broken, the floors were covered (literally speaking) with glass, even the phone was torn from the wall. In the basement we gathered two tubs of broken glass from the floor. My car was stolen and most of my large rugs were taken.

The fire, moving east along Archer Street, cast a reddish hue in the gray light of early morning. Rows of homes were ignited, and the raiders could be seen in the glow of crackling new fires as the houses burst into flames. Telephone and power lines were toppled, wires whipping about and sparks flying in every direction. On other streets, telephone poles stood like burned matchsticks, lifeless wires dangling in the street. All power was soon shut off in Greenwood.

Dense clouds of smoke began to rise as the torchers moved north on Elgin and Detroit avenues, the latter a western boundary between white and black Tulsa. The arsonists looted and ignited the black homes on the east side of Detroit while carefully avoiding the white homes on the other side. As the warm sun rose, the heat and smoke created a stifling, airless environment. Perspiration soaked men's shirts. Flower gardens wilted. Cats keeled over.

Eighteen-year-old Otis Clark lived on Archer Street with his mother and grandmother as well as his bulldog, Bob. He had seen the blacks shoot out the streetlights in Greenwood to deter whites from invading at night, and he awoke on June 1 assuming the troubles were over. He hoped the ruckus hadn't disturbed his grandmother's vegetable garden, whose tomatoes he sold to the white prostitutes sitting on their porches on First Street, their lace underclothes draped over their knees. He decided to visit a friend who ran Jackson's Funeral Home down the street, but before long he heard more shooting. Jackson's had its own ambulance, and Otis accompanied an attendant to get it from a garage. As the attendant turned the key to open the garage, a rifle blast sounded and a bullet crashed into his hand, spilling blood like water from a fountain. A sniper was on the grain elevator. As Otis and the attendant ran for cover, bullets whistled by their ears, kicking up dust and splitting wood on the building. They made it back to the funeral home, where Otis saw Mr. Jackson tending three or four bodies on tables.

He left the funeral parlor and headed home; but bands of whites blocked his route, so he ducked into an alley and went to his cousin's instead. She and her husband were preparing to flee by car, so Otis joined them to go to Claremore, twenty-nine miles away. Before they got there, white men with guns stopped the vehicle and demanded that they give up their arms.

They returned to Tulsa the following day. Otis found his home destroyed, the vegetable garden covered with ash, his mother and grandmother heartbroken, his bulldog gone. Otis wanted nothing more to do with this city; he decided to go to Milwaukee and live with his father. That night he hopped on a freight train, climbed to the top of a boxcar, and never looked back.

As the morning sun climbed higher, the first buildings burned on West Archer had begun to disintegrate while new fires were running east through Greenwood, then north. At 9 A.M. a white lawyer named Luther Jones stood on top of the Hotel Tulsa and saw thirty or forty separate fires, each with a different dance and shape, the smoke varying in texture and tint. Some blazes produced brownish gray clouds of vapor that turned white as they died out; others unfurled a black haze that settled heavily over the city. A light eastern breeze created an eerie half canopy: west of Cincinnati Avenue was a cerulean southwestern sky, while east was a dark cumulus cover of dust and smoke.

The police appeared more intent on helping the mob than protecting life and property. According to a black deputy sheriff, V. B. Bostic, a white police officer drove him and his wife from their home and then "poured oil on the floor and set a lighted match to it." A white witness said that "a uniformed [white] policeman on East Second Street went home, changed his uniform to plainclothes, and went to the Negro district and led a bunch of whites in Negro houses, some of the bunch pilfering, never offered to protect men, women or children."

A white judge named John Oliphant, testifying after the riot, offered a similar account of the police force. "They were the chief fellows setting the fires," he said. "They were not in uniform, but they had stars on. They had badges on." Henry Pack, the black officer, also testified that he saw about a dozen "special police" knocking down doors and setting fires. Pack subsequently quit the force and moved to Muskogee.

Chief Gustafson, in later court testimony, did not implicate his own officers but suggested that the civilians with special commissions started the fires. "We were unable to limit the commissions to our choice," he said. "I usually talked to the men and those I thought would remain cool-headed I commissioned. But of those who might have lost their heads — they might have applied the torch. But that was positively in contradiction to orders."

The National Guard squared off against blacks in some of the riot's most heated gun battles. Between 8 and 9 A.M., the police urgently requested that two units of the Guard stop black gunmen on the northwestern edge of Greenwood from firing at white homes on Sunset Hill. A force of up to one hundred thirty-five guardsmen, carrying Springfield rifles, .45 Colts, and pistols, advanced in a "skirmish line" to the "military crest" of the hill but were met by blacks firing from the base. The guardsmen, shooting from the prone position, fired back as blacks took cover in "out-buildings"; the battle raged for twenty minutes. Overwhelmed, the blacks began to retreat, using frame buildings to gain better cover, followed by the guardsmen in hot pursuit. The encounter ended badly for the blacks. As Captain John McCuen of Company B wrote in his report of the incident: "Little opposition was met with until about half way through the settlement when some negroes who had barricaded themselves in houses refused to stop firing and had to be killed." He also wrote that in a different battle, "at the north-east corner of the negro settlement," ten or more blacks barricaded themselves in a concrete store, and a "stiff fight ensued between these negroes on one side and guardsmen and civilians on the other." The description suggests that in some cases little difference existed between the Guard and the mob — both were in Greenwood to fight blacks.

The Tulsa Fire Department did not join in the riot, but it was cowered by the mob. The station on North Main Street responded to its first call at 2 A.M., sent a truck to Main and Archer, and had hooked its hose to a water plug when several whites pointed their guns at two firefighters. As the Archer fires roared in the background, the firemen disengaged the hose. "They told us to get away from that hose or someone would get killed," the driver, C. H. Moore, later testified. "We went back to the fire station and we went to sleep."

When the next alarm sounded, the fire truck didn't move. "We had orders not to respond," Moore said.

Even after daybreak, when the department tried to do its job, it was no match for the arsonists' gas-soaked rags. At about 7 A.M. Moore responded to a call that the black district's Frissell Memorial Hospital on East Brady was on fire. With bullets whizzing overhead and the streets packed, Moore laid out the water hose. "I put out [the hospital fire] and by the time I got it out, the house on the corner was afire." As he tended that blaze, the hospital was set on fire again. So he put it out a second time — only to have the mob set the hospital on fire a third time. It too was finally destroyed.

At several turns, whites were thwarted from helping blacks. Edward L. Wheeler, who joined the National Guard that day, rode out to Detroit Avenue with a dilapidated machine gun, hoping to frighten the blacks into surrendering. A large group of whites hid behind a boiler, waiting for the blacks to appear. Wheeler, carrying a small pistol in his hip pocket, dismounted from the truck and pleaded with the whites to stop shooting. A man stepped out from behind the crowd, drew his gun, and placed it against Wheeler's abdomen. Declaring that the captain was trying to protect the Negroes, he shot once. The bullet went through Wheeler's right side and broke his arm, but he survived. At forty-five, he was a veteran of the Spanish-American War and the world war who had moved to Tulsa, according to the *Tribune,* "several months ago from the north with the hope of benefiting his health."

As the assault continued, the overwhelmed blacks had few options. Some continued their armed resistance while others tried to hide in abandoned iceboxes or dirty hog pens. One person tried to leave Greenwood through an underground sewer line. Many escaped by foot, walking nine miles or more under the hot sun to Sand Springs and other communities. For those who stayed in Greenwood, saving family heirlooms or assets became unrealistic. Survival was the best most could achieve.

"You could hear shooting everywhere in town, boom, boom, boom," said C. F. Gabe, whose piano was struck by a bullet. "People were saying, 'The white folks are killing all the niggers and burning all their houses.'"

Men and women ran down Greenwood Avenue in their nightclothes and bare feet, carrying their dazed children. One woman had put her stillborn baby in a shoebox, to be buried that morning. But when the riot broke out the woman, running, bumping, tripping down Greenwood Avenue, lost the box. As she desperately searched the ground, shots rang out and her husband yelled for her to get out of the street. "Where's my baby?" she screamed. "Where's my baby?" Watching the futile search was twenty-three-year-old Rosa Davis Skinner, who vividly recalled the incident at the age of ninety-nine.

"They never did find that child," she said softly.

Most blacks peacefully submitted to the guardsmen before their homes were looted and burned, but surrender did not guarantee survival. When A. C. Jackson, one of the most prominent black surgeons in America, walked out of his house on Detroit Avenue with his hands raised, a band of menacing white men approached him. "Here I am," he said. "I want to go with you."

John Oliphant, the white judge, lived a block away and saw trouble coming.

"That's Dr. Jackson," he said. "Don't hurt him."

Two of the whites fired their guns, and Jackson fell with the second shot, a bullet in his chest. The shooters walked away, but not before one of them fired another shot to break the doctor's leg. He died later that day. His house was splashed with gas and coal oil, then torched.

Blacks who resisted arrest or whose homes had firearms — both evidence of being a "bad nigger" — were the most likely to be executed, but the invasion of Greenwood was less about mass killing than about the physical and spiritual destruction of a community. Even acts of mercy were gestures of hate. In one instance, a white man who entered a black home was going to shoot a defenseless resident, but another white stopped him so that the black man could tell others "what happens to niggers who hunt trouble." That same message was delivered by postcards depicting a devastated Greenwood.

With black homes defenseless, whites entered at will — not just men but women and children, who rummaged through drawers and cabinets, stuffed belongings in pillowcases and sheets, and celebrated their good fortune. When the black deputy sheriff, Cleaver, left the courthouse on Wednesday morning and returned to Greenwood, he met two white women carrying a bundle of clothes.

"What have you got there?" he demanded.

"Who wants to know?" one asked.

"Those are my wife's clothes."

"Yonder goes a man on a truck with the rest of the stuff."

In some cases, whites justified the looting on the ground that black wealth was amassed in the underground economy or through some kind of chicanery that would allow an inferior race to prosper. Black success was an intolerable affront to the social order of white supremacy, so taking their possessions not only stripped blacks of their material status but also tipped the social scales back to their proper alignment. This reassertion of authority, expressed through ransacked homes, was a cause for celebration.

"Some [looters] were singing," Judge Oliphant later testified. "Some were playing pianos that were taken out of the building, some were running Victrolas, some dancing a jig, and just having a rollicking easy good time in a business [in] which they thought they were doing what was upright."

The invasion of Greenwood had another chilling dimension — airplanes, flown by whites, swept over Greenwood in the morning hours. Exactly what they did has been debated ever since but numerous black witnesses have said the aircraft were used to assault Greenwood: pilots either dropped incendiary devices like "turpentine balls" and dynamite or used rifles to strafe people from the sky. If true, Tulsa was the first U.S. city to suffer an aerial assault. But police officials said the planes were used only to monitor the fires and to locate refugees. Walter White, the journalist from the NAACP, wrote: "Eight aeroplanes were employed to spy on the movements of the Negroes and according to some were used in bombing the colored section." Even if the planes were not used for offensive purposes, their presence emphasized the total-war atmosphere of the raid and seared another harrowing image into many blacks' memories.

At 9:15 A.M. Adjutant General Charles Barrett arrived on a special train from Oklahoma City with one hundred nine white soldiers and officers under his command. The National Guard's reinforcements had arrived, although much of the destruction was well under way. Barrett later wrote that his train "halted in the midst of fifteen to twenty thousand blood-maddening rioters" (a probable exaggeration) and that "no civil authority could restore order." Barrett then ordered additional troops from Muskogee, Vinita, and Wagoner, and rumors continued to circulate about invasions of blacks from other parts of Oklahoma.

While many black Tulsans widely praised the "state troops," Barrett could not take control of the city without following certain protocols. He needed first to report to the local authorities, which included a fruitless effort to find Sheriff McCullough, and precious minutes passed before martial law could be declared. Later, critics of the National Guard would attach great importance to the apparent decision of the state troops awaiting orders to eat breakfast while homes and businesses were being destroyed. Wherever the fault may lie — with local officials in their delayed request for state help or with the state troops for failing to act with urgency — martial law was not imposed until 11:49 A.M., when the riot was effectively over.

The local guard had a key role in one of the most dramatic moments of the riot.

The new Mount Zion Baptist Church was rumored to be a warehouse for armaments among whites. As the *Daily Oklahoman* reported, the church "was said to have been the rendezvous of the Bolshevik element of the Negroes who are responsible for the outbreak." Word was that twenty caskets had been taken to the church, each filled with high-powered rifles. After the riot, blacks ridiculed this claim — "that church was built to glorify God," said Mabel Little — and assumed that the accusation reflected the resentment toward blacks who built a place of worship as elegant and beautiful as any white church in Tulsa.

With or without ammunition, the sturdy building provided blacks with one of their best fortresses, and any white who charged it or the surrounding houses was repelled by gunmen inside. One firefight lasted an hour. As fire and smoke enveloped nearby streets, Mount Zion stood strong. Seeking greater firepower, the whites called in local guardsmen. They arrived on Elgin Street in a flatbed truck, stopping less than a quarter mile from the church. One soldier jerked back a canvas cover from a machine gun, which was placed on a tripod. Another pulled the lid from a box, withdrawing belts of ammunition. He fit the shells into the grooves of the gun while the gunman adjusted the sights of the barrel. His cap pulled backward, he shifted into a comfortable position, aimed the gun at the church, and pulled the trigger. As bullets flashed from the muzzle, a smoky haze enveloped the men. One witness said the gun started "chattering [in] a stream of bullets" (although the National Guard reported that the gun could only fire one bullet at a time).

Chunks of mortar and brick flew from the belfry, where blacks had been firing through narrow slits. The rioters who had been held at bay swung around the back of the church, taking shelter behind a rim of houses and firing away with their own guns. In five or six minutes, the machine gun had created large jagged holes in the side of the church, and bricks flew wildly about. The gunfire from the church had stopped as windows shattered and the belfry collapsed.

The surrounding homes that had been protected by the gunmen in the church were then torched. So too was Mount Zion. Smoke poured out of the top, and fire flashed from every hole "like flaming tongues of dragons." An estimated seven or eight blacks were killed.

The three guardsmen dismounted the machine gun from the tripod, wrapped it in canvas, and laid it on the flatbed. They rolled up the belts with empty shell casings, stored the unused rounds, and drove away not more than ten minutes after they arrived. The battle of Mount Zion was over, leaving nothing left but scorched brick walls and smoldering embers buried beneath piles of rubbish.

Black Tulsa's final humiliation was its exodus from Greenwood.

Removed at gunpoint from their homes throughout the day, the African Americans were lined up on the street, their hands raised above their heads, and slowly marched out of the district. Others were taken in trucks or cars. E. W. Woods, the principal of the high school and perhaps the most respected man in Greenwood, left his home with one arm held high, the other carrying his three-month-old baby. Three whites holding guns urged him forward. Men, women, and children carried bundles of clothing on their heads and backs and pulled wobbly carts with clothes, phonographs, and household goods. Skinny mules lugged wagons carrying ice-filled trunks, huge boxes of food, and tubs of coffee. One aged woman clung to her Bible; young girls held white stuffed dogs and wax dolls. A sickly old man wrapped in quilts and blankets was finally placed in a car and taken to a hospital.

With the city jail full, the blacks were detained at the Convention Hall, a few blocks beyond Greenwood's western boundary. Some whites had already been given the day off — a grocer released his clerk because it was "nigger day" — and the white crowds had to be held back by armed guards as the blacks were brought in. They were ordered through the front door, guarded on both sides by men with bayonets, pistols, and rifles. Before reaching the entrance they were searched, with every knife, pistol, and cartridge taken from them. Inside, the men with families were allowed to try to calm their crying children. The rest went to a balcony, the men on one side and the women on the other. The guards were brusque to the "surly Negroes," especially if they were carrying ammunition. "You're the sort that has caused all of this," said one officer to a black lawyer as he took a handful of pistol cartridges out of his pocket.

Not all blacks went to the hall voluntarily. Officer Leo Irish "captured" six Negroes in the burned district, roped them together in single file, and made them run behind his motorcycle to the detention center. J. W. Hughes, a schoolteacher, was initially taken with his family to the city jail, then forced to march to the Convention Hall. "Many people cheered and clapped their hands as we were marched four abreast with our hands above our head," he said. "A man was shot at the door of the Convention Hall while both hands were above his head. Many men who were shot out in the city were brought in the hall and we heard their cries and groans."

When the Convention Hall was full, blacks were taken through the heart of downtown Tulsa, where spectators were given a further view of the prisoners. The guards shot at the heels of those who couldn't keep pace. Many were taken to McNulty Park, on Tenth and Elgin streets, where the baseball locker rooms were used to separate the men and women, and blacks huddled from one end of the grandstand to another. By Thursday, June 2, 6,000 blacks had been consolidated at the fairgrounds, about one mile northeast of Greenwood, where platforms used to groom cows were transformed into sleeping areas.

Seated on the floor at the fairgrounds was an old woman, a gray handkerchief knotted about her wrinkled face, rocking gently back and forth. In her hand she held a cup of hot vegetable soup. Tears fell from her eyes. "Oh lawdy, me, an old woman that has worked so hard all her life, and now everything is gone. My house burned, my clothes burned, my chickens burned. Nothing have I but the clothes on my back! Oh lawdy, that I should live to see such a day."

Back in Greenwood, a white man surveyed the ruins. Small frame houses had been reduced to charred chimney columns and gateposts. Electric wires and telephone lines hung in tangled loops across pavements and between the shattered walls of brick buildings. Office chairs, sewing machines, trunks, pieces of cars, and piles of clothing and household goods lay in trails of ruin.

"Everything has been destroyed except the earth on which the town was built," he said. "I guess that if there had been any way to set fire to the soil, it would be gone too."

While many white Tulsans acted with depravity, other whites behaved magnanimously, even courageously. They volunteered their services at first-aid stations or tried to douse the raging fires; others stood their ground against armed white vigilantes who went from door to door in search of black cooks, maids, and butlers. White homeowners hid their domestics in basements and attics or smuggled them out of town. When Charles and Amy Arnold refused to release their housekeeper, the marauders yelled "Nigger lovers" and heaved a brick through their front window. A young white stenographer named Mary Jo Erhardt heard the gunshots at night from her room at the YWCA at Fifth and Cheyenne. In the morning, she was heading downstairs when she heard the familiar voice of a black porter who worked there.

"Miss Mary! Oh, Miss Mary!" he said. "Let me in quick." Armed whites, he said, were chasing him.

Erhardt quickly directed him to a walk-in refrigerator and had stashed him behind the beef carcasses when she heard a pounding on the door. She saw three white men with revolvers.

"What do you want?" she asked.

"Where did he go?" one asked.

"Where did who go?"

"That nigger! Did you let him in here?"

"Mister, I'm not letting anybody in here!"

The men left, although ten minutes passed before Erhardt felt the black man could be safely released.

Many blacks sought refuge in Tulsa's white churches, sometimes leaving a trail of blood on their steps. The Holy Family Catholic Church received four hundred refugees on the first day of the riot, twenty-five of them babies. They were bathed and clothed, and the adults were also given clothes and food. The First Presbyterian Church used its basement to shelter mothers with infants, children separated from parents, and terrified women and children. Five dead bodies were also deposited outside the church, perhaps because its pastor, the Reverend Charles Kerr, was known to be sympathetic to African Americans. The First Baptist Church set up cots for the wounded, but many victims had to lie on the floor or on wooden benches. The YWCA opened a Hostess House on Archer Street, which included baths, "disinfection," sewing machines, restrooms, and employment registration.

These acts of kindness could not erase the images of horror for others. Ruth Avery, a white girl in first grade at the time, would often recall two truckloads of dead black bodies riding down the street, their arms and legs protruding through the slats. "I saw a boy on top of the bodies," she told a television interviewer in the 1980s. "He was wearing brown pants and a blue shirt. When the truck hit a pothole, his head flipped over and his mouth was open and his eyes were open. It looked like he was frightened to death. I screamed."

Lucille Kittle, then a white teenager from Sand Springs, recalled in the 1980s how she tried to comfort the destitute Negroes who appeared in her town:

> There must have been two hundred blacks from Tulsa, mostly women and children, who walked that north road out to Sand Springs. I felt so sorry for those people. All I could do was cry, but they were crying too, so that didn't help anyone. But they were terrified, and I was appalled. I'm not sure I even knew what "appalled" meant at age fifteen, but I was appalled at how horrible it was. There was no complaining, no griping, no doing, no nothing. They simply were shocked and stunned into silence. Children, little kids walked those nine miles. It wasn't pleasant, and it's not pleasant to talk about now either.

Some witnesses were less sympathetic. Paul Haggard, who was twelve years old in 1921, was a friend of Don Adkison, the police commissioner's son. The morning after the riot, the commissioner took the two boys with him to inspect Greenwood. "Whoa boy, what I saw," Haggard said in the 1970s. "There was a store whose front had been knocked out, and Don and I found two boxes of Crackerjacks. So we're eating those, and then we came across them colored boys who were down there on the tracks and they'd been shot, and the sun

was on them and all that stuff. And that's where we threw the Crackerjacks." He chuckled at the memory.

The ruins of Greenwood were a grim display of racial hatred, but
prejudice alone does not explain the motives of a white community
that depended on blacks for so many service jobs. It was also clear, in
retrospect, that each side misunderstood the actions of the other and
made fateful decisions as a result. The riot was not only an expression of hostility between the two groups but also a reflection of the
isolation and mistrust each community felt for the other.

White Tulsa's central miscalculation was that blacks were trying to
take over the city, a blunder partly engendered by their own racism.
Whites who assumed that blacks were inclined to be violent could
believe that a relatively small Negro population would defy all logic
and launch a raid against white Tulsans, even though such an attack would be suicidal. Blacks, of course, were not suicidal, but savages were, at least the black savages in the imagination of white
America. As blacks in Oklahoma and elsewhere began using force to
resist oppression, white Tulsans' anxieties were reinforced by headlines shouting FEARS OF NEGRO UPRISING, which recalled the early
slave rebellions.

The armed blacks who drove through white Tulsa and marched to
the courthouse were undeniably militant, but the whites assumed
that they represented all black Tulsans as well as blacks in Muskogee and the other towns that were supposedly preparing to attack.
If such an assault had occurred, then a full-throttle counterattack
would have been appropriate. But these assumptions were all wrong.
The blacks who left Greenwood hardly formed a monolith of Negro
opinion; the whites' bigotry blinded them to the obvious fact that diverse opinions exist among African Americans just as they do among
whites.

Most white Tulsans were ignorant of this logic, but the armed
blacks were also oblivious of the panic that their actions would create. Segregation imposed an invisible wall between the two communities, making blacks and whites strangers. Even whites who employed black servants often did not know their employees' last
names. This isolation and the absence of communication prevented

the two sides from comprehending each other's actions in the early evening hours of May 31. The whites did not realize that blacks had legitimate fears that Dick Rowland would be lynched, even after the sheriff reassured them. But the blacks didn't realize that their actions — driving in large groups into white Tulsa, occasionally firing guns in the air — would be interpreted as an attempt to take over the city.

Oddly enough, the safest black man in Tulsa during the riot was Dick Rowland. He stayed in the jail under guard that night, was spirited out of town the next morning, and was never seen again in Tulsa.

III. The Legacy

Blame and Betrayal

ONCE THE RIOT ENDED, Tulsa's white elite was not sure how to react. While prosecutors began court proceedings against the "Negro instigators," other white leaders voiced contrition and urged the city to rebuild Greenwood. A judge said that the city and county were "legally liable" for all damages, and the *Tulsa World* began its lead editorial on June 2: "Proud, matchless Tulsa comes before the bar of Christian civilization this day and, with head bowed, the mantle of shame upon her cheek, and, we sincerely hope, with deep regret in her heart, asks that she be pardoned the great offense some of her citizens committed." Even Richard Lloyd Jones, publisher of the *Tulsa Tribune*, expressed sympathy to "thousands of colored people, most of whom are innocent."

But this view was soon replaced by a consensus that blamed the riot on the blacks and shifted the responsibility for restoring the Negro district to the victims. In fact, the betrayal of Greenwood after the riot was as great a crime as its destruction, because it was carried out not by a faceless white mob but by the men who led the city's most important business, political, and religious institutions.

Tulsa's bad faith was revealed early on, in its tabulation of the dead. Immediately after the riot, officials issued wildly conflicting figures that kept reducing their number. On June 1, the *Tribune* reported that 9 whites and 68 blacks had died, but a bulletin in that same issue said about 175 were known dead. The *Kansas City Star*, citing Major Daley of the National Guard, also reported on June 1 that 175 were killed. But the next day the *Tribune* significantly pared the number down to 30 deaths: 9 whites and 21 blacks. The same day, the *New York Times* said 77 people had been killed, including 68 blacks, but then five days later it too lowered its number, reporting that only 33 people had been killed. These dwindling estimates raised suspicions among black Tulsans while producing a comical headline in the *World:* RIOT DEAD DECREASE. Ultimately, the Bureau of Vital Statistics in the Oklahoma Department of Health settled on 10 whites and 26 blacks killed in the riot, but that number was never accepted by Tulsa's blacks or by many black journalists, including Walter White.

White's account of the riot in the *Nation* was noteworthy for its dispassionate analysis. He argued that the conflagration was caused by the whites' envy of blacks' success, ineffectual law enforcement, and black "radicals" demanding equality; he concluded that between 200 and 250 people had died, with blacks accounting for 75 to 80 percent of the total. Even white observers agreed with these higher numbers: O. T. Johnson, the head of the Salvation Army in Tulsa, said a minimum of 150 blacks were killed, and Maurice Willows, the director of the Red Cross relief effort in Tulsa, who spent seven months in the city, wrote in his final report: "The number of dead is a matter of conjecture. Some knowing ones estimate the number of killed as high as 300, others estimate [its] being as low as 55. The bodies were hurriedly rushed to burial, and the records of many burials are not to be found."

The numbers would have been even higher if they had included those who died from disease or exposure while living in tents after the riot. In the first week, 384 army tents were erected, many of which had wooden floors and screen doors. Some refugees lived in tents for well over a year, combating floods, heat, and cold. Pneumonia, typhoid fever, malnutrition, smallpox, and stress all took their toll. So too did broken hearts. The Red Cross reported that 8 premature births resulted in stillborn babies. At least one newborn did survive, named June Riot.

Three hundred became the widely accepted upper estimate of riot dead. But even accepting the Tulsa officials' understated body count of 36, the disaster ranked as one of the deadliest riots in American history. Only the New York City draft riots in 1863, with an estimated 105 deaths, were definitively worse.

Determining the number of casualties was complicated by Adjutant General Barrett's decision to deny funerals for the deceased. Barrett justified his order on the grounds that "many of these churches" were being used as shelters for refugees. But it was the white churches that were being used as shelters, and most of the bodies that needed burial were black. This denial of proper funerals was one more indignity against black Tulsa, and it further scrambled the already bewildering task of counting and handling the corpses. Where did all the bodies go? It would be one of the most controversial legacies of the riot. For generations, stories persisted that African Americans were "stacked like cordwood" on flatbed trucks ("dead wagons") and driven out of town; that they were dumped in mass graves; that they were thrown into incinerators, coal mines, or the Arkansas River. Tulsa's children, white and black, grew up hearing stories that their elders once "smelled burning flesh" or that "the Arkansas ran red."

No mystery surrounded the destruction of physical property. The buildings in most of Greenwood were either looted, burned, or both. The commercial district was now a brick and stone skeleton surrounded by mounds of ash and cinder. Gone were the Dreamland and Dixie theaters, the Liberty Café and Elliot Hooker's clothing store, B. C. Franklin's law office and Mabel Little's beauty salon. Gone also were at least a half-dozen churches, a public library, a public hospital, a junior high school, and most of Greenwood's 191 businesses. The Red Cross reported that 1,256 houses burned while 215 others were looted but not torched. The Tulsa Real Estate Exchange estimated that the property damage amounted to $1.5 million ($12.5 million today), a third of which was in the business district. The commission also estimated the loss of personal property at $750,000. Between June 14, 1921, and June 6, 1922, Tulsans filed riot-related claims against the city for more than $1.8 million.

The pattern of the riot was not unique. In East St. Louis, Illinois, and Elaine, Arkansas, and other towns, whites had invaded, robbed, and torched black areas. But given the commercial development of Greenwood, it is unlikely that any previous race riot had ever produced such dramatic economic losses. What's more, no conflict had resulted in the liquidation of virtually an entire black community and the institutions that held it together. It was reminiscent of the pogroms of czarist Russia and an omen of the ethnic cleansing that would, decades hence, sear central Africa and the Balkans. What began as a "riot" or a "war" in Tulsa had concluded as a massacre.

Race relations in America had been relatively calm since the "red summer" of 1919, when battles wracked dozens of towns and lynchings surged. But the Tulsa riot — or THE ERUPTION OF TULSA, as Walter White's story in the *Nation* was headlined — was a bracing reminder of a profound nationwide racial division.

The *St. Louis Post-Dispatch* said: "We have in this country an ugly race problem, and to ignore it is only to postpone the day of reckoning." The *Houston Post* warned: "The race problem is not being solved in any part of the country," while the *New York World* added: "So long as the negro is denied . . . the rights and immunities guaranteed him . . . the way is open to the repetition of such tragedies." But such warnings were disregarded by the federal government, which did little in response to the disaster. Attorney General Harry M. Daugherty ordered a general inquiry into the riot, but the Department of Justice concluded that no federal question was involved. A Senate subcommittee holding hearings on a "riot investigation bill" considered looking into the Tulsa incident but also failed to act. Representative L. C. Dyer of Missouri hoped the riot would help his antilynching bill — which would, among other things, impose $10,000 fines on the counties in which lynchings occurred — but the bill died anyway. Many members of Congress opposed the legislation on the ground that it interfered with the police power of a state.

Even after the riot was over, white Tulsans continued to believe that they would be invaded by armed Negroes from other towns as the police fielded dozens of panicked calls to that effect. City leaders formed the Business Man's Protective League of two hundred fifty men to deploy armed patrols on the roads leading to Tulsa as well as key streets within city limits. In what a later age would call "racial profiling," they were instructed to halt any African American who looked suspicious and to fire if the individual refused to stop on command. Seeking further information on a possible invasion, a Tulsa police captain used an airplane to reconnoiter the black towns of Boley, Red Bird, Taft, and Wybark, as well as black neighborhoods in predominantly white towns. Nothing unusual was sighted.

But white fears were not placated. Despite the city's disastrous experiment in deputizing civilians, Tulsa County issued special commissions to new deputies after the riot. This time, Major Patrick J. Hurley, an army veteran who later became U.S. secretary of war, organized a force of a hundred men to assist the sheriff. Most of the new deputies had been Rough Riders in the Spanish-American War and were supposedly chosen for their fearlessness and their ability to handle a gun. They faced little opposition; the blacks were in no position to initiate a fight and the whites had nothing left to destroy.

Despite their fears, white Tulsans tried to return quickly to business as usual. Seidenbach's, for example, had closed during the riot; the next day it ran an ad in the *World:* "Our Great June Sale of Underwear, advertised in Wednesday's *World,* will be held today."

But for many whites, routine could not be so easily restored. For all the pride they took in their felt superiority and their segregated lives, they relied on blacks to wash their clothes, sweep their restaurants, and provide myriad other services. The *Tribune* wrote that the riot had produced "white mourners as well as colored ones [because] nearly all [whites] who had their family wash in the destroyed negro huts lost their clothes." Indeed, the riot created a crisis among "society women," who, as the *Tribune* reported, "found it necessary to cook their first meals in years while in the Maple Ridge and Sunset Park district, women of the house could be seen putting out their family wash. It was a strenuous day in many a Tulsa home."

Merchants were donning overalls and pushing brooms. Hotel

clerks doubled as porters. Virtually every restaurant window displayed signs advertising for cooks and dishwashers. Employment offices were swamped by calls for laundresses. At the fairgrounds, whites searched for their former servants, but most of them knew their employees only as "Annie," "Luella," or "Aunt Lizzie." This was a problem, according to the *Tribune,* because "there are dozens of 'Annies' and 'Lizzies' in darkeytown."

Almost a month after the riot, the *Tribune* reported that the sounds of "rub, rub, rub" from washboards in Greenwood indicated that Negro women were busy once again. "There are scores of women in whom the news will incite devout thanksgiving," the newspaper said, "because it has a very real and economic value to them. It implies that once again the washing can be taken away from the house, kept a few days and returned in the state of virginal whiteness that was its weekly habit in the days before the riot."

With these inconveniences surmounted, white Tulsans turned to the task of assigning blame for the riot. The city's establishment, including the press, the courts, the politicians, and the church, quickly created a narrative of black responsibility for Greenwood's immolation. In an echo of the "old Negro–new Negro" construct that followed Reconstruction, the "bad Negroes" had started the riot while the "good Negroes" humbly submitted to their white saviors. According to the *World*'s article "Negroes Shuffle to Safe Retreat": "The men walked, and as they passed up the city's most traveled street, they held both hands high above their heads, their hats in one hand, in token of their submission to the white man's authority."

Local newspapers that had previously ignored the city's black residents were suddenly depicting them at length as simpletons. Under the headline NEGRO WOMAN GIVES GUARDS PHONOGRAPHS, the *Tribune* reported:

> The grim shadow of death and desolation that broods over Tulsa today took on its first hint of a softer tone this afternoon when an old gray-haired negro mammy climbed haltingly up Standpipe hill from the charred embers that had been her home, with a big, wooden box in her arms. Straight she came to a group of men in [the] khaki garb of National Guardsmen, heavily armed, who tramped watchfully

about a machine gun trained on the valley of smoldering ruins out of which she had emerged. "I jes saved mah talkin' machine an' mah Bible records," the worn old woman explained plaintively, as she surrendered herself and her burden to the soldiers. "Ah wants you all to use it, kase I hain't got no place tuh keep it now."

A black man named W. C. McDonald received four days' pay from his white employer to tide him over. According to the *Tribune,* he "rattled the four silver dollars down on the desk of Carl Pleasant and said, 'Yo all give me foah dolla's too much. Ah thot the best time to bring it back was whilst ah had it.'"

These were the good Negroes — grateful, penitent, defeated — and they condemned not whites but blacks.

"De good Lawd has sent terrible punishment on us niggahs!" an "old negro mammy" was quoted in the *World.* "I sho hopes dey kills dem bad niggahs dat is responsible fo' dis misery. Thank de Lawd all de onions ain't gone. Jes de tops scorched. Land sakes, I sho don' know what we's gwine to do."

Accordingly, detention centers for Negroes were not a deprivation but a blessing. Blacks "were pathetically grateful to the white folks who had come for them and brought them to a place of safety and who were caring for them," the *Tribune* wrote. "In the afternoon, trucks guarded with uniformed and armed men carried the negroes at McNulty Park and Convention Hall to the fair grounds, where the air was better."

The *World* observed that "the unquenchable humor of the negro race manifested itself even in this dire extremity of the innocent ones who suffered most heavily. 'Dem shooters took $40 out o' my trunk,' one negro woman confided to another today as she was inspecting her house . . . 'You'll can't blame dem cause dey wasn't gettin' paid nothin' for their work,' the other negro sympathized."

At first the *World* published editorials strongly denouncing the white rioters (although calling them "members of a superior race"). It also established a relief fund that raised $5,642.50, including $250 from the Kansas City Waffle House with thirty black employees. But the newspapers' infantile depictions of blacks after the riot dovetailed with their standard coverage of Negroes as drunken, divorced, lynched, or murderous. Visiting Greenwood, perhaps for the first time, reporters discovered an alien land — or, as the *World* said, "a foreign country."

> The whole district is so different from the city Tulsans think of as their city that it might be in a foreign country as far as any resemblance it may have to the real Tulsa. The streets were unnamed, the houses unnumbered, barns were built in the streets in the same line with the houses, and general confusion instead of order was the predominant characteristic of the district before the flames reduced most of it to charred ruins.

These bleak images made the mob's destruction seem less heinous, as if rioters had merely turned blight into ruin. Some whites, most notably Richard Lloyd Jones, even argued that Greenwood's demolition represented a net gain for Tulsa.

Before the riot, Jones had launched a hostile campaign against the city administration, accusing the police of ineptitude and the mayor of corruption. His attacks stemmed in part from an unrelated issue, the future water supply of Tulsa; his patron, Charles Page, had a financial interest in one plan, and the mayor favored a competing plan. At stake were millions of dollars for one of the most ambitious municipal projects in American history. Jones's attacks were designed to weaken the city officials politically, and the riot gave him a chance to renew his charges.

Thus, he initially blamed the riot on the authorities. On Friday, June 3, he wrote, "City and county authorities are responsible for this distressing story and this appalling loss of property." He also urged Tulsans to donate clothes, food, and money to the Red Cross for the victims.

But this generosity quickly vanished. The following day, his lead editorial wove together political attacks on the city administration with a racist screed. In "It Must Not Be Again," he wrote:

> Such a district as the old "Niggertown" must never be allowed in Tulsa again. It was a cesspool of iniquity and corruption . . . Anybody could go down there and buy all the booze they wanted. Anybody could go into the most unspeakable dance halls and base joints of prostitution.
>   In this old "Niggertown" were a lot of bad niggers and a bad nigger

is about the lowest thing that walks on two feet. Give a bad nigger his booze and his dope and a gun and he thinks he can shoot up the world. And all these four things were to be found in "Niggertown" — booze, dope, bad niggers and guns.

The Tulsa Tribune makes no apology to the Police Commissioner or to the Mayor of this city for having pleaded with them to clean up the cesspools in this city.

Commissioner Adkison has said that he knew of the growing agitation down in "Niggertown" some time ago and that he and the Chief of Police went down and told the negroes that if anything started they would be responsible.

That is first class conversation but rather weak action.

Well, the bad niggers started it. The public would now like to know: why wasn't it prevented? Why were these niggers not made to feel the force of law and made to respect the law? Why were not the violators of the law in "Niggertown" arrested? Why were they allowed to go on in many ways defying the law? Why? Mr. Adkison, why?

Jones's tirade would give him a measure of immortality as future scholars and journalists cited it to capture the visceral bigotry of Tulsa. His accusations were particularly scurrilous in light of the number of whites outside Tulsa who held his own newspaper partly responsible. General Barrett attributed the conflict to "an impudent Negro, a hysterical girl, and a yellow journal reporter." He later wrote that the article implied "a sex impulse" as the basis of the attack, and many Tulsans "drove to the county jail after dinner engagements in the hope that they might witness a form of Roman holiday in the way of an attempted lynching." Maurice Willows of the Red Cross, in his official report, wrote on the origins of the conflict: "A newspaper headline — some local irritations — a band of negroes, a larger band of whites — plenty of guns, and a riot was on." The *Kansas City Star,* which published some of the most balanced coverage of the riot, said on June 4 that its origins were the misuse of a single word. "An afternoon newspaper . . . used the word 'assault' . . . The public got the meaning that rape had been attempted, which was untrue. But 'assault' in connection with a white girl and a young negro was enough to fan the flame of race feeling that was existent between the semi-idle young men of both races in Tulsa." Loren Gill, who interviewed both black and white leaders of Tulsa in his 1946 thesis on the riot, concluded bluntly: "This highly discolored and illusory news-paper article precipitated Tulsa's race riot."

White civic organizations also condemned black Tulsans for the riot. The Kiwanis Club praised "the actions of those citizens of our city who during the late emergency risked their lives in overcoming, ar-resting and disarming the Negro ruffians who sought by force of arms to intimidate officers and citizens and impose their will on our fair city." Just as some blacks would allege that whites had carefully planned the riot, the same charge was also being leveled against blacks. The Tulsa Silver Plume Lodge Knights of Pythias, which billed itself as "one hundred percent American," said, "We believe the awful tragedy . . . was a premeditated, unlawful uprising of a large number of armed Negroes who appeared in the heart of the business district . . . and without cause fired upon white men, women and children." The Tulsa Ministerial Alliance was more catholic in its criticism, blaming the disregard of moral and criminal codes, public dancing, and uncensored motion pictures, among other scourges. Several ministers specifically blamed the blacks. Bishop E. D. Mouzon, in an angry sermon at the Boston Avenue Methodist Church on June 5, said that W.E.B. Du Bois was "the most vicious Negro in the coun-try" and suggested that his March speech in Tulsa had a bearing on the riot. J. W. Abel of the First Methodist Church said, "Every Negro accessory to the crime of inciting and taking part in the riot last Tuesday must be run down and brought to trial."

Politicians, too, blamed Greenwood's destruction on Greenwood it-self. Mayor Evans, in a statement to the city commissioners on June 14, was particularly insensitive and graceless. "Let the blame for this Negro uprising lie right where it belongs — on those armed negroes and their followers who started this trouble and who instigated it," he said. "Any person who seeks to put half the blame on the white people are wrong and should be told so in no uncertain terms." Noting reports that armed blacks had twice before made incursions into white Tulsa, the mayor said that they had come only once in his administration. "We are not prophets, but we wager that trip num-ber two will not take place soon."

Echoing the sentiments of Richard Lloyd Jones, Evans claimed that the "destruction" might have been a positive development because, according to "many wise heads in Tulsa," the "uprising" was inevitable. "If that be true and this judgment had to come upon us, then I say it was good generalship to let the destruction come to that section where the trouble hatched up . . . All regret the wrongs that fell upon the innocent Negroes [but] the fortunes of war fall upon the innocent as well as the guilty."

Three days later Oklahoma's attorney general, S. P. Freeling, spoke at the Hotel Tulsa, pining for the "old Negro" and voicing concerns about blacks' exaggerated notions of equality. "The cause of this riot was not Tulsa," he said. "It might have happened anywhere for the Negro is not the same man he was thirty years ago when he was content to plod along his own road accepting the white man as his benefactor. But the years have passed and the Negro has been educated and the race papers have spread the thought of race equality. Then came the war and in the army the Negro learned the value of organization . . . and in this organization there lies a force that is liable to start trouble any time."

On November 2 Freeling wrote to the assistant attorney general of Minnesota, James E. Markham, seeking to extradite a black man accused of inciting the riot. The letter revealed Oklahoma's chief law enforcement officer to be either delusional or disingenuous. "In my opinion," Freeling wrote, "there is no prejudice in Tulsa County . . . The white citizens immediately began to repair the damage which had been done and the very best men in Tulsa County took charge of the situation." Markham apparently did not believe the accused could get a fair trial in Tulsa County; the fugitive was never returned to Oklahoma.

Freeling played a critical role in a grand jury's investigation of the riot. The governor named District Judge V. W. Biddison as the presiding jurist and Freeling as his assistant. On June 9 twelve jurors began their work behind closed doors, then issued an invitation for testimony. It came as no surprise that the grand jury, on June 25, issued a lengthy report that blamed the Negroes for starting the riot. It said in part: "The [white] crowd assembled about the courthouse being purely spectators and curiosity seekers . . . There was no mob spirit among the whites, no talk of lynching and no arms. The assembly was quiet until the arrival of armed negroes, which precipitated and was the direct cause of the riot."

The grand jury found as indirect causes "agitation among the negroes for social equality" and poor police work by the city and county. It recommended that "colored town" be policed by white officers and urged a more stringent enforcement of segregation laws, specifically citing as harmful the "indiscriminate mingling of white and colored people in dance halls."

The grand jury indicted eighty-eight people, mostly for rioting, carrying weapons, looting, and arson. (The racial breakdown of the indictments was not disclosed.) Dick Rowland was indicted for "unlawfully, violently, forcibly, and feloniously, and against her will, attempt[ing] to ravish, rape and carnally know her, the said Sarah Page . . . of previous chaste and virtuous character."

Freeling, however, was displeased with the proceedings because he wanted to indict several county and city officials. He apparently tried to indict Sheriff McCullough, who testified that he went to sleep after he refused to give up Dick Rowland to the white mob. "I didn't know there had been a riot until I read the papers the next morning at 8 A.M.," he said. Though McCullough signed the telegram to Governor Robertson requesting the National Guard, the sheriff claimed he thought its purpose was to protect the prisoner, not suppress a riot.

The penalty for inciting a riot was death or life imprisonment, but despite all those who were indicted, only one was convicted. Garfield Thompson, a black, was arrested on the night of the riot for carrying a concealed weapon, and he was sentenced to thirty days in the county jail. Most of the indictments never came to trial but were simply dismissed by the county attorney, who may have thought the punishment already meted out by the white mob was sufficient. On September 28 the indictment against Dick Rowland was dismissed, according to court records, "for failure of prosecutrix" — Sarah Page — "to appear and prosecute the case."

The grand jury did hold one white man responsible for the riot — Police Chief John Gustafson, who was charged with neglect of duty and was removed from office. The following month, he faced a grueling two-week trial on charges related to the riot as well as his involvement in a car theft ring. It was a historic event: the lead attorney for the state was Katherine Van Leuven, Oklahoma's assistant attorney general, who became the first woman to address a Tulsa jury. If black Tulsans thought that a female official would be more sympathetic to them, Van Leuven dispelled that hope. In charging Gustafson with negligence, she granted blanket immunity to all the whites who murdered and looted. The state, she said, "has never contended that any law was violated after that trouble at the courthouse. After those armed Negroes had started shooting and killed a white man — then those who armed themselves for the obvious purpose of protecting their property and lives violated no law. The [police] chief neglected to do his duty and the citizens, after seeing their police fail, took matters into their own hands. No, we don't contend that they violated the law."

Her comments had no bearing on Gustafson's innocence or guilt, but they sanctioned the lawless attacks against black Tulsans. The *Louisville News*, a black newspaper, wrote that Van Leuven's statement was "a conscious effort to clear the skirts of the white citizens of Tulsa of all measure of guilt."

The trial was sensational front-page drama. In addition to riot coverage, there was evidence of the city's top police officer's shaking down car thieves for his own profit. After six hours of deliberation, the jury found Gustafson guilty of failing to take proper precautions for the protection of life and property during the riot and for conspiring to free automobile thieves and collect rewards. For white Tulsa, Gustafson's conviction fit the unfolding storyline of the riot: it was triggered by insubordinate blacks, and then it spun out of control because of a corrupt and incompetent police chief. White Tulsa was blameless: the hooligans, the state said, were not violating the law but acting in self-defense.

Richard Lloyd Jones, who had condemned Gustafson even before the riot, felt a measure of redemption and praised his ouster and conviction. But Gustafson had his revenge on the publisher. Despite his conviction, he never served time in prison. Instead, he returned to his work in the private detective business, and his agency was hired by one of Jones's enemies to gather information about the married man's trysts with an editorial assistant at the Hotel Tulsa. The snoops camped out in an adjacent room, witnessed the "hard loving" through a keyhole, and gave a full account to investigators. The scandal failed to drive Jones out of Tulsa, but the hypocrisy of the man who wrote "sermonettes" on trust and honesty had been laid bare.

The state's leaders were no more sympathetic to the black victims' plight. Governor Robertson refused to consign about a hundred National Guard tents to Tulsa, forcing the Red Cross to find its own tents for the homeless. He also refused the offer of fifty Black Cross nurses from the president of the Chicago chapter of the Universal Negro Improvement Association, and he made no offer of state funding or resources for relief or reconstruction. Instead, he asked the city to pay the state $12,750 to cover the costs of sending the National Guard. When the city stalled, Robertson became infuriated, paid the expense from his own budget, then dashed off this withering note to Tulsa on August 23: "I would not have [paid the expense] at all but for the fact that these soldier boys had to be paid. They are all poor and can't understand why the State doesn't pay them after they have performed their duty, and we are liable to need them in the future . . . The next time Tulsa gets in a pinch and begs for troops, I will be compelled to think twice before incurring any indebtedness."

While outraged over his unpaid troops, he expressed no concern over the thousands of homeless blacks, including many children, who were slogging through mud during rainstorms, desperate for food, medicine, and building materials.

Some of those needs would be filled by Maurice Willows of the American Red Cross, a pallid forty-five-year-old social worker and an outspoken advocate for black riot victims. Perhaps his outsider status — he was born in Canada and worked in the Red Cross Southwest Division Headquarters in St. Louis — enabled him to contradict the information provided by local officials. In addition to estimating that as many as three hundred were killed, he refused to use the phrase "negro uprising" in his reports. He called it "civil war-fare" in the official summary of his work, "Disaster Relief Report."

That the Red Cross was even involved in these relief efforts was highly unusual. It was the first time the U.S. agency, founded in 1881, had assisted victims of a manmade disaster, although the International Red Cross regularly aided war casualties. The American Red Cross was also strictly nonpartisan, so the highly charged atmosphere of a race riot made its officials nervous. "Unquestionably there is a big opportunity for misunderstanding any action taken by the Red Cross in connection with race riots," wrote James Fieser, manager of the agency's Southwest Division, to the chairman of Tulsa County's chapter. The agency, he wrote, must act "with unusual caution."

It was also telling that Tulsa would cede basic relief services to an agency accountable to no one in the city. Though Tulsa touted itself as having the highest per capita income in America, it had no public hospital, poor public services, and permanently underfunded social service agencies. Mayor Evans all but fled from the task. On June 2, he wrote to the local Red Cross director, "The responsibility [for all relief work] is placed in your hands entirely."

Ironically, Willows's last day at the Red Cross was to have been May 31; he was scheduled to start a new job in Kansas City in June. Accepting the emergency assignment, he was initially hesitant about moving the agency into such a volatile environment. When he arrived in Tulsa by train early in the morning of June 4, he saw a crowd of blacks being fed in front of the YMCA, the headquarters for the local Red Cross relief effort. But Willows, finding no "providential causes" for the disaster, called Red Cross headquarters in Washington for guidance. He was also concerned about the "race issue." The director told him, "We will take your advice . . . We will back you."

Willows's misgivings soon gave way to his concern for the riot victims and his distrust of the local officials. In his memoirs, he wrote that he ordered "the incumbent city officials," including the mayor and police chief, to "abdicate for a period of sixty days." They gave Willows free rein to provide food, clothes, shelter, and medicine to the riot victims and to distribute funds to help patients pay for care. (The city and county contributed $200,000 for relief efforts.) He assembled a team of about three hundred people, mostly white, including physicians, nurses, social workers, a purchasing agent, an accountant, county and state officials, and many volunteers. He moved the relief headquarters from white Tulsa to Booker T. Washington High School in Greenwood, which inexplicably had not been touched by the mob. There, 2,000 people were temporarily sheltered, with men and women sleeping on opposite sides of the building and long lines waiting for sandwiches and coffee. The school also housed a central hospital, where the black patients were eventually consolidated. It included a dental clinic, a "dispensary" for medicines, and a venereal disease clinic. With abysmal sanitary conditions contributing to an outbreak of smallpox, Willows brought in vaccines from nearby communities and inoculated 1,800 refugees against tetanus, typhoid, and smallpox.

With no public hospitals, the sick and the wounded were initially taken to six private hospitals; a large residence was also commandeered and equipped. According to the Red Cross records, 163 operations were performed in the first week after the riot, and the agency provided care to 763 wounded patients while giving first aid to 530. The numbers understated the riot's true toll. The Red Cross assisted only 48 wounded whites because, Willows wrote, many injured white people avoided the agency; they did not want to be identified as riot participants. All the patients had to explain how they sustained their injuries; the whites who sought assistance often wrote that they had been "innocent bystanders." When a teenager with a gunshot wound invoked that phrase, Willows wrote, a record keeper confronted him with a picture showing "the same young man in the middle of the riot district with a shotgun over his shoulder and high powered rifle in his hand. He has not been seen at the Red Cross office since."

The Red Cross injury list also understated the number of black wounded, who showed up at nearby towns like Muskogee and Sapulpa and as far north as Kansas City, and records showed an unspecified number of "maternity cases" involving complications due to the riot.

More than a decade before the New Deal organized government welfare, public "handouts" were considered odious, even in extreme cases such as Tulsa's. Willows himself believed that riot victims should not simply be given handouts; he set up tents with sewing machines, and women were given cloth and other materials to make clothes, quilts, cot pads, sheets, pillows, and pillowcases. "We furnished all necessary items for the negroes to rehabilitate themselves, requiring themselves to work it all out!" he wrote.

Some white Tulsans who themselves were struggling financially resented what little assistance was given to the downtrodden blacks. A young widow who was earning $15 a week and was about to lose her job wrote to the *World* on June 13: "Yes, give the negroes work, clothes, money, assistance of any kind, but, oh! Fair minded Tulsa, look at the white men and white women who are struggling, begging for a chance to even 'get by,' and they do resent going down and cleaning up the debris in Little Africa when that race has so many idle members."

By June 7, most black men who had lost their jobs after the riot had found employment, in part because white businesses and other organizations had agreed to pay them twenty-five cents an hour. As money began to trickle into the fairgrounds, where many refugees were billeted, the Red Cross started charging twenty cents a meal, but it continued to give away food to the unemployed and the ill. This latter group, along with women with infants, continued to receive relief supplies, but in less copious amounts. They now got "clothing and grocery permits" on an individual basis. As tents with wooden floors were hastily erected around the high school, the fairgrounds rapidly cleared out. On the evening of June 2 it held more than 4,000 people. By June 15 the camp was empty.

In the wake of the riot, contributions poured in from across the country. The Reverend Adam Clayton Powell Sr., one of America's leading black ministers, donated $75 to riot survivors, while the black inmates at the Wisconsin State Prison contributed $116.50. Both checks, funneled through the NAACP, were sent to the Red Cross. Many cities sent telegrams offering aid. Unfortunately, Tulsa's officials quickly adopted the policy that the riot "was strictly a Tulsa affair and that the work of restoration and charity would be taken care of by Tulsa people." Cash contributions would be accepted by the Red Cross for relief, but no donations, cash or otherwise, would be used to reconstruct Greenwood. According to Walter White, all financial contributions to the city were rejected, the donors told "in theatric fashion that the citizens of Tulsa 'were to blame for the riot and that they themselves would bear the cost of restoration.'"

The city's position seemed inexplicable — Greenwood's needs were enormous. But Tulsa, whose swashbuckling boosterism had been central to its growth, put civic pride above the interests of its black citizens. Accepting help would have been a humiliation, an acknowledgment of the scope of its losses. If Tulsa didn't need help, then how bad could the riot have been? The city promised to heal itself.

On June 1 Mayor Evans appointed a Citizens Committee to care for the refugees, a responsibility that was quickly ceded to the Red Cross. The following day, at a meeting of forty business and civic leaders at city hall, General Barrett lambasted his audience for allowing mob law to flourish, and he urged that a more permanent committee be established to restore Tulsa to "normal conditions." In response, the city leaders created the Board of Public Welfare and elected Judge Loyal J. Martin as its chairman.

Martin had been a crusading law-and-order mayor of Tulsa from 1910 to 1912. He closed liquor stores, denounced "harlots," and gave the city its first traffic officers. But nothing had prepared him for the lawlessness he witnessed on June 1 when he went to the Convention Hall and saw two armed whites clenching a black prisoner.

"What are you going to do with him?" Martin demanded.

"We're going to shoot this nigger," one said. "He killed a white man."

"No, you can't do that," the judge said.

"Who's going to stop us?"

"We will." Martin turned to a group of whites and asked if they would stand for this. Many hollered, "No."

Undeterred, the two whites loaded their prisoner into a car and drove to the river. As Martin recalled, "I heard afterwards that they did shoot him — I don't know, for I never saw him again."

The responsibilities for the new group included protecting and rehabilitating the city. An experienced politician, Martin made sure he had the public behind him. He asked through the local newspapers that citizens sign statements of support — he received a thousand — while he also gained endorsements from many clubs in Tulsa. Martin needed that support for his righteous but contrarian advocacy of black riot victims. In his acceptance speech, he proclaimed:

> Tulsa can only redeem herself from the countrywide shame and humiliation into which she is today plunged by complete restitution and rehabilitation of the destroyed black belt. The rest of the United States must know that the real citizenship of Tulsa weeps at this unspeakable crime and will make good the damage, so far as it can be done, to the last penny . . . We have neglected our duties and our city government has fallen down. We have had a failing police protection here, and now we have to pay the costs of it. The city and county are legally liable for every dollar of the damage which was done.

It was a remarkable, even stunning, statement — an appointed official accepting legal liability for the riot and promising restitution, which could cost the city and county millions of dollars. Martin, a Democrat, probably enjoyed berating the Republican mayor, but the statement sent a clear message that Tulsa — white Tulsa — accepted responsibility for Greenwood's destruction.

Martin quickly followed through on his promise. On June 7 he proposed creating a "housing corporation" to finance the rebuilding of homes in the black district. By offering low-interest loans, the corporation would not only allow the homeless to rebuild but would also stimulate black employment. Martin's motives were not entirely altruistic. The businessmen connected to the Board of Public Welfare had agreed to finance the corporation and, indeed, would profit from its success, but that mattered little to homeless blacks desperate for capital.

At the same time, Martin urged Tulsans to donate money for food and shelter, setting a goal of $100,000, and the president of the Chamber of Commerce, Alva J. Niles, announced that the city's leading businessmen were working "not only for the succor, protection, and alleviation of the suffering of the Negroes, but to formulate a plan of reparation" to rebuild Negro homes. At stake was the reputation of Tulsa, he said, which contributed more than $33 million for the war and "can be depended upon to make proper restitution and to bring order out of chaos at the earliest possible moment."

Unfortunately, these promises proved hollow: other members of the city's elite had entirely different plans. On June 3 the Real Estate Exchange, a powerful trade organization, surveyed Greenwood and recommended to the mayor and other officials that an industrial or commercial zone replace the Negro district, which would be moved farther north. The commission also asked for temporary orders that forbade the construction of wooden shacks and prohibited the transfer or sale of property in the "burned district." General Barrett complied with the latter request, instructing the county registers of deeds not to accept any papers of record for property in Greenwood.

Merritt J. Glass, president of the real estate group, said the "burned district's" proximity to the railroads made it ideally suited for industrial use. A union depot, with expanded rail service, was also recommended for the site. Commerce, however, was only part of the reason to expel the blacks from Greenwood. "We further believe," Glass said, "that the two races being divided by an industrial section will draw more distinctive lines between them and thereby eliminate the intermingling of the lower elements of the two races, which in our opinion is the root of the evil which should not exist . . . You must remember that the first impression of men entering our city is lasting." And the sight of black faces was not the first impression the real estate men wanted to give.

But the men had a problem: how to compel blacks, who owned at least one third and probably close to one half of the land in Greenwood, to vacate their own district? Initially, white Realtors held a number of meetings with black representatives, including O. W. Gurley and Barney Cleaver, and offered either to buy black-owned property or exchange it for land north of Greenwood. One black leader was offered a $35,000 commission to negotiate a deal with other African American property owners. At one point, these blacks offered to sell their land at its value prior to the riot, but the whites rejected the idea. The two groups reached an impasse. Some blacks opposed moving because a few important structures, like the high school, had survived, and moving them would be onerous. This resistance was strengthened by an unlikely source — Maurice Willows, who believed he had to protect the blacks against not only disease but also predatory businessmen. According to Frances Dominic Burke, who interviewed black and white Tulsans for a master's thesis on Greenwood (1936), "The deal was never negotiated, [and] much credit must be given to a representative of the American Red Cross, who through his work in that disaster had acquired the confidence of the Negro people and had advised the Negroes against entering into any such [real estate] agreement."

Rebuffed from acquiring the land legally, the real estate men asked city officials to use more perfidious methods. On Monday, June 7, the mayor and the city commissioners extended Tulsa's fire ordinance to include Greenwood. As a result, frame houses could not be constructed — and fire-resistant structures were prohibitively expensive for most blacks. The ordinance would not apply to the proposed Negro resettlement area north of Greenwood.

Neither city officials nor the press tried to justify the fire code as a safety measure for blacks; in fact, they were forthright in explaining the purpose of the ordinance. As the headline in the *Tribune* announced: NEGRO SECTION ABOLISHED BY CITY'S ORDER. The first sentence read: "Thirty-five blocks of the negro district south of Standpipe Hill, now in ruins following the fire of last Wednesday morning, will never again be a negro quarter but will become a wholesale and industrial center." It appeared that Richard Lloyd Jones's stance — that Greenwood "must not be again" — was coming true.

The city's move, however, caused outrage among many blacks and prompted speculation that the riot had not been a spontaneous outbreak but part of a conspiracy to grab valuable land from African Americans. In a letter to the *World*, Ira E. Moore wrote: "Some plot is it not? Could it be possible that such a scheme could be pre-meditated and pre-arranged? . . . We have read of such means being used to acquire the Indian lands in the early days of this great country of ours. Could it be possible? Very likely it could."

At first blacks ignored the order and continued building wooden houses on their burned lots. They had little to lose, a jail cell being no less uncomfortable than a tent. C. F. Gabe, asked if he feared arrest for violating the order, said, "They had better get the jail ready for us, because we are going to keep on building. Negroes are not waiting for winter to come and not have any place to live."

B. C. Franklin, the lawyer, urged his clients to flout the law and build on their property, promising that he would secure the release of anyone arrested. At least one client was arrested a dozen times for defying the new ordinance. But Franklin did far more than release prisoners. After the riot, he and two other black lawyers, I. H. Spears and T. O. Chappelle, opened an "office" in a tent on Archer Street. This arrangement produced one of the most memorable photographs of the riot: two dignified black lawyers in spotless white shirts sitting at a wooden desk, their law books stacked around them, framed by the folds of the canvas tent. The image captured the duress under which the black Tulsans had fought for their rights and the faith they retained in a legal system that had so often betrayed them. On August 12, Franklin filed a suit in district court against the city to prevent its enforcement of the fire ordinance. To do so, he argued, was tantamount to taking property from his client, Joe Lockard, without due process.

By the time the suit was filed, Mayor Evans had already shown his hostility toward blacks. A thin man with dark hair and a narrow face, the fifty-one-year-old Evans was a proud pioneer of Tulsa, having moved to the city from Iowa in 1906. A lawyer by training, he was a partner in a real estate firm, but he had no experience in politics. His term as mayor, from 1920 to 1922, was his only time in elected office, and his political clumsiness showed. On June 14 he disbanded the Public Welfare Board, which had been sympathetic to blacks, charging it with usurping his authority. He also tried to oust the Chamber of Commerce from the municipal building because it had helped the welfare board. The mayor replaced the board with yet another board, a group of cronies who formed the Reconstruction Committee. The mayor's truculence was "like a thunderclap out of a clear sky," according to Maurice Willows's official riot report. Evans had stripped the power of Greenwood's most ardent advocate — Loyal Martin, who now devoted his time to the Red Cross.

The mayor had his own men in charge, and the Reconstruction Committee undid what little progress had been made for Greenwood. While the Public Welfare Board had raised $26,000 for riot victims, contributions all but stopped under the Reconstruction Committee. Its goal was neither relief nor rebuilding but clearing obstacles for the industrial district. It allowed the proposed housing corporation to die, and it rejected a proposal by the Chamber of Commerce to help Negroes rebuild on their own land. As Willows wrote in his report, the committee was "politically constituted and is chiefly interested in maneuvering for the transfer of negro properties and the establishment of a new negro district." The city government, he added in his memoirs, "was not what one might call a 'virtuous' one [and] was shot through with political corruption and inter-racial connivances."

In the end, Tulsa failed to create an industrial district and to move its black residents. On September 1 B. C. Franklin won his lawsuit: three judges declared the fire ordinance unconstitutional on the grounds that it took private property without due process of law. It was a decisive legal victory, rescuing black Tulsans from betrayal by their own government. Less clear was the relationship between the riot and the city's putative "land grab," as it became known. Had the riot been a conspiracy to swindle land from blacks — a belief that persisted in pockets of black Tulsa for the rest of the century — or simply a spontaneous explosion of racial violence? The answer was probably somewhere in between.

The riot occurred in two phases: the downtown firefight at the courthouse and the invasion of Greenwood at daybreak. The evidence is overwhelming that the riot began because blacks believed that a lynching was about to occur and whites interpreted their advance into South Tulsa as an uprising. But certainly the second phase of the riot required organization and planning among the whites. In her thesis on Greenwood for the University of Oklahoma, Burke wrote:

> It is still rumored about Tulsa that one of the immediate causes of the conflict of 1921 was an undercurrent of agitation carried on by a number of white industrialists and financiers who hoped to secure these properties and develop them profitably. Four informants, prominent businessmen of Tulsa today, stated that there was [a] definite organized effort to displace the Negroes from the south portion of Greenwood . . . and that on the night of the riot, a number of business men participating in this plan, actually did much to stimulate the rioters to destroy completely the community.

Burke, a social work student, wrote that the efforts by the white real estate men to buy the burned-out property were then thwarted by inflexible Negro homeowners. Her assessment that the white industrialists and financiers stimulated the rioters — but did not start the riot — seems reasonable. The businessmen had coveted the land for years. After the first phase of the riot, with fears of a Negro uprising riding high, someone had to coordinate and organize thousands of whites for the invasion. Why not the men who had the most to gain by Greenwood's annihilation? If true, it would not mean that the riot had been a conspiracy to grab land, but it would suggest that the incident involved more than random acts of destruction by drunken hooligans.

Rescinding the fire ordinance also brought about the demise of the Reconstruction Committee, which seemed better able to insult the victims than to help them. One of its few accomplishments was a resolution calling for all local civic organizations to donate "old and unnecessary furniture to the relief of negroes," calling the initiative "old furniture day."

A black doctor named Charles Wickham was the first person to file a claim against the city of Tulsa. In light of Gustafson's conviction for negligence, the plaintiff seemed to have a powerful case. The mayor asked a committee — the city attorney, a private attorney, and a lawyer for East St. Louis, Illinois, which had dealt with its own liability claims two years earlier — to evaluate Tulsa's legal standing. On August 6 the committee reported that Tulsa was not liable for "an unlawful uprising of Negroes, unless there is specific negligence shown." The lawyers concluded that negligence had not been shown — even though the police chief had just been convicted on that charge. No matter; neither Charles Wickham nor any other riot victim successfully sued the city. The victims had the same experience with insurance companies that denied claims because of a riot exemption clause in their contracts. By July 30, 1921, plaintiffs had filed 1,400 lawsuits for claims of more than $4 million on property, including household goods, jewels, office equipment, and money. The suits dragged on for years; most were dismissed by the middle 1930s.

While the white mob that invaded Greenwood had been anonymous, the men who betrayed the black Tulsans after the riot occupied prominent positions at city hall and in the community's courthouse, press rooms, churches, and office buildings. Tulsa's leading institutions not only created a white narrative of the riot but also failed to keep its promises for restitution. This betrayal was as unsettling as the assault on Greenwood because it was legal and open. But black Tulsans were not grieving over their betrayal; they were rebuilding their community and writing their own history of the riot.

8

Rising from the Ashes

THE RAINS CAME on June 2, putting out the last of the fires, and with martial law in place, the National Guard had little difficulty imposing order on an exhausted and embarrassed city. Most blacks found themselves homeless, with few resources. Many had lost their businesses. Whites had destroyed their community, yet blacks now relied on white people more than ever. Initially, they were allowed to leave the fairgrounds only if a white employer vouched for them. The *World* observed: "Sullenly and shiftlessly, the negroes stood in line, not looking directly at employers from the race that all but exterminated them yesterday."

Under General Barrett, blacks became wards of the state. Leaving the fairgrounds, they had to wear a green tag that included the individual's name and address, an employer's signature, and the words POLICE PROTECTION. Any African American without proper identification would be arrested and returned to custody. All 7,500 tags were issued by June 7. They were, to blacks, another sign of subjugation, but whites saw them as long overdue. "The green card does something more than help the city get rid of the bad negro," Richard Lloyd Jones wrote. "It is a certificate of industry and decency to every negro who carries it."

Barrett ordered Mayor Evans to withdraw the "special police commissions" after concluding that those bearing them were ringleaders of the mob. The general forbade any cars, except for police, physicians, and the Red Cross, on the street at night. He also shut down most businesses by 6 P.M., and he outlawed carrying a gun on the street without military or police authorization. After the governor visited Tulsa, martial law was lifted the next day, June 3, two days after it had been imposed.

While many blacks praised certain guardsmen for securing their safety, Barrett's rule forced African Americans to endure unnecessary indignities. In addition to prohibiting funerals for riot victims, he effectively compelled forced labor for the blacks in detention camps. All "able-bodied negro men" were required to work, caring for refugees or cleaning up the city, as mandated by the military authorities or the Red Cross. Black women without children were covered by the same order. Those who were able but unwilling to work were arrested on vagrancy charges. The order served a vital purpose for a city that could not find workers to remove the massive debris in the "burned district." So the blacks were paid twenty-five cents an hour to clean up the ruins of their own community.

Some blacks in the detention centers returned to Greenwood believing their homes were still intact. Most were stunned by the scorched chimneys, the charred cement foundation blocks, and the blackened onion tops and cabbages in vegetable gardens. Red Cross relief workers occasionally found signs of life. On the outskirts of Greenwood, two workers on horseback reached a row of houses that had been pillaged but not burned. From a tumbledown, vine-covered hut hobbled a white-haired man named Ofie Page, who had been born a slave. "I always said white folks and cullud people won't never get along," he told the workers. "There's misery 'cause of what's happened today. Crazy niggers and crazy white folks." An old woman carrying her only remaining possession, a guitar, trudged along the road toward the heap of ashes that had been her house. From another hut stumbled an old woman trembling with fright, weakly waving a white rag. She stopped and watched the relief workers in their pressed white shirts. When she heard who they were, tears rolled down her wrinkled face, and she praised the Lord that the terror of the night was over.

C. L. Netherland, who owned a barbershop, later described his losses: "From a ten-room-and-basement modern brick home, I am now living in what was my coal barn. From a five-chair white enamel barber shop, four baths, electric clippers, electric fan, two lavatories and shampoo stand, four workmen, double-marble shine stand, a porter, and an income of over $500 to $600 per month, to a razor, strop, and folding chair on the sidewalk."

Returning refugees began searching desperately for valuables. Two blacks who had just purchased an eight-room house and car had converted their remaining $300 into gold and silver coins. Their home was burned in the riot, their car stolen, and with their remaining cents in their pockets, they sifted through the ash in search of their gold and silver. Meanwhile, scores of blacks swarmed around police headquarters to identify stolen property that had been recovered by the authorities. The loot was piled in the station's basement, and each item — carpets, Victrolas, stoves — had been tagged with the address from which it had been confiscated.

The search for people was even more desperate. Under its "Lost and Found" column, the *World* ran classified ads from blacks looking for their loved ones. The *Tribune* on June 4 reported: "R. E. Love, negro, has searched for his family since Wednesday morning [June 1]. He has not seen or heard from his wife and four children, one a baby a month old."

An estimated 10,000 African Americans lived in Tulsa at the time; with 60 to 80 percent of them placed in detention centers, 2,000 blacks — and perhaps twice that — left Tulsa for some period of time. Hundreds bought one-way train tickets to places as far away as New York or San Francisco, while others were seen walking to Bartlesville, Broken Arrow, Claremore, Collinsville, Dewey, Muskogee, Owasso, Sapulpa, and Sperry. Riot postcards were mailed around the country; one featured a wide-angle shot of a half-dozen blacks walking down an empty dirt road, the sky blackened by a sweep of dark clouds. "Running the Negro Out of Tulsa," the card read.

The riot had other repercussions. The following Saturday, the city's clerk issued twenty-three marriage licenses, mostly to blacks, and "the run on the hymeneal altar was continuing unabated today," a newspaper reported on Monday. A "black cupid" was "perched on the smoking ruins of the negro district," but his arrival was no cause for celebration. Young women who had rejected matrimony were now accepting "the protection of their dusky suitors since [the women] face the future penniless and without a roof to cover their heads."

The first month after the riot, the scheming real estate men had far less impact on black Tulsans than the weather did. It rained like hell. Heavy storms from June 18 to June 28 caused massive floods on the Arkansas River, which sometimes rose two inches an hour. Sewers everywhere were clogged with water and debris. Low crossings were turned into lakes; two feet of water stood in some intersections. Cars bobbed helplessly down streets. On August 5, a particularly vicious downpour lasting only forty-five minutes dumped an inch of water on Tulsa, blew down trees, toppled electric wires, paralyzed traffic, and caused two fires. The following night, another storm forced more than fifty black women and children to seek protection in the Red Cross headquarters. The driving rain blew down their tents and soaked their bedding, and their stoves and firewood were so drenched that they could not start fires until the following afternoon. Maurice Willows said the storm served notice of what might be expected in the fall.

Black Tulsans were obviously ill prepared to handle such conditions. According to a report from Willows on June 30, only seventy tents had lumber floors; more than two hundred others had only canvas separating their occupants from the ground. Willows also said that about 3,500 blacks were still "without adequate housing, tentage, bedding, and clothing. These are for the most part women and children without breadwinners to provide income."

Willows also noted forcefully: "The extent of relief work necessary will not diminish until some authority, municipal or otherwise, sets in motion plans whereby these thousands of homeless and destitute people can be restored to homes and earning power."

Once the city's fire ordinance was declared unconstitutional, black Tulsans could rebuild in earnest. Money began to trickle back into Greenwood the same way it always had — through the wages of black servants — and some blacks had savings. But most did not have the necessary funds to reconstruct their homes and businesses. Those who had credit borrowed money, many from white employers, and they built shacks with one or two rooms. Although Willows claimed in his report that the Red Cross did not take part in reconstruction efforts — a task for the city, he said — he disclosed in his memoirs that the agency did help in rebuilding. With lumber in short supply, Willows dispatched his purchasing agent to nearby mills, which gave him two carloads of lumber. "Local negro carpenters were provided the lumber, they did the work of building homes," he wrote.

Plank by plank, nail by nail, Greenwood rebuilt, and the resourcefulness and energy of the community was a source of pride across black America. But the price, as Mabel Little discovered, was also high.

Little had spent seven years building her beauty salon, while her husband, Pressley, ran a café. At the time of the riot, they also owned their own house and two rental properties — emblems of success in the community — and they had just paid cash for a shipment of new furniture, but their property was now easy prey for the white mob. The Littles stayed in their house on the night of the riot, but the next morning, with the mob bearing down, they fled on foot with Mabel's mother, who had followed her daughter to Tulsa. (Their Model T Ford was either damaged in the fighting or stolen.) With other blacks, they began walking north to the town of Turley, but they were soon stopped by National Guardsmen in a truck.

"We're going to take the men back," a guardsman said.

Mabel Little was not about to be left behind. "If you're going to kill us, kill us all together. You are not going to leave my mother and me in an out camp."

They were all put in the truck and taken to the First Presbyterian Church, where white volunteers brought them food, clothes, and comfort — "Christian women with blood on their sleeves," as Little described them. Some of these women let refugees stay in their homes temporarily.

With all of their property destroyed and only fifty dollars to their name, the Littles stayed briefly in the house of a white man, then moved to the fringe of Greenwood, Marshall Street, more than a mile north of the business district. They cut cornstalks to clear the ground and erected a three-room shack. There was no electricity, no water, and no gas. They had to clear mounds of debris, cook outside with wood, and dig wells for drinking water. The labor wore down Pressley. Without the resources to open another café, he spent the next three years doing carpentry and reconstruction work, toiling in the heat of summer, in pools of sewage, and on frozen ground during winter. One day Pressley came down with the flu, which soon turned to tuberculosis.

The doctors told Pressley that he was going to die. Only one tuberculosis sanitarium in Oklahoma accepted blacks, but Mabel could not get her husband admitted. For three years he suffered and withered. He did get into a home in Colorado Springs, Colorado, where the clean air was a balm. But the separation from Mabel, who had reopened her salon, was too painful for him, and he went home. "It was hard to see him in such pitiful shape, lying in bed just dwindling and wasting away," Little wrote in her memoir. "You could see the terror and misery in his eyes as they slowly began to sink into their sockets. At times he could sit up for awhile, but his body would wretch continually with a chronic hacking cough, and his chest was always wracked with pain."

In 1927 Pressley was admitted to the Clinton sanitarium, two hundred and twenty miles away on winding dirt roads, and Mabel worked day and night to pay for the expense. He died three months after his admission.

Pressley Little's name did not appear on any list of riot victims, but it was the riot, Mabel believed, that killed him. "He was forced into outdoor work to which he was unaccustomed, cleaning up debris which undoubtedly exposed him to the tubercular germs so rampant in those days," she wrote in 1990. "He was my one and only true love, my pride and joy, my shining black knight; and I have clearly discovered that I could never love another man the way I loved him."

While Tulsa's white establishment created one explanation for the riot, the city's blacks drafted a very different story, which was voiced in newspapers and journals across the country. The Negroes in Tulsa were hailed as heroes for preventing a lynching and for fighting back. If the death count for blacks was high, so too for whites. In the worst of the early race riots — in Wilmington, North Carolina (1898), Atlanta (1906), and Springfield, Illinois (1907) — no whites were killed. But that had changed in recent years. In the riots of 1919, five whites had been killed in Elaine, and fifteen died in Chicago. "The Afro-American is fighting back — meeting violence with violence," reported the *St. Louis Argus,* a black newspaper. "And one may be pretty certain that, taking the cue from Tulsa, the Afro-American will fight fire with fire in future riots."

When W.E.B. Du Bois visited Tulsa in 1926, he could barely contain his pride. Tulsa, he wrote, "is the most astonishing case of Negro grit of which I ever heard. I know the softer side of my folk; they cringe, they give up. But now and here in Tulsa, they fight back; they kill and die and rise again and they do not know when they are whipped. I stand before Tulsa with uncovered head." Black Tulsans, Du Bois asserted, were not acting in self-defense but they were the aggressors. He wrote:

> Black Tulsa started that riot. It went gunning for lynchers. It said, "There shall be no lynching"; there was none. But there was war. A flying squadron of black riflemen rushed into white Tulsa. Driven back, they sniped and killed the white invaders from the housetops. White Tulsa and all the countryside armed for war. They came down to black Tulsa with machine guns and airplanes. It was real war: murder, fire, rape, theft . . . Black Tulsa rose triumphant from the dead. Black Tulsa will fight again if fight it must and white Tulsa knows it.

Several truths animated the black version of the battle. Black Tulsans would have won the riot, except that an aerial assault — "fire bombs" or "turpentine bombs" or "liquid fire" — rained terror on Greenwood. Dead bodies were hidden in mass graves, coal mines, incinerators, or the river. The blacks who went to the courthouse were not whiskey-drinking, gun-toting outlaws whose reckless behavior began the riot. They were heroes who prevented a lynching, army veterans who had fought for the very freedoms in France that they were denied in America. Those who did not make it back to Greenwood died as martyrs for a noble cause.

As the *Wilmington Advocate*, a black newspaper, wrote:

[Black] men fought with utter abandon against the human devils above and around them. As the scorching, white fire from airships above was poured upon them, the defenders of their homes made a valiant effort to stave off the blood-thirsty passion of the hounds who killed them. Men slipped and fell in the blood of their brothers. White men died cursing "niggers." Railroad property on the tracks was utterly demolished. One man, leaning far out from an airplane, was brought down by the bullet of a sharpshooter and his body burst upon the ground. Men were hideous. Women were evil. Judgment was in the air and the multitude perished.

Breathless embellishments occasionally gave way to absurd fabrications. The *Washington Eagle* reported that, according to one black witness, the riot actually began on May 29 after a white dairyman killed a "colored girl" who had spilled a pail of milk. More typical were newspaper accounts that the riot had been organized by white oilmen to grab valuable land. Eight black Oklahomans in New York claimed that African Americans were told to leave the state by June 1 through newspaper announcements and on little cards pasted to the doors of Negro homes.

Tulsa's two black newspapers were destroyed in the riot, but the *Star*'s publisher, A. J. Smitherman, wrote a lengthy poem, "The Tulsa Riot and Massacre," that distilled the black community's narrative of the event. Protecting Dick Rowland, he wrote, was a matter of "Negro manhood," and after blacks stopped the lynching, the whites called in reinforcements and prepared to invade.

> But our boys who learned the lesson
> On the blood-stained soil of France
> How to fight on the defensive
> Purposed not to take a chance
>
> Like a flash they came together
> Word was passed along the line:

"No white man must cross the border;
Shoot to kill and shoot in time!"

"Ready, Fire!" And then a volley
From the mob whose skins were white
"Give 'em hell, boys," cried the leader,
"Soon we'll put them all to flight."

But they got a warm reception
From black men who had no fear,
Who while fighting they were singing:
"Come on Boys, the Gang's all Here."

Rapid firing guns were shooting,
Men were falling by the score,
'Till the white men quite defeated
Sent the word "We want no more."

Nine P.M. the trouble started,
Two A.M. the thing was done,
And the victory for the black men
Counted almost four to one.

But the tide turns when Greenwood is attacked by aerial bombs
and mounted machine guns. Women and children are killed, while
"Black men, like the ancient Trojans, / Fought and died to save a
cause."

White hoodlums enter a house with a mother and children hiding
in the basement. But before the rioters torch the home, they pause to
play a record on the phonograph, "One Day in June." Then the coal
oil is poured out, the blazes erupt, and the family is momentarily
trapped.

Through the smoke and almost stifled
Groping, grasping for their breath
Mother saved herself and children
From a cruel and fiery death.

But the mob still murders an aged couple, who had lived together for
fifty years, before the fighting ends and the blacks are taken to detention camps "at the points of sword or gun." The poem ends:

Tulsa with her teeming millions
Paid the toll for racial strife
But her black men won a victory
With their blood they paid the price.

Nobly they had stopped a lynching
Taught a lesson for all time,
Saved a man the Court has since found
Innocent of any crime.

Though they fought the sacrificial
Fight, with banners flying high,
Yet the thing of more importance
Is the way they fought — and why!

While the white narrative was steeped in fears of Negro aggression, the black account also blended fact and fiction; it was Sheriff McCullough, for example, who prevented the lynching. But for a community that had been disenfranchised, segregated, marginalized, despised, invaded, shot at, looted, and burned, the black version of history validated its own struggle, and it was closer to the truth. Both narratives survived in the oral histories of the two communities.

Just as some white Tulsans dissented from the majority's interpretation, some prominent blacks blamed members of their own race for starting the melee.

O. W. Gurley, for example, told the *Tribune* that he went to the courthouse to try to persuade the blacks to return home. "They were nearly all dope users or 'jake' drinkers with police records," he said. "However, there were a few more intelligent ones in the lead." They included a tall brown-skinned fellow named Mann, who with his brother owned the largest grocery store in Greenwood. "They stand well in the community, but this boy came back from France with exaggerated ideas about equality and thinking he can whip the world ... They started the trouble and this fellow Mann fired the first shot. They brought calamity on us." Gurley identified several blacks by name, then addressed whether black Tulsa's foremost citizen was involved. "It has been charged that John Stradford, proprietor of the

Stradford hotel, was a ring leader. This may be true, but was not to my knowledge, as I did not see Stradford" at the courthouse.

Barney Cleaver, the black deputy sheriff, told reporters that the "Negro mob" was made up largely of men "without employment . . . Army vets who wanted to show whites that they could not be bluffed into submission." He identified by name about a half-dozen whom he thought responsible for starting the riot and said, "I am going to do everything I can to bring the Negroes . . . who are responsible for this outrage to the bars of justice. They caused me to lose everything that I have been years in accumulating."

Cleaver had been affectionately known as "Uncle Barney," but his testimony earned him the derogation of "Uncle Tom" for years to come. He was, nonetheless, a sympathetic figure on the night after the riot. He walked back to the county courthouse carrying his belongings in a handkerchief. The rest of his property, including three two-story buildings valued at $20,000, had been destroyed. He hadn't seen his wife since the riot began and didn't know where she was. He sat at his desk, quietly removed her trinkets from the handkerchief, and cried.

While the statements by Gurley and Cleaver were incriminating, they may have also been self-serving. As a deputy sheriff, Cleaver was beholden to white interests for his job, and both men were negotiating with white real estate agents willing to pay large commissions to blacks to facilitate the purchase of burned lots. Both men may have wanted to curry favor with white Tulsans to move those transactions along.

While white Tulsans blamed the anonymous "bad Negroes," they still needed a specific black villain, and they found one in J. B. Stradford.

Stradford went to the courthouse on the blacks' first trip; convinced that Dick Rowland would not be lynched, he tried to calm the group and saw no reason to fight. But the next morning, he stood in his hotel, gun in hand. To Stradford, the building represented not only a considerable financial investment but also black equality — Negro travelers now had comparable accommodations — and he was willing to fight to his death to protect it. As flames began to consume other buildings on Greenwood Avenue, Stradford and several other blacks tried to keep the rioters at bay by firing their guns from a second-story porch that circled the building.

But the hotel was not a fortress. The three-story structure of brick and stone had become a refuge for black families, and they could all be killed by bullets or in a fire. A machine gun had already knocked out the windows on the west side of the hotel. About six men had been shot and needed medical attention. At least one was dead. And as the shooting dragged on, some of the women began to plead with their husbands to surrender and beg for mercy. The entreaties prevailed.

"Stradford, I'm going to leave you," one man said. "If we are trapped here, all of us will be killed. If we leave now, we may have a chance for our lives. Here is your gun and shells."

Most of the other men also left, and soon Stradford's wife, Augusta, begged him to do the same. "Oh, papa, let us go too," she said, crying.

"I intend to protect my hotel," he said. "If you want to go with the crowd, then go."

She stayed. The battle would have continued, but the blacks who left the hotel returned with an important message: the state militia had arrived and promised to protect the hotel. In exchange, Stradford had to surrender. He agreed, and when the guardsmen arrived at the hotel, he opened the door. They assured him that his hotel would not be burned and that it would be used as a refuge as long as he agreed to go into custody. During this discussion, a black man ran across a lot near the hotel, and a white rioter, in full view, began shooting. Stradford screamed for him to stop as the leader of the Guard yelled at the gunman, "Don't shoot in that direction! You might hit one of the soldier boys in that yard!" As Stradford wrote in his memoirs, "The militia had been ordered out to take charge of the affair, but instead they joined the rioters."

Stradford, with no other options, still surrendered to the Guard. As he got into a car, the "raiding squad" arrived to break into a nearby drugstore to steal cigars, tobacco, and money. Driven to Convention Hall, he saw a great many of "our group" walking with their hands above their heads, and anytime their hands were lowered, a guardsman would yell to raise them or shoot at their feet.

Stradford did not remain at Convention Hall. The next day, June 2, General Barrett ordered that he be arrested and held for the impending grand jury investigation. It was believed that the carloads of armed blacks had left from his hotel and that he had encouraged them. City officials also confiscated $2,000 of Stradford's money. With the authorities closing in, Stradford reached the depot and boarded a northbound train.* As the rains put out the last of Greenwood's fires, the train departed, and Stradford leaned back in his segregated car. The community he had lived in for twenty-two years lay in ruins, his hotel a pile of charred brick, broken glass, and ash.

That evening he reached Independence, Kansas, where his brother lived; but the authorities were tracking his whereabouts. Early the next morning, he had not yet dressed when the city's chief of police came to the house. He had orders to arrest Stradford on charges that he had incited the riot, and he asked if he would turn himself in.

"Hell, no," Stradford said.

The officer arrested him and took him to the jail. Stradford, who had a law degree, knew that he had a measure of protection as long as he stayed out of Oklahoma. Kansas did not have jurisdiction over what happened outside its borders. He told the police that he had had nothing to do with the riot but otherwise refused to answer any questions. He also said that if they wanted to return him to Oklahoma, they would need to get extradition papers. In a similar case the previous year, Kansas's governor, Henry Allen, had denied a request by Arkansas to extradite a black man accused of inciting the race riot in Elaine. The governor doubted that man could get a fair trial, and a guilty verdict could bring the death penalty.

Despite this precedent, Stradford wasn't going to let others determine his fate. He called his son, Cornelius, a Columbia Law School graduate who understood Tulsa's racial climate. He was deeply involved in trying to overturn the city's segregation ordinance of 1916 and appeared ready to follow his father's footsteps as a Negro civic leader. But he recoiled at the city's racism, and his wife, whose frilly

* It is unclear what happened to Stradford's wife, but it does not appear that she left Tulsa with him.

clothes and eastern upbringing earned her the name "Belle of New York," hated Greenwood's muddy streets. "She cried for a year," her daughter said. The couple moved to Chicago, where Stradford gave them a monthly allowance until his son began to earn a living. When Cornelius got the call from his father, he immediately headed for Independence by train.

On Monday, June 6, the assistant county attorney for Tulsa, John Goldsberry, filed an "information" formally charging Stradford with inciting the riot, the first person so charged. He said that even if Stradford did not murder, loot, or rob, he would be guilty of those charges if he "abetted a riot" that produced those crimes. The county attorney's office prepared extradition papers and sent them to Oklahoma's governor for approval. Goldsberry told reporters that he hoped Stradford would be back in Tulsa on Wednesday or Thursday.

By then, Cornelius Stradford had reached Independence, where a jailer led him to his father.

"Don't be afraid, Papa," he said. "I will have you out of here in a few days."

He filed for a writ of habeas corpus, which allows a federal court to release a suspect detained illegally, and it was granted. But Stradford still faced extradition charges, so bond was posted at $500. Cornelius paid the fee and father and son left the jail — with the instruction that J. B. was to stay in Independence and return to the authorities on June 10.

A hearing before Governor Allen was set for Thursday, June 16. The Oklahoma authorities, however, were concerned that the Kansas governor would reject the request for extradition on the same grounds that he had rejected the previous year's request from Arkansas. So, in an unusual move, on the night of June 15 Oklahoma's attorney general and Tulsa's county attorney went to Topeka, Kansas, to appear at the 10 A.M. hearing. In addition to the extradition papers signed by Oklahoma's governor, they had letters from "prominent men" in Tulsa assuring Governor Allen that Stradford, if returned, would receive a fair trial and would be protected from mob violence. Also at the hearing was a delegation of black lawyers from Oklahoma, who planned to argue that Stradford's life would be endangered if he were sent back to Tulsa.

The hearing would have been a legal and political showdown —
but it never took place because the star witness did not appear.
Stradford never returned after posting bond, and he could not be
found anywhere in the city. He was now no longer a suspect for starting a riot but a fugitive from justice. Governor Allen promptly issued
an executive warrant for his arrest, but it was too late. Stradford was
long gone from Kansas.

After he made bail, he and his son fled by train to Chicago, where
the chance of being returned to the South was much smaller. By
then, the risk of defying the law (jumping bail) was less than the risk
of obeying it (returning to Tulsa). Kansas officials searched for several days but soon gave up; neither they nor their Oklahoma counterparts had any idea where Stradford had gone.

The entire drama was played out in the Tulsa newspapers, often on the front page. STRATFORD SKIPS RIOT CHARGE was the
Tribune's eight-column banner headline after he jumped bail. (His
name was often misspelled.) While no one in Greenwood was a
household name to white Tulsans, Stradford's was the most familiar.
The newspapers had covered his lawsuit against the Midland Valley
Railroad and his opposition to the segregation ordinance, both of
which placed him squarely against the values of white Tulsa, and his
eponymous hotel cemented his profile as a man of ambition. His position as Greenwood's Republican Party boss — or "henchman,"
as one newspaper put it — further reinforced his role as a leader.
If the riot was a "Negro uprising," who better to be the ringleader
than one of Tulsa's wealthiest, most outspoken, most defiant black
men?

His behavior after the riot allowed whites easily to assume his
guilt. He had something to hide. *He fled the law.* He was just a two-
bit fugitive.

But the claim lacked evidence as well as common sense. There is
no public record or newspaper account of Stradford's inciting a riot,
and Stradford, without clear evidence of a lynching, would not have
encouraged acts of provocation. After all, he had the most to lose in a
riot, which he did. As recorded in the late 1920s by Mary E. Jones
Parrish in *Events of the Tulsa Disaster*, Stradford's losses added up to

$125,000, 32 percent more than the person with the second highest losses. He lost almost twice as much as Gurley, probably Greenwood's second leading businessman.

But Stradford's motives and denials didn't matter. Just as the Gustafson conviction ratified the corruption of the police department, Stradford's flight from justice affirmed the lawlessness of black Tulsa.

Once in Chicago, Stradford moved in with his son. Though he was a fugitive, he did not stay underground. In September he filed a suit against the American Central Insurance Company, seeking to recover $65,000 in insurance. He filed the suit in Chicago because he believed he couldn't get a fair trial in Oklahoma, but it was unlikely that a black outlaw in 1921 would have had much standing in any court of law. In fact, none of the riot victims, including Stradford, was able to collect on insurance claims because a riot clause exempted the insurers from paying.

Stradford lived in Chicago for the rest of his life. He was never apprehended by the authorities and he never set foot again in Oklahoma, but the success he once enjoyed in Tulsa eluded him. He tried to build a new hotel, but it was never completed and he had to return money to his investors. He opened a small pool hall, a candy store, and a barbershop; he worked on his memoirs and he would tell his grandchildren, "Not many fathers can credit their lives to their son." But he also nursed a grudge for having lost everything at the hands of a "blood thirsty mob." His losses were not just financial. As one of the pioneers of Greenwood, he saw its success as a model of black initiative and independence, and its demolition turned his dreams into dust, a heartache from which he never fully recovered. "It is incredible to believe that in this civilized age that a white man could be so void of humanity," he wrote. "My soul cried for revenge and prayed for the day to come when I could personally avenge the wrongs which had been perpetrated against me."

He died in 1935, still a fugitive, at the age of seventy-four.

Stradford was not the only man Oklahoma tried to extradite. A. J. Smitherman was the second most prominent "race man" of Greenwood. He arrived in Tulsa in 1913 and founded the *Tulsa Star*, a megaphone for his own "radical" views. He tried unsuccessfully to get blacks placed on election boards alongside whites. He was outspoken in his belief that blacks should fight to protect their suffrage and their civil rights, and he had contrarian instincts. He was, for example, a Democrat, even though that party was the architect of Jim Crow and most blacks favored the party of Abraham Lincoln. He probably recognized that the Republicans in Tulsa were not much different in their attitudes toward race than the Democrats. Smitherman wore several hats: he was a justice of the peace and an inspector of elections, but he was best known for his zealous investigative work. In 1917 he went to Dewey, Oklahoma, to look into the torching of twenty black homes and wrote a report for Governor R. L. Williams. His work contributed to the arrest of thirty-six men, including Dewey's mayor. The governor also selected Smitherman to be the only black in a delegation of Oklahomans who greeted President Wilson at Oklahoma City in 1919.

After the riot, it was not surprising that Oklahoma tried to extradite him as well, although in a less public fashion than Stradford. With the destruction of his newspaper plant, valued at more than $40,000, Smitherman took his wife and five children and left Tulsa. After a stay in St. Louis, they ended up in Boston, and in January 1922 Smitherman wrote an article about the riot for the *Boston Herald*. It concluded: "In Tulsa, as in many other parts of our country, the calloused spots of indulgence on the souls of black men have been rubbed off by the friction of race hatred, leaving the raw, bleeding sores of injustice and contumely of a half century's accumulation, and they are now smarting under the sting of a growing national indifference to their cause."

Before publishing it, the *Herald* sent the article to Richard Lloyd Jones, the leading newspaperman of Tulsa, who telegraphed back: SMITHERMAN FUGITIVE FROM JUSTICE EXTRADITION PAPERS GRANTED BY THREE GOVERNORS STOP BAD ACTOR STOP WRITING. The *Herald* published the article anyway, perhaps concluding that Smitherman could not be wanted for crimes in three different states. Smitherman later moved to Buffalo and started a newspaper; he never returned to Oklahoma.

*   *   *

The blacks who stayed in Tulsa received some long-needed medical care for problems unrelated to the riot. Within a month, doctors diagnosed 225 cases of tuberculosis and 2,500 cases of sexually transmitted diseases, affecting about a quarter of the entire black population. The county superintendent of health recommended that it operate a permanent hospital in Greenwood. Maurice Willows agreed to provide Red Cross funds and look for a suitable location. The county commissioners turned over an empty lot, once occupied by the Dunbar School, and a small hospital was built, including an operating room that cost $65,000. It opened in September, allowing the patients in the high school to leave so that classes could begin at their normal time. The new building was given a fitting name, the Maurice Willows Hospital.

The Red Cross wrapped up its work at the end of the year, and a reporter made a rare visit to Greenwood to interview Willows. With winter at hand and many black Tulsans still lacking basic amenities, the director could barely contain his anger at Tulsa's indifference to human suffering.

"The people of Tulsa can't realize conditions as they exist out here," Willows said. "We are fighting pneumonia from the exposure that is inevitable. Sixty percent of riot sufferers are still sleeping on cots issued last June." He explained that 18,000 quilts were burned in the riot, and relief workers had been trying to find warm bed covers. "The Negroes haven't thought in terms of pillow cases or sheets yet. It has been a question rather of a place to sleep and something to cover them. Now they are getting to the place where they can think of pillows."

The Red Cross was planning a Christmas Eve celebration, but the muddy ground made it imperative for the children to find shoes and stockings. "We can get them stockings, but shoes come too high for us to buy," Willows said. "Our aim, and just about all we can do, is to keep the suffering down and the morale up."

Twenty-four patients were in the Negro hospital, including a boy who had been hurt in the riot and was not yet out of bed. Exposure caused a little girl to contract pneumonia; she died a day before the interview. An operation had taken place every day of the previous week.

By Christmas, much of Greenwood's housing infrastructure had been rebuilt, with 664 frame shacks, 48 brick or cement buildings, and 4 frame churches. But 49 families still lived in tents.

The white relief workers and black adults wanted the children to enjoy Christmas Eve. They were able to buy raw material at cost, and the black women, working at the hospital, rapidly sewed quilts, pillows, underwear, dresses, and other garments. A large Christmas tree was placed in front of the hospital, its branches holding white bags filled with nuts, oranges, and candy. Capping the tree was a blazing lighted star, a gift from a local industrialist. As the cool night fell, the children and their parents, 2,200 strong, held hands and gathered around the tree. They stood amid the remnants of comfortable homes replaced by one-room wooden shacks, large piles of brick and stone, and twisted metal. But there they stood. Greenwood had survived, and that night it sang.

"Never has the writer witnessed a more spontaneous outburst of Christmas fervor than on this occasion," one observer wrote. "Whole families were there — men, women and children. 'Swing Low, Sweet Chariot,' 'Down by the River Side,' 'Standing in the Need of Prayer,' coming from the throats of these people revibrated throughout the night air and attracted most of the crowd gathered in the business section over on Greenwood Street. It seemed as [if] the whole negro population could not resist the chance to sing."

Twenty-seven hundred white bags of goodies were distributed; so too were bedsprings, pillows, underwear, a heating stove, cotton, and other useful items. The climax of the evening occurred when a leader of the community stood before the crowd and said, "Let us remember the old Negro tradition: 'There is no room in our hearts for hatred.'"

The celebration was soon called "the greatest night in the history of Tulsa Negroes." It was a fitting culmination to the work of the Red Cross, which would forever be remembered in Tulsa as "the angels of mercy."

White Tulsans ended 1921 in high style on a brisk starlit night. Revelers with gaudy paper hats raced their cars along Main Street, making them backfire, and yelled joyfully at each explosion. The Hotel Tulsa sponsored the city's most elaborate party, with more than five hundred guests sitting around tables, their elbows touching. Exclusive parties for "society people" were held on the mezzanine. A fifteen-piece orchestra provided the dance music in the main lobby, and vaudeville performers appeared throughout the night. Each table bore a dainty display of cut flowers, and as midnight approached the hotel management distributed paper caps and ribbon confetti, which were quickly strewn among the guests and the tables. On all sides were costly ornaments.

Throughout the city, everyone agreed that the depression in the oil industry had made 1921 a difficult year, but still the champagne flowed. A formal military ball was held at the National Guard armory; parties were held at the Country Club and the Oakhurst Country Club and the Kennedy restaurant. Dozens of "watch parties" and slumber parties were held in churches and private homes. The *World* wrote: "The onlooker concludes quickly there cannot be a serious business depression here. It appeared that every class of citizenship, from the humble bookkeeper to the millionaire oil producer, joined heartily in the festivities — and possessed plenty of money to enjoy the pleasures that appealed to his tastes."

Promptly at midnight, a bombardment of "light artillery" erupted over the river, briefly lighting the sky, then fell like dust into the water.

The Rise of the Secret Order

THE RIOT WAS a godsend to one group — the Ku Klux Klan. Oklahoma's fledgling organization used the upheaval to transform a sinister fringe group into a mainstream phenomenon, making Tulsa itself a redoubt of Klan menace. This outcome was one of the riot's tragic ironies: an event that could have radicalized black Tulsans radicalized their white counterparts instead. While blacks focused on rebuilding their community, many whites found a new outlet for their bigotry and fanaticism.

Oklahoma was fertile ground for the Klan. The state held many whites who had migrated from the Confederacy as well as original Klansmen, who appeared in the Deep South immediately after the Civil War and had lived in the Indian Territory since the 1870s, passing their regalia down to younger generations. In 1915 *The Birth of a Nation,* showing the alleged depravities of the emancipated blacks, helped spur the revival of the Klan, and the film was enthusiastically received. A few Klansmen appeared in the state during and immediately after World War I; in 1917 the *World* called the black-robed "Knights of Liberty" who flogged suspected Wobblies in Tulsa the "modern Ku Klux Klan." But until 1920 the Invisible Empire, in Oklahoma and elsewhere, was more invisible than empire.

Unlike the original Klan, which was born of sectional strife and was devoted to the restoration of white supremacy in the South, the new Klan combined racial and national loyalties with an avow-edly patriotic appeal. It exploited the social disorder to advance its own nativist agenda, maligning blacks, Jews, and Catholics for their "un-American" ways, and promised to reestablish Anglo-Saxon he-gemony. But it needed an issue to make potential supporters fear that their way of life was in jeopardy, and the "red summer" of 1919 provided that spark. The race riots, labor strife, and political turmoil created a vacuum of law and order that made the Klan's promise of swift retribution far more appealing, and it expanded from its head-quarters in Atlanta to cover sixteen states, including places like Ore-gon and Indiana, outside the South.

The Klan arrived in Oklahoma City in the summer of 1920. Un-like the Reconstruction Klan, the Hooded Order was now a money-making machine, charging each new entrant ten dollars. Tulsa, with a history of mob vigilantism, racial antagonism, crime, and oil wealth, proved profitable for the Klan. Its recruiters, known as "Kleagles," were active in Tulsa before the riot, promoting themselves at churches, fraternal lodges, and other organizations. But Tulsa did not have a "klavern," a local organization and building where rituals were held.

Determining the Klan's role in the riot is like shaking hands with a shadow; the very nature of a secret society is to conceal its member-ship. But it is doubtful that the Klan played a central role because it was still in its embryonic stage in Tulsa. While individual Klansmen were anonymous, their activities were quite public — marches, ral-lies, whippings, cross burnings. The press later covered these exten-sively, but they had not done so on the eve of the riot. The *World*'s publisher, Eugene Lorton, who strongly opposed the order in part because it used violence to flout the law, warned on May 25, 1921, that he sensed the Klan was moving in. "If the Ku Klux Klan has attained such proportions in Texas, you can rest assured that it is in existence in Tulsa, because Tulsa does not lag in anything." Still, there were no signs. According to the best scholarship on the subject, Carter Blue Clark's "History of the Ku Klux Klan in Oklahoma," it is unlikely that the Klan triggered the riot, although "some of its members had an intimate relationship to the event [and] some policemen were Klansmen."

But the clash had a galvanic effect on its recruitment in Tulsa and throughout Oklahoma. A "Negro uprising" crystallized fears of a militant black underclass, and the Klan promised to protect white Protestants against black violence and to maintain the purity of southern womanhood. Its campaign against immoral conduct also received a boost from the *Tribune's* focus on vice in Greenwood. If the police couldn't stamp out the opium dens and brothels, why not give the nightriders a chance?

On August 10 more than 2,000 whites, mostly men, jammed into a muggy Convention Hall to hear Caleb A. Ridley, an Atlanta Klansman, urge his audience to join the hooded brethren. Ridley, who was also a Baptist minister, said the riot "was the best thing that ever happened to Tulsa and judging from the way strange Negroes were coming to Tulsa, we might have to do it all over again." A white man's job, he added, "is to see that civilization comes under no inferior race so long as he lives." Ridley had been introduced by Wash E. Hudson, a Tulsa lawyer who would become the majority leader in the Oklahoma senate and one of the state's most prominent Klansmen.*

Three weeks later, on August 31, about three hundred white Tulsans were initiated in a Klan ceremony held outside town, and three days later nightriders kidnapped an alleged bootlegger named J. E. Frazier, hauled him to a remote spot outside Owasso, and beat him severely. The county attorney announced that no action would be taken against the Klansmen and suggested that the victim got what he deserved. That same month, Convention Hall showed the reissue of *The Birth of a Nation,* which celebrated the exploits of the original Klan.

More whippings followed, as did Klan parades, Klan funerals, and Klan fundraisers; car raffles were popular. By December, the local Klan claimed to have 3,200 members, who bankrolled its ambitions. The Klan paid an estimated $60,000 for an abandoned church, tore it down, and built a $200,000 brick building called Beno Hall. The name was an abbreviation of the local Klan's official title, the Tulsa Benevolent Association, but Beno Hall more commonly stood for

---

* Hudson also had a tie to the riot. After Dick Roland was arrested, a judge assigned Hudson to be his lawyer, a moot point after the charges were dropped.

"Be no Nigger. Be no Jew. Be no Catholic." With three stories and a seating capacity of 3,000, it was among the largest assembly halls in the state and one of the largest in the Southwest. The hall rituals, the prayers, and even the bizarre acronyms were designed to create feelings of solidarity and strength. When a Klansman entered, a "nighthawk," or guard, said, "Ayak," which stood for "Are you a Klansman?" The response was "Akia" — "A Klansman I am." The nighthawk said, "Kigy" — "Klansman, I greet you."

Dressed in spectral robes, they stood on oak floors and balconies and tried to glimpse the altar, the cross, the Bible opened to the twelfth chapter of Romans, and the flag. Always the subject was the preservation of American civilization, white supremacy, and Protestant ideals. Before leaving, they might sing "Rock of Ages" or "The Old Rugged Cross," although their anthem became "Onward, Christian Soldiers."

Beno Hall was a fortress of bigotry unlike any in America, and it was Tulsa's.

Support for the Klan was certainly not unanimous. In addition to its obvious opponents — blacks, Jews, and Catholics — many of the city's elite recognized the damage of a vigilante group not only to its victims but also to the Magic City's reputation. Certainly Eugene Lorton was mindful of those repercussions in his paper's denunciations of the Klan. Nor did it receive support from the roughnecks whose very behavior — drinking, gambling, carousing — was deemed abhorrent by the Klan. As the historian Danney Goble noted, "Neither princes nor peasants, Tulsa's Klansmen were the squeezed middle class, squeezed on one side by an economic aristocracy they could never enter, squeezed on another side by a caste whose morals they could never accept." In addition, the Klan was opposed by some politicians and law enforcement authorities, who feared that its tactics could trigger broader violence, even another riot. Sheriff McCullough, for one, openly opposed the order.

Some of these tensions surfaced before a proposed Klan march through downtown Tulsa on the evening of April 1, 1922. Mayor Evans, fearing a bloody confrontation, had denied the group permission to march, and rumors circulated that the National Guard would return with machine guns to block the procession. As evening fell, an estimated 15,000 people packed the streets.

Suddenly an airplane arched across the dark sky, lit by two strings of electric lights on its underside in the shape of a cross. The plane dipped low above the city, made "weird gyrations in the air," banked, and vanished. It then returned and roared right over Greenwood.

Within a few minutes, the Klansmen emerged from Convention Hall in their masks and robes and walked three abreast in a line that extended a mile and a half. Leading the way were mounted horses draped in white robes, followed by a Ford truck carrying an eight-foot-high "burning cross" illuminated by gas that burned through perforated pipes. The marchers, some carrying torches, took long, quick strides and headed south on Cheyenne to Archer, turned east, and went straight toward the black district. When the column reached Main Street, it veered south and skirted the outer edges of Greenwood.

The parade through downtown lasted sixty-nine minutes. The estimated 2,000 to 5,000 participants carried banners (WE PUT BI-BLES IN THE PUBLIC SCHOOLS) and threw out inscribed red cards (PURITY AND WOMANHOOD). The crowd, quiet and deferential, occasionally burst into cheers. At one point, the spectators watched the Klansmen walk up a slight hill on Main Street, then disappear into a rolling mass of blue and brown clouds — created by smoke machines used in theatrical performances. There were no National Guardsmen and no confrontations, but there was praise from the *Tribune:* "Probably there has never been a march so spectacular in the history of Oklahoma. So absolute was the awe that gripped the crowd that one could almost hear a pin drop among the massed thousands as the advance guard of the long white line swept through the city."

At one rural ceremony in July 1922, more than a thousand new members were initiated. Tulsa had Klan auxiliaries for both women and teenagers. The organization endorsed political candidates in the newspaper, and its members occupied the highest offices in the city. In December 1921 three bandits killed a top police official, Harry Aurandt, who was Commissioner Adkison's "secretary," or chief assistant. Aurandt's association with the Klan surfaced at his burial when twelve Knights, their white robes whipping in the wind, appeared at the grave, each dropping a rose on the casket.

The following year, before the first election after the riot, the Klan published its ratings of city and county candidates (favorable, neutral, opposed); every candidate opposed by the Klan lost in the primaries. Sheriff McCullough was defeated and Mayor Evans didn't run, to be replaced by H. F. Newblock, a Klansman and Democrat. In 1923 three out of the five members of the state house of representatives from Tulsa County were Klansmen, and Tulsa was also used as a launching pad to set up other klaverns. At the Klan's peak in the early 1920s, the state had between two hundred and three hundred klaverns and an estimated 150,000 Klansmen, making the Oklahoma Realm one of the strongest in the nation. One out of every ten white Protestant males in Oklahoma belonged to the order; Klansmen were more numerous than organized labor or any single political party.

In 1923 Governor John Walton learned how strong the Klan was. Its brutal whipping of a Jewish movie projectionist in Tulsa prompted the governor to impose martial law on the city once again, this time for six weeks.

"There cannot be two governments in Oklahoma while I am governor," he said. "When the sheriff, the county attorney, the district judge, and the jury commission are all in the hands of an organization responsible for mob activities, what can be done? You have no law, and you have no courts worthy of the name." The state indicted thirty-one Klansmen, although only four were punished. Ten months after his inauguration, Walton was impeached and removed from office in a move orchestrated by the Klan.

By the end of the decade, the Klan's strength had markedly diminished both in Tulsa and across the state. Its excesses eventually alienated many supporters, and corruption among its leaders further crippled its standing. The damage, however, had been done. Oklahoma would have been Klan country in the 1920s under any circumstances, but Tulsa's "Negro uprising" was a clarion call to complacent whites, giving America's most virulent protest movement a milestone to rally around.

A Culture of Silence

THE RIOT disappeared from sight. There were no memorials to honor the dead, no public ceremonies to observe an anniversary or express regret. Tulsans, black and white, made no public acknowledgment of the riot. Greenwood's damaged buildings were evidence of the assault, but in time they too were toppled or rebuilt. The riot was not mentioned in Oklahoma's history books from the 1920s and 1930s, including *Oklahoma: A History of the State and Its People, The Story of Oklahoma, Readings in Oklahoma History, Oklahoma: Its Origins and Development, Our Oklahoma,* and *Oklahoma: A Guide to the Sooner State.* Angie Debo was a fearless Oklahoma historian — she was known as a "warrior scholar" — who chronicled how federal government agencies and business interests swindled land from the Indians. In 1943 she published *Tulsa: From Creek Town to Oil Capital,* but even this popular history made only brief and superficial reference to the riot. The *Chronicles of Oklahoma,* a quarterly journal on state history published by the Oklahoma Historical Society, has never run a story on the riot. It began publication in 1921.

Efforts to cover up the riot were rare but unmistakable. The most egregious example was the *Tribune's* decision to excise from its bound volumes the front-page story of May 31, "Nab Negro for Attacking Girl in Elevator." Equally irresponsible was the shredding of that day's editorial page. Years later, scholars discovered that police and state militia documents associated with the riot were also missing.

These efforts to suppress information, however, do not account for the lack of serious scrutiny given the riot. Any scholar, journalist, or interested citizen could piece together the incident through court records, newspaper articles, photographs, and interviews. But such an investigation rarely happened. For most white Tulsans, the disaster was as isolated as Greenwood itself. One of America's most distinguished historians, Daniel J. Boorstin, grew up in Tulsa and was six years old at the time of the riot. He graduated from Central High School and devoted his professional life to studying history, writing some twenty books and winning a Pulitzer Prize for *The Discoverers,* about man's quest to know the world. But Boorstin never wrote about what may have been the greatest race riot in American history, even though his own father might have been a rich source of information. In 1921 Sam Boorstin was the lawyer for the *Tulsa Tribune.* In an essay about the optimistic ethos of Tulsa in *Cleopatra's Nose* (1994), Daniel Boorstin mentioned the city's "dark shadows — such as the relentless segregation, the brutal race riots of the 1920s, and the Ku Klux Klan. But these were not visible or prominent in my life." *

The white Tulsans' response to the riot has been called "a conspiracy of silence" or "a culture of silence." The subject was certainly ignored in schools, newspapers, and churches. During the middle 1930s, the *Tribune* ran a daily feature on its editorial page describing what had happened in Tulsa on that date fifteen years earlier; but on the fifteenth anniversary of the riot, the paper ran a series of frivolous items. "Central high school's crowning social event of the term just closed was the senior prom in the gymnasium with about 200 guests in attendance," the *Tribune* dutifully reported. "The grand march was led by Miss Sara Little and Seth Hughes."

Many whites viewed the riot as one of those inexplicable events,

---

* Boorstin, through his secretary, declined to be interviewed for this book.

an act of nature. A brief article in the *Tulsa World* on November 7, 1949, proclaimed the incident as the "top horror of city history . . . Mass murder of whites and Negroes began on June 1. No one knew then or remembers now how the shooting began."

But the incident survived as a kind of underground phenomenon, a memory quietly passed along and enhanced by the city's pioneers at picnics, church suppers, and other gatherings. In time, the riot acquired new shades of meaning: it was viewed as a healing event in the city's history, a catalyst for progress between the races, and an opportunity for magnanimous outreach.

This revisionism was captured in *Oklahoma: A Guide to the Sooner State,* written for the Federal Writers' Project around 1940. (Its reports became the American Guide travel series.) The report said that vigilantes invaded Greenwood and laid it waste by fire, but after two days of martial law, "The whites organized a systematic rehabilitation program for the devastated Negro section and gave generous aid to the Negroes left homeless by the fires. Nationwide publicity of the most lurid sort naturally followed the tragedy, and Tulsa's whites and Negroes joined in an effort to live down the incident by working diligently — and on the whole successfully — for a better mutual understanding."

Nothing could be further from the truth. Whites not only avoided rehabilitation but were also engaged in systematic discrimination in the 1930s (when the *Guide* was researched). Most southern and southwestern cities routinely assigned public service jobs to African Americans, but not Tulsa. Eight black policemen patrolled Greenwood, but the city otherwise did not have a single black employee. Tulsa and its private utility companies hired only whites as meter readers in black neighborhoods. Tulsa was also one of the few cities to have only white carriers deliver mail in the black community. The city not only segregated its schools but used different-colored checks to pay white and black teachers. In the federal building, the U.S. government had 425 employees, only 8 of whom were black: 4 men swept the floors during the day, and 4 women scrubbed them at night. The Mid-Continent Petroleum Corporation operated the world's largest inland refinery in Tulsa, employing more than 3,000 people. It had no Negro employees. There were also no Negro Girl

Scouts. A director for the organization explained, "If the Negro girls wore Scout uniforms, the white girls would take theirs off."

The riot receded from memory as Tulsa returned to what it did best, making money, and the 1920s saw the city solidify its reign as the Oil Capital of the World. With crude oil surging through a network of pipes into refineries across the Arkansas River, petroleum production (as opposed to exploration and discovery) became Tulsa's leading industry. Around the country, as millions of automobiles rolled off assembly lines and factories hummed all night, the demand for "Tulsa oil" pumped new riches into the city.

Rising from downtown lots were new hotels with terracotta exteriors, multimillion-dollar office towers with Art Deco designs, movie palaces with Renaissance décor. When the Ritz Theater opened in 1926, featuring life-size marble statues and a ceiling of "twinkling stars," a reporter wrote: "As if by magic, the patron is transplanted from familiar streets to the languorous land of the blue Mediterranean." The Orpheum opened in 1924 as a vaudeville theater, where Mae West, Sally Rand, and Jimmy Durante would perform. The Mayo Hotel (1925) eclipsed the Hotel Tulsa in size and grandeur. The Exchange National Bank stretched across an entire block and stood more than twenty stories high. The Philtower (1927), costing $2.5 million, featured a sloping tile roof, two gargoyles above the Boston Avenue entrance, a chandelier in the lobby, and a magnificent second-floor mall. For a city associated with Indians and oil, the ornate buildings struck some as bizarre — casting "their twenty-two-story shadows across the barren plain," one writer observed — but they were a permanent expression of Tulsa's wealth and maturation.

"It was estimated that during 1927 more than a million dollars a month was spent on downtown building," Angie Debo wrote.

> Tulsans at this time erected skyscrapers not so much because ground space was at a premium, but because they liked to see them rise. The skyline reached balanced proportions due to the rapidity of its erection and the unity of forces that produced it . . . The rolling timbered hills to the southeast and up in Osage County became an area of landed estates laid out in the exuberant spirit of a people to whom wealth was a new and exhilarating experience. In all directions street

after street ringed the city with smooth lawns and finished residence sections, to the rows of little houses, everything was new, and — thanks to the clear Southwestern atmosphere and the use of natural gas as fuel — everything was clean. Tulsa no longer looked like something in the throes of creation.

Tulsa also burnished its reputation for visionary leadership, technological derring-do, and philanthropy. In 1924 it solved its principal obstacle to growth — a lack of water — by building a dam across Spavinaw Creek in the western foothills of the Ozarks, blasting tunnels through the hills, sending water fifty-three miles through concrete pipes, and storing it in massive concrete reservoirs. Despite warnings of a boondoggle, the voters approved $8.3 million in bonds to finance the project.

The greatest needs in the city were often funded by its oil barons, even if commercial self-interest motivated their benevolence. In 1928, for example, Tulsa needed a new airport to accommodate an air tour sponsored by the auto magnate Henry Ford. With no time to vote on a bond issue, forty-seven businessmen raised $172,000 to buy a 390-acre lot northeast of town. The Tulsa Municipal Airport opened in time for the tour and, at the dawn of commercial air travel, became an asset to the city.

Tulsa's benefactors also gave the city its first university. In 1907 they rescued a Presbyterian school named Henry Kendall College, which had gone bankrupt in Muskogee, and placed it on grasslands east of town. In 1921 it was chartered as the University of Tulsa, and its buildings of buff limestone were a roll call of Tulsa's oilmen — McFarlin Library, Chapman Building, Kemp Hall. Another oil magnate, Waite Phillips, built an Italian villa in South Tulsa, surrounded by twenty-three acres of landscaped grounds and botanical gardens; in 1938 he turned it over to the city as the Philbrook Art Center and Indian Museum. Its collection included Renaissance paintings, galleries of classical and modern art, and collections of southwestern Indian art and craftsmanship.

Thomas Gilcrease used his oil wealth to acquire one of the greatest collections of the American West and Indian culture ever assembled. It consisted of more than 4,000 paintings by European and American artists, 20,000 rare books and documents, and 10,000 pieces of clay, gold, and jade artifacts. But in the early 1950s Gilcrease's oil business fell on hard times and, facing insurmountable debts, he wanted to sell the collection. Tulsans feared that the buyer would move it out of the city, so a bond issue was called and voters approved, by a 3–1 margin, the use of $2.25 million to pay off Gilcrease's debt. In return, he deeded the collection to the city in 1955, later donating his museum buildings and grounds to the city as well.

But the money lavished by the oil princes — and the occasional lifelines extended by taxpayers — rarely found its way to Greenwood.

The strong economy of the 1920s helped the district rebuild. Despite the riot, the number of black Tulsans during the decade increased by 71 percent, to 15,203. Fueled by dollars earned by domestic servants, Greenwood's economy revolved around recreation and personal service — pool halls, bowling alleys, domino parlors, and card rooms, as well as barbershops, beauty shops, and shine parlors. The Dreamland Theatre was rebuilt, with a different movie every day and Westerns on Saturdays. Drugstores served ice cream and soft drinks, giving them an advantage over the ones in South Tulsa that would not permit blacks to sit at the counter. By 1926, Tulsa had more hotels for blacks than were in Harlem, and Greenwood flourished as a jazz and entertainment mecca. Count Basie supposedly began his career by playing the piano on a Greenwood sidewalk, while Nat "King" Cole, Duke Ellington, Ernie Fields, and many other black performers passed through the Small Hotel, a three-story brick building that became a legendary stop for black bands across the Southwest's "chitlin circuit."

When Jesse O. Thomas, a noted black writer and social worker, visited Greenwood in 1929, he observed that many old frame houses had been replaced by substantial brick buildings. The bustling business district had about twenty-five grocery stores, six garages, three jitney lines, a life insurance company, undertakers, tailors, architects, contractors, restaurants, lawyers, doctors — in short, the whole panoply of businesses that existed before the riot.

"There is probably no other case in the history of America," Thomas wrote, "where a group of people in a similar hostile community so quickly and so completely rebuilt a 'new Jerusalem upon the ashes of a fallen city' with so limited financial resources."

But the thriving business district masked deeper problems in Greenwood, some of which stemmed directly from the riot. The community rebuilt rapidly for the purpose of shelter; shacks were made of crates and other threadbare material. On twenty-five-foot lots, houses were commonly stacked four deep. City policies contributed to the congestion. Tulsa's covenants prohibited blacks from moving outside their district, and a comprehensive zoning plan in 1923 designated Greenwood to be used for industrial purposes, enabling factories, a large steel foundry, and other small industrial concerns to shoehorn into the district. The overcrowding drove up rents, forcing families to pay sums that averaged 10.2 percent of their house's value. That made Tulsa, in the 1920s, the most expensive city for African Americans with a black population greater than 10,000. Black homeowners were similarly victimized by having to pay exorbitant mortgage rates, between 10 and 20 percent.

The Depression devastated Greenwood when wages for black domestics were cut, reducing the revenue that fueled the other businesses. One entrepreneur who felt the pinch was Mabel Little, the beauty salon owner. In 1936, after falling behind on her mortgage payments, she received notice from Sooner Federal that it would have to foreclose on her house, and she was asked to meet with a bank officer.

"Mrs. Little, we want to be sure you understand we are not taking this action because you are black," he said.

"I don't feel that way," she said. "I know I owe money."

The banker pointed to a stack of papers on his desk. "These all represent good parts of town on whom we've had to foreclose," he said. "Mrs. Little, do you have any money?"

"I have a dime after paying a nickel to come down here," said Little, by then a widow caring for several children.

The banker then told her that Sooner Federal had concluded she was "too good a woman" to lose her home, and the bank had decided it would pay her back taxes and cut her monthly mortgage payments to $17.50. "Can you manage that?" he asked.

"Praise the Lord, I will," she said.

Little was among the lucky ones. By 1936 white lenders owned more than 30 percent of all the property in Greenwood.

The city's neglect of Greenwood was appalling. During the 1930s, most of its streets were unpaved and without running water, city sewers, or regular trash pickup. Surface wells would overflow after hard rains and become polluted with water that had passed through the toilets and privies from higher residential sections. The garbage that was not burned was tossed into backyards and alleys and became breeding places for flies and maggots. Outdoor privies were prevalent. For white Tulsans, thirty-four parks and playgrounds covered more than 3,000 acres. The blacks had one small park of less than 20 acres.

Streetlights were another problem. There were only six lights along the thirty blocks of Greenwood Avenue. With the exception of three main thoroughfares, the bulbs appeared only in front of the occasional business address. Where the houses owned by whites began on Pine Street, a light stood on every corner. Most of Greenwood was in the dark. The rates for homicide, tuberculosis, infant deaths, and other disorders were all inordinately high. Tulsa's two large hospitals accepted a minimal number of blacks, one in basement quarters, the other in the furnace room.

These problems were directly related to the riot, according to a study in 1945 by the National Urban League. "The blighted conditions in this most densely populated area are due largely to the necessity for the Negroes to provide some shelter for themselves after the disastrous race riot of 1921," the report said. "When tranquility finally prevailed . . . Negroes began to erect makeshift shacks, many of which still stand. Present conditions are due to the failure of the city to properly plan and aid in the rehabilitation and maintenance of the Negro residential area."

World War II not only revived Tulsa's economy but relieved its dependence on the oil industry. The War Department gave the city a $15 million Douglas Aircraft bomber plant, generating 20,000 new jobs, including some for African Americans. After the war, Tulsa became the principal maintenance base for American Airlines, which became its largest employer by the middle 1960s. Other technological companies, such as makers of precision instruments and electronic devices, made Tulsa their home and attracted educated scientists, engineers, and technicians, as well as attorneys, accountants, and bankers. Chamber of Commerce representatives boasted that Tulsa had the highest percentage of skilled labor of any city in the country. "Oil Capital of the World" no longer fit a city that was promoting its clean air, beautiful parks, rose gardens, and stout oaks. "Driving in from the north," the *Saturday Evening Post* reported in 1947, "you pick it up twenty-five miles out. Soft coal defiles most cities between Pittsburgh and Kansas City. Burning oil and gas, Tulsa is smokeless, and looks as new as an angel-food cake fresh from the oven."

Suburban sprawl, shopping centers, and a construction boom seemed to make the drive for money even more frenetic. Elevators bore a sign: MEN OR WOMEN NEAREST THE DOOR GET OFF FIRST. During the downtown rush hour, traffic cops blew their whistle just before the lights flicked to green to give drivers a split-second jump. The clocks at the Mayo Hotel ran five minutes fast — and not by accident. Once an oilman staying there missed a million-dollar deal because he got to his appointment five minutes late. The Mayo's management said that mustn't happen again and moved all its clocks five minutes ahead.

Tulsans flaunted their wealth with gaudy stunts and memorable parties. When the First National Bank dedicated its new building in 1950 it built a special platform, ordered searchlights to stab the sky, and called on the Tulsa Philharmonic Orchestra to perform in front of 25,000 people. The Philharmonic was part of another ambitious gimmick at the International Petroleum Exposition and Congress, an annual event where the industry displayed its new equipment. In 1953 the Standard Oil Company erected an operating derrick on the grounds and encased it in glass. Philharmonic musicians, wearing tin safety hats, played inside the air-conditioned structure, the rotary table spinning to the rhythms of Bartók.

The race riot? Most white Tulsans ignored, forgot, or never knew about the tragedy. In fact, it seemed that most of them ignored, forgot, or never knew anything about blacks in their city. In 1957 the Tulsa Chamber of Commerce commemorated Oklahoma's fiftieth anniversary by publishing a 120-page souvenir program that described virtually all aspects of Tulsa's life and history: aviation, religion, electricity, telephones, water, housing, and culture. Also featured were different groups of citizens, such as bankers, oilmen, children, and women. ("The women of Tulsa are a unique breed. Besides their physical beauty, they have proven that they are a breed capable of . . . homemaking, business and civic promotion.") It even featured various animals in the zoo — the monkeys got a full-page spread. But there was not a single mention of Tulsa's black residents.

In this environment, it was possible even to deny that the riot had happened, and it took persistent reminders from whites like Nancy Feldman to ensure that did not happen.

Feldman moved to Tulsa in 1946 to marry a fellow student at the University of Chicago Law School. She was young, Jewish, and liberal, a board member of the NAACP in Chicago, and she was sickened by the city's humiliation of blacks as well as women. On one occasion, she and a black lawyer, Primus Wade, were denied entrance to a meeting of the Tulsa Bar Association at the Mayo Hotel; the organization did not accept women or minorities. Wade was not even allowed on the elevator. But he asked a hotel waiter for a white linen napkin and wrapped it around his head. He then attached Feldman's lapel pin, which had a fake gemstone, to the cloth. With his conservative dark suit and coal-black skin, he looked like a foreign dignitary. He and his "female assistant" confidently rode up the elevator, walked into the meeting, and sat down unmolested. "We couldn't look at each other because we were giggling so much," she later recalled. But they were not served lunch; even a black "foreign dignitary" could not touch the silverware.

Assisting blacks in their push for better housing, health care, and other services, Feldman quickly learned about the riot and promptly raised the matter in an inappropriate place — the University of Tulsa, where she taught sociology. (No Tulsa law firm would hire a female lawyer.) When she mentioned the race riot to her class — all white — she was shocked that none of her students, including the older war veterans, had ever heard of it. As she described it in more detail, some students adamantly denied that it had ever taken place.

To convince them, Feldman brought to class one of Greenwood's most respected citizens, Robert Fairchild. A smallish man with a degree from the University of Nebraska, a warm smile, and sad eyes, he had been seventeen at the time of the riot and now worked at the Tulsa County Health Department. His father died when he was ten years old, and on his deathbed he told the youngster, "There are two things I want you to learn how to do. Pay your debts and say your prayers." His mother then sent her children to an orphans' home in Taft, where he lived for six years. Fairchild returned to Tulsa in 1920, attended high school, and worked downtown at a shoeshine parlor.

"The owner had arranged for me to use toilet facilities across the alley," he told Feldman's class in the fall of 1946. "There was a Negro, rather handsome, something of a lady's man, shining shoes with me. His name was Dick Rowland." He explained that on May 30, 1921, Rowland allegedly made improper advances to a girl operating an elevator. "I doubt very strongly that he did. He might have kidded her, but at that time, Negroes didn't bother much with integrated relationships.

"And of course they had him arrested," Fairchild continued. "That happened at 10 A.M. the next morning. That evening the *Tribune* came out and told what had happened, and said there was going to be a lynching in Tulsa tonight. And when the Negroes saw this, they said, 'Ohhh no, not in Tulsa.'"

He told the story without emotion and with little inflection in his voice. He often used the phrase "of course," as if racial hatred were taken for granted. He explained that several years before Rowland's arrest, a Negro woman had been lynched in Wagoner and dragged through the street. After that, Fairchild said, Tulsa's blacks commented, "Whenever they come over here to lynch somebody, we're going to be in the middle of it."

He said that on the night the riot began, he was at a theater, rehearsing a singing performance for his high school graduation. Someone came in and told the instructor that trouble was brewing, and the students were dismissed at eight-thirty. "Greenwood was packed with people," he said. "Some of the men had been drinking and were cursing and shooting their guns in the air, and someone said, 'Don't waste your bullets, you may need them later.'"

"Well," he continued, "they went to the courthouse, and of course when they got there, there were white people too. I wasn't there, but I'm told that an old white man walked up to a six-foot-four Negro, black as tar, who had an army .45 automatic in his holster. And the white man said, 'Nigger, what are you doing with that pistol?' And he said, 'I'm going to use it if I need to.' And the man said, 'No, you give it to me.' And he tried to take it, and the scuffling set off the riot."

Chaos soon overcame Greenwood, Fairchild said, as people began "shooting wildly and scattering and running for cover." The commotion continued throughout the night; he said he was later told of the stand that the Negroes had made at the Frisco railroad tracks. "But I was scared," he told the students, "and of course I went home and, being close to my mother, I told her, 'We got to get out of here. We got to leave before they come and kill us.' But she said, 'No, we'll wait until morning and see.' Well, the next morning we were awakened by gunfire, and we saw black smoke coming out of buildings."

He again told his mother he was leaving, and his mother again resisted. This time she couldn't stop him. "'No, I'm not going to stay around and let these white folks kill me,'" he recounted. "'I haven't done anything wrong.' But we had nothing to eat, so my mom said, 'You take that loaf of bread and stick of butter, and put it in a sack.' And with that, I went down to the Midland Valley track, and as far as you could see on the track were people walking north, and so I started walking too. I met up with some friends, and they said, 'Bob, we're going to Kansas City, why don't you come with us.'

"So I took off with them, going east, and we got to Lewis when up came a touring car filled with white people. And of course naturally we just scattered, and they just died laughing. They thought it was the funniest thing, I guess, to see twenty-five or thirty Negroes, youngsters too, scattering." But the whites didn't bother them, and Fairchild and his friends continued walking until the National Guard stopped them and instructed them to go to the fairgrounds. "We weren't afraid of them," Fairchild said. "They had guns, but near as I remember didn't threaten us."

He said he stayed in one of those "animal buildings," where they keep the livestock during the fair, and slept on hay. He found the "man in charge of the camp" and told him the name of his employer at the shoeshine stand, Mr. Simon, who was then called in. Asked if he would take the youngster, Mr. Simon said, "He ain't going to bother anybody. Send him on down."

When he returned home, Fairchild was surprised to see it standing. "There was a lady we were renting from," he recounted, "and she stayed there, and when the white people came, they told her to leave, and she said, 'No, you're not going to burn my house.' She said, 'If you're going to kill me because I stay here, then help yourself, because I'm going to stay here.' And she stayed, and they didn't set anyone's house on fire on that side of the block because at that time the houses were so close together that if you set one on fire, you set them all on fire."

It took Fairchild three days to find his mother, who had been at the Convention Hall. Their house had still been ransacked — beds turned over, belongings stolen — and together they tried to get their lives back in order. "Everything was a mess," he said. "Everything was burned. The churches, the schools, the buildings, everything." He said the "Klansmen were prevalent" during the riot, and they had boasted they could "intimidate the Negro. But we had a different breed here than we had in Alabama or Mississippi. We had one that would stand up and fight back. I don't think they had taken that into account. And that was the story of the race riot."

Feldman was certain that Fairchild's detailed account would convince her skeptical students that there had indeed been a riot. "I said to them, 'Go home and ask your parents,'" she recalled years later. "But some came back and still said, 'It never happened.'"

Her renegade style brought a sharp rebuke from the dean, who explicitly told her not to talk about the riot. She ignored his warnings and again invited Fairchild to speak to her class. The dean relented, so in at least one classroom in Tulsa, the race riot was not denied.

Black Tulsans relied on the oral tradition to pass down the riot story quietly, but for many years Greenwood also had a glaring reminder of the battle — Mount Zion Baptist Church. Known as the "church that faith built," it was completed with a $50,000 loan at the eleventh hour of construction. The riot not only destroyed the new building but placed it under a cloud of suspicion when rumors spread that the church had been a warehouse for armaments to be used against whites. After the riot, the Reverend R. A. Whitaker stood vigil over the ruins and demanded that a delegation of city officials and white ministers witness the clearing of the rubble. No evidence of weapons was found.

The church was insured, but like the rest of the policies covering Greenwood, a riot exemption clause made it worthless. The riot not only destroyed the building but also divided the congregation and almost killed the church. A dispute arose between the congregants who felt obligated to pay off the $50,000 debt and those who did not believe the debt was legally binding and could be ignored. In 1928 the congregation split, with one group opening a new church and the remainder slowly scraping money together to pay off the debt but doing little to rebuild. Mount Zion went through a rapid succession of ministers, and as the rest of Greenwood recovered, its ruins stood as a haunting reminder of bigotry and discord.

This "half-built, half-completed" church made an indelible impression on the young John Hope Franklin, who in 1925 moved from the black town of Rentiesville to Tulsa with his mother and sister. They joined his father, B. C. Franklin, who had arrived in Tulsa shortly before the riot, but it took four years for Greenwood to stabilize enough for his family to join him. John Hope was ten years old when he arrived, and he saw few remnants of the riot, save the ruins of Mount Zion and several other black churches. "It really struck me, because they were so obviously unfinished," he later recalled. "They would go up to a certain point — and then flat. No superstructure, no arches, no towers, no belfries." These wrecked houses of worship were "the best example we had of man's inhumanity to man." They also taught the youngster, whose later scholarship as a historian would help redefine the black experience in America, a lesson about the country's racial divide. Tulsa's white churches were impressive, even breathless, structures, particularly the Boston Avenue Methodist Church, a towering Art Deco masterpiece built for $1.5 million in 1929. "The white churches were built and the black churches were not built," Franklin recalled. It was a religious as well as a social paradox for the precocious youth. "I don't know," he said, "if that began my searching criticisms of Christianity."

For a time, Mount Zion's congregants gathered and prayed in the house of Mabel Little, but by 1937 they could convene in the church's basement, which was now covered. The seats were planks laid across wobbly sawhorses, which sometimes fell to the dirt floor during sermons. But under a new leader, J. H. Dotson, the ceiling was plastered, one hundred fifty metal chairs were brought in, and the membership grew. More important, the Reverend Dotson went on a mission to raise money, starting with the White Elephant Drive. The whiteness of each elephant represented a debt of $1,500, and brown patches to cover the debt cost $3.25 apiece. Patch by patch, the white elephants began to disappear. Congregants were also given envelopes for their weekly donations, which could be dropped in one of three boxes. Two were ordinary containers, for the regular Sunday offerings and for tithes. The third was made of rough wood, sealed with a padlock, and trimmed with tin bands and gold letters — "like the Joash chest in the Bible," the Reverend Dotson said. Every member was supposed to contribute at least a dollar a week to that chest. As the Depression gave way to the more prosperous war years, the contributions got larger, and on November 23, 1942, twenty-one years after the riot, the debt was erased.

Services were still held in the basement, which had a low ceiling, a twelve-inch podium, a choir stand, and a piano. The congregants prayed, sang, and dressed no differently than if they had been in a finished church. The men wore suits and ties, the women, gloves and long dresses, and everyone wore hats. "You should never go before God," the elders would say, "with your head uncovered."

But Mount Zion was determined to build a new church that would be more beautiful than the previous one. Plans were drawn up for a three-story Gothic structure with two spires, a full gable, and stained glass windows, and the fundraising efforts continued. In 1945 *Time* magazine ran a story about its struggle, attracting contributions from around the country. One man enclosed a dollar and asked if he could "buy one brick." Another wrote that religious intolerance had driven him from his own church and he was giving Mount Zion his yearly donation of $52. Another woman wrote: "In the midst of so many pages of magazines and newspapers given over to hatreds and wars and desolation in these bitter times, the courage

J. B. Stradford, the wealthiest man in Greenwood in 1921, was wrongly accused of starting the riot.

Richard Lloyd Jones's newspaper, the *Tribune*, printed the incendiary article that triggered the courthouse confrontation, and after the riot Jones wrote racist editorials.
State Historical Society of Wisconsin

The *Tribune* article steered white Tulsans ("the picture show crowd," according to one observer) to the courthouse in anticipation of a lynching.
Courtesy of the Greenwood Cultural Center

Mount Zion Baptist Church symbolized black affluence, but the rioters believed it was used to store ammunition. *Courtesy of the University of Tulsa*

BURNING OF CHURCH WHERE AMUNITION
WAS STORED - DURING TULSA RACE

On the morning of the riot, smoke quickly engulfed Greenwood.
Courtesy of the University of Tulsa

The National Guard used a machine gun on a tripod to topple Mount Zion.
Courtesy of the University of Tulsa

Black victims typically
did not receive immediate
assistance. *Courtesy of
the University of Tulsa*

After the riot, blacks were marched to detention centers like prisoners.
Courtesy of the Tulsa Historical Society

Many black victims were carted through town on flatbed trucks.
Courtesy of the Tulsa Historical Society

The rioters destroyed 1,256 houses across 36 square blocks.
Courtesy of the University of Tulsa

At least 2,000 blacks left Greenwood, temporarily or permanently.
Courtesy of the Tulsa Historical Society

Tulsa's officials reneged on promises to help rebuild Greenwood.

Courtesy of the Tulsa Historical Society

After the riot, B. C. Franklin (right) ran his law office from a tent.
Courtesy of the Tulsa Historical Society

In 1996 the Black Wall Street Memorial was unveiled at the Greenwood Cultural Center, but the "eternal light" had a short lifespan. *Courtesy of the Greenwood Cultural Center*

Cornelius Toole, a great-grandson of J. B. Stradford's, was determined to exonerate his patriarch. *Courtesy of the Tulsa World*

Beryl Ford, whose collection of Tulsa memorabilia included vintage newspapers, was determined to defend the city's honor.
Courtesy of the Tulsa World

Mabel Little, shown here in the 1970s, was outraged not only by the rioters but by the "good whites," who did not protect Greenwood.
Courtesy of Oliver Thompson

The riot prevented Veneice Sims from attending her first prom, but she got a second chance 80 years later. *Courtesy of the* Tulsa World

George Monroe's personable style—and his story of a white rioter's stepping on his hand—made him a beloved survivor. *Courtesy of the* Tulsa World

Mayor Savage reached out to Otis Clark and other black survivors, but she did not advocate reparations for them. *Courtesy of the* Tulsa World

Currie Ballard showed an enlarged postcard of a black being lynched to explain the racial hatred that contributed to the riot. *Courtesy of the* Tulsa World

Vivian Clark-Adams believed that the riot showed how black voices are often ignored in the writing of history. *Courtesy of Vivian Clark-Adams*

Scott Ellsworth began doing research on the riot as a college student and was later the state commission's lead consultant. *Courtesy of the* Tulsa World

One state legislator, Don Ross, needed all of his oratorical skills to build support for a riot and reconciliation bill. *Courtesy of the* Tulsa World

The neighborhood that once surrounded Mount Zion Baptist Church has been replaced by an expressway. *James S. Hirsch*

and quiet faith of your congregation is an abiding tribute to all that is free and gentle in human kind. Surely the Almighty must look with a kind and happy eye on the people of your congregation."

Faith was not going to rebuild Mount Zion, nor would money alone do it. It was the carpenters, bricklayers, plasterers, and electricians who toiled on weekends and at night to construct the new building on the site of the old one. The Latimer brothers, W.S. and J.C., architects who had graduated from the Tuskegee Institute, oversaw the work, barking out "more mortar, more mortar" to the volunteers. The church could not borrow money from a bank but did borrow from the Broadhurst Foundation, established by a Tulsa businessman. The loan was retired early, in 1959.

On Sunday, October 21, 1952, dedication services were held for the new Mount Zion Baptist Church. Costing $300,000, it had buff bricks and stone masonry and a stained glass window of the River Jordan aligned so the "water" appeared to be flowing into the baptistery at the base of the window. The church's revival was a testament to the sacrifice of its members; one elderly woman's many contributions eventually drained her savings for her own burial. "She loved the church so much, she made the supreme sacrifice," said the Reverend Calvin McCutchen, who has been the pastor of Mount Zion since 1957. "When she died, we had to receive an offering for the family to help bury her." To other congregants, their test was one that Jesus himself might have faced, and the new church was a triumph of faith over hatred, a repudiation of the mob that tried to destroy Greenwood's spirit.

"You can do all things through Jesus Christ," said Julius Pegues, who as a teenager helped rebuild Mount Zion. "That leaves nothing out. You can even overcome a race riot."

A culture of silence may have surrounded the riot in many parts of white Tulsa, but a palpable fear haunted other parts of the community — the fear of a second riot. When Nancy Dodson, a junior college teacher, arrived in 1950, her white friends would not talk about the event. "I was admonished not to mention the riot almost upon our arrival," she later wrote. "Because of the shame, I thought. But the explanation was, 'You don't want to start another.'"

Ironically, those fears served to calm racial tensions. In 1957, three years after *Brown v. Board of Education* struck down segregated schools, black Tulsans began to trickle into white neighborhoods. They were met initially with cross burnings. Then, in January 1958, the house of a black family was bombed when an explosive was thrown from a passing car, landing one yard away from the front porch. All the windows were shattered, and the walls in the living room and kitchen were cracked; a fourteen-year-old girl who was typing in the dining room was treated for shock. Suspicion fell on the White Citizens Council, which had been organized to preserve the city's Jim Crow laws. Its placards had appeared in the windows of white Tulsans' homes, but after the bombing, many whites removed them and rallied behind the black family. These whites were still not pleased about living near a black family, reported the *Oklahoma Eagle,* Tulsa's black newspaper, but according to one white Tulsan, "We don't want anything like this [bombing] to happen and we don't want a recurrence of 1921 when we had a race riot." No one was ever arrested for the bombing.

The shadow of the riot was felt in the 1960s, when black activists used the possibility of a second clash to advantage in their demands for public accommodations, open housing, and other civil rights. Tulsa's black leaders were less militant than those in many other cities — there was never open warfare in the streets during the civil rights movement — and many believe that the city averted violent demonstrations because both white and black leaders were willing to compromise to preclude a replay of 1921.

But the riot also left deep wounds in the city. It made the black and white communities more distrustful of each other and intensified their segregation. In a 1962 master's thesis for the University of Oklahoma, Karl Thiele interviewed Tulsans of both races. "Fear, generated by the race riot, which has existed in the minds of many people cannot be underestimated," he wrote. "This is the intangible result of the riot which was most often mentioned in the interviews . . . It is generally agreed that the race riot . . . has made it very difficult for the Negro and white communities to communicate. Most of the fear has been in the minds of Negroes who felt the total force of the disaster in 1921 . . . 'What happened once can happen again,' is the very real fear in the minds of many."

Thiele wrote that white Tulsans could not be friendly with the blacks who were blamed for causing the disaster. It was, perhaps, the most painful legacy of the riot: a race war that erupted because two communities distrusted and misunderstood each other had driven a wedge even more deeply between them.

"Negroes wished to be left alone," Thiele wrote, "and the white community was happy to oblige."

"Money, Negro"

THE COUNTRY's major race riots in the first quarter of the twentieth century became, in time, obscure events to most Americans,
and Tulsa's upheaval, for all its destruction, would have been another anonymous tragedy but for the impassioned efforts of several
residents, black and white. No one played a more crucial role in
this endeavor than Don Ross, a black journalist-turned-politician
who spent more than four decades trying to summon the event from
history.

As a young boy in the late 1940s, he lived in the small agricultural
town of Vinita, Oklahoma, where he learned the doctrine of separate
and unequal. His house was across the street from the white River-
side School, but he had to walk several miles to the Attucks School.
Run out of the "white" park, ten acres of clean slides, a manicured
ball field, and a pond, he was restricted to the "colored" park, which
was half the size and had worn benches and rusted equipment. He
heard old folks talk about the Grand Café, which once posted a neon
sign: NIGGER FRIED CHICKEN. When he asked his grandmother
what it meant, she said, "Racism is a cross that Negroes have to
bear." He read Gene Autry comic books but could not see the singing
cowboy's movies. For some reason, only the Aztec Theater, which
banned black patrons, showed Gene Autry films. Don had to sit in
the balcony of the Center Theater, which featured Roy Rogers films.

Although neither entertainer was to blame for this arrangement, Ross would hold a lifetime grudge against Gene Autry.

When his family moved to North Tulsa in 1952, the eleven-year-old thought he had landed in paradise. He saw a prosperous, self-sufficient black community happily insulated from the white world, an image that was not simply the conjuring of a small-town youth coming to the big city. Despite Greenwood's chronic housing, health care, and infrastructure problems, World War II had energized black Tulsa as well as the rest of the city. Hundreds of African Americans had been industrial workers, mostly in defense plants, while the shortage of white labor had opened up jobs at oil companies. By 1945 there were 242 black-owned businesses — the most ever in the community — as well as uncounted illegitimate enterprises.

Greenwood had skating rinks, drugstores with soda fountains serving 7Up, and the teen canteen, a social club where Robert Fairchild, wearing Bermuda shorts and socks up to his knees, collected twenty-five cents for admission. He allowed Don to sneak in because he knew the youngster didn't have a spare quarter. Greenwood Avenue wasn't pretty, but the tin-and-tar shacks housed profitable businesses: Madison's and Isaac's shoestores, Jackson's and Jack's mortuaries, Jarrett's grocery, Caver's and Farley's cleaners, and the Royal Hotel. There were also pool halls — Spann's and Big Ten's — which gave Don his first calling in life: he wanted to be a pool shark.

And the movie theaters! The Peoria, Regal, Rex, and Dreamland all brought Hollywood's grainy fantasies to town. Even Gene Autry's grade-B Westerns appeared in Greenwood — proof that this place was special. Greenwood was a comfort zone, where the only whites Don saw were the bootleggers selling their half pints of "white heat" from the trunk of a Buick. On weekends, he would sit on the porch of his apartment building — a low-income housing project — and listen to men who would sip their good scotch and tell the stories of Greenwood. They would talk not about the riot but about the heroic black pioneers who settled Tulsa, built their homes and businesses, and overcame the petty slights and institutional bigotry of their city.

Don saw his father only twice — once, he said, when he was twenty-three and once at the man's funeral. His mother was a domestic; his stepfather worked at a foundry but was a weekend alcoholic. There was no middle or upper class. There were houses with indoor toilets, houses with outdoor toilets, and the projects, where he lived. He slept with his brother on a rollaway bed in the kitchen, which was heated by a gas stove in the winter, the cold air sealed out by rags shoved under the door and through cracks in the ceiling.

His family was on welfare, even if they had to use subterfuge to secure payments. As he recalled, "If you were on welfare in the fifties, there were three no-no's: no man in the house, no TV, and no telephone. Our apartment was a source of excitement because we violated all three, and we also had a caseworker who never knocked. My brothers and I would take turns as lookouts. When the caseworker came, we generally spotted her and would throw the old man's clothes under the bed, put the television in the garbage can, and set the phone under the sofa pillows, hoping no one would call while she was there."

His family may have cheated on welfare, but their poverty was real. When Don wore a hole through a shoe, he used cardboard to cover it. Only when the top of the shoe came off did he get a new pair. When he graduated from Booker T. Washington High School in 1959, his mother couldn't buy him a suit and nice shoes, so the principal's wife took him to see several sympathetic white Tulsans and asked for contributions. The money came in, and Don Ross wore a fine sharkskin suit and black shoes for his graduation.

That he graduated at all was no mean accomplishment. He had little respect for authority and was a terrible student who preferred the pool hall to the classroom, craved attention as the class clown, and was frequently reprimanded for his tardiness and misbehavior. As his eighth-grade teacher, Juanita Hopkins, recalled, "I don't think he ever learned where to put the period." Ross later wrote of his schooling: "I refused to learn. I was obstinate, undisciplined, crude. A near-illiterate trouble maker . . . I was often sent to the dean's office and read comic books." He avoided *Tom Sawyer* and *Huckleberry Finn* because they didn't have pictures.

He also shunned school sports and extracurricular activities because they interfered with pool, but it was not a completely misspent youth. As a high school sophomore, he had a crush on a girl who was on the yearbook staff. Seeking her attention, he reluctantly joined the staff — it met after school, which he resented — and encountered W. D. Williams, a history teacher who had ambitious plans for the yearbook. "This isn't just a history of Booker T. Washington," Williams told the students. "This is a history of the community." He then told the story of the riot.

Don Ross sat in disbelief. The story violated every idea he had had of Greenwood — a town of strong, defiant black men who could fight like hell and commanded respect from everyone. They built thriving businesses and good schools and were unified. Any black community that showed Gene Autry movies wouldn't let a bunch of crazy whites destroy their homes and churches. White people? Who even cared about white people? The boy didn't believe a word he heard, and he leaped to his feat. "Greenwood was never burned. Ain't no three hundred people killed. We're too old for fairy tales," he said angrily.

Openly disputing a teacher was dangerous — a student could get paddled for less — but Don was spared. Instead "Mr. W.D.," as he was called, invited his skeptical student to stay late after his next class. He showed him an album with photographs, postcards, and newspaper articles confirming everything he had said. Don saw the singed corpses and blacks being marched to detention camps and wicker coffins stacked on flatbed trucks heading to unnamed gravesites. "What do you think now, fat mouth?" Mr. W.D. asked Ross.

Speaking in labored tones, Williams also told him about his own experience as a sixteen-year-old watching his father, John, "defend Greenwood" in the riot. John Williams owned several businesses, including the Dreamland Theatre, and on the morning of the riot, he stood on the top floor of his three-story brick building on Greenwood Avenue, a .30-.30 rifle perched on exposed pipe. His positioning gave him a clear shot, but his adversaries soon homed in on the building, riddling it with bullets. When a low-flying airplane roared overhead, Williams vainly shot at it. With the whites inching closer, he bounded down the stairs, grabbed his family, and fled on foot up Greenwood Avenue. His son could hear the bullets whizzing past his ear. While his wife left for her mother's house on Detroit, father and son sought refuge in a pool hall, where the elder Williams again positioned himself with his rifle on the second floor. With another man, he held his ground for about an hour but once again had to flee, this time escaping down the back stairs of the building. Williams and his son decided to split up and reconvene on the northern edge of Greenwood, but after a few blocks, three armed whites stopped W.D. He was taken to Convention Hall, where he joined his parents. When they returned home, the Dreamland Theatre was a heap of bricks and cinders.

This story made an impression on Don Ross, and he wanted to learn more. He returned to the old men and women in his neighborhood and along Greenwood Avenue and began asking questions. Thirty-five years had passed, but they all confirmed that white marauders had raced through their streets and torched their homes. These survivors, however, did not tell Ross a story of defeat and despair but of honor and pride. They described how Peg Leg Taylor stood on Standpipe Hill and mowed down the white invaders, how the blacks were winning the war until the National Guard arrived, and how even those units needed air cover from planes firing on innocent blacks. They told Ross how the city promised to rebuild Greenwood but never followed through and that the pride and strength of black Tulsans rebuilt the community — with no help from outsiders.

Seeing the teenager's interest, W. D. Williams took him to the home of Seymour Williams (no relation), Greenwood's legendary high school football coach. He was also a history teacher and a survivor of the riot. He sat Ross on his front-porch swing and explained that Oklahoma's public schools purchased their textbooks from white southern publishing companies, so that meant he had been reading one-sided history, distorted history, *white* history. In these books Robert E. Lee was a hero, the Confederates were defending a noble cause, and black slaves were anonymous. To dramatize his contempt for this official narrative, Williams held up a textbook about the Civil War and ripped out the pages. "And you can rip them out of your book also," he said. "It's a damn lie." If you wanted black history, he said, you had to read the black press, and the same was true for the riot. Even liberal newspapers like the *New York Times*, he said, didn't go to the concentration camps and talk to victims. It interviewed the mayor, the police chief, the sheriff — all members of the establishment aligned against the blacks.

Ross asked why no one in Greenwood talked about the riot, why it was kept a secret.

"Blacks lost everything, and they're afraid it could happen again," Williams said. "There were a lot of big-shot rednecks at that courthouse who ran the city and still do. Sinclair Oil Company owned one of the planes used to drop firebombs on people and buildings. The killers are still running loose, and they're wearing blue suits as well as Klan sheets."

Williams placed the riot in the broad context of the white subjugation of other races. He told Ross about the history of slavery, the Trail of Tears, and the federal government's abrogation of treaties with the Indians and its confiscation of their lands. The riot was less a historical aberration than a violent spike in a continuum of oppression against dark-skinned people.

These stories were revelations to the teenager. He continued to solicit the oral histories of his community, and he carried them like a sack of thorns across his back. Don Ross the pool shark, the class clown, the kid who barely had the grades to graduate and couldn't afford to buy a suit — he of all people would compel Tulsa to confront its history.

After high school, Ross spent four years in the air force, then returned to Greenwood. He took courses at the University of Tulsa — once again, white patrons who recognized his potential footed the bill — and worked as a busboy, a baker, and at other odd jobs. He also began attending civil rights meetings and realized that he could be part of historic change in Tulsa. In 1963 he wrote his first article for the weekly *Oklahoma Eagle*, "Who's Uncle Tom?" It urged militancy for equal rights and ridiculed accommodating African American leaders. The article also launched his own column, "From the Ghetto Line," and established him as one of Greenwood's most important voices.

Ross blended whimsy and ire. He tweaked Tulsa ("the city with a Questionable Personality"), Oral Roberts ("the only man I know who made a million dollars slapping people"), Governor Ronald

Reagan ("Negro Tulsans for Reagan will meet Friday night . . . in a phone booth"), even landings on the moon (which would become "just another white antiseptic suburb"). He wrote that he bought his son a membership to NIGGER (the National Institute for God-given Equal Rights) and that he was a card-carrying member of BANG (the Black African Negro Group). Asked why he wrote humor, Ross said, "I don't write humor. I write about hypocrisy that some people find funny." He was called the "black Art Buchwald," and in the 1970s he sent his clips to the famed humorist. The two became friends, and they joined Russell Baker, Andy Rooney, and Erma Bombeck in an Academy of Humor Columnists, a club that never convened but supported one another through phone calls, letters, and good-natured needling. "We needed an ethnic," Buchwald later explained in why they included Ross. "We told him he'd be better off writing *Roots.*"

Despite his relative anonymity, Ross gained the respect of his peers for his ability to turn a phrase. Noting the unequal distribution of park space for white and black Tulsans, he wrote, "South side kids play on *grass.* North side kids play on *glass.*" Responding to white leaders who urged blacks to get an education but were indifferent to their hunger, he observed, "It's hard to concentrate with wrinkles in your belly."

His wit disarmed his critics. "He's the only person who could call our police chief a racist and the chief would laugh at it," said James Goodwin, publisher of the *Oklahoma Eagle.* But Ross's jokes, funny or flat, were usually tinged with anger. "White folks are asking me questions again," he once wrote. "Would you have your daughter marry a white man? Sure, if he was wealthy and had 24 hours to live. (And I would be her assurance that he made his deadline.)" Sometimes he chucked the one-liners to vent his rage more clearly at whites for resisting black demands for equal rights and economic opportunity. "The residents of the Ghetto hardly believe that America exists," he wrote. "We are, in fact, exaggerated Americans. We cling to objects . . . in the dread of nothingness. We've sat in [white people's] meetings, visited your homes and watched you worship your rights, your freedoms, your materialistic heavens." Ross also aimed barbs at the black community, once defining the black church as "a seat of power and wealth built with Bibles and led by men who have a monopoly on sending people to heaven and who are governed by a guaranteed annual income."

His stridency was unnerving in a city where black doormen in downtown office buildings still greeted whites, "Good morning, mas'sah." Most white Tulsans resisted open housing, public accommodations, and other landmarks of racial progress. In 1964 the city was the nation's largest to vote for the Republican presidential candidate, Barry Goldwater, who opposed civil rights, and that same year saw the arrest of dozens of protesters who tried to integrate white restaurants. Ross was often on the front lines, and his jug ears, his profanity, and his raspy voice — which, in his words, was like "the sound of rusty nails being pried from the floor of a sinking ship" — made him hard to miss at sit-ins and demonstrations. He specialized in making white politicians uncomfortable. At a meeting in the late 1960s, Mayor James Hewgley told Ross he was going to have to end the discussion because he had a luncheon.

"Where is it?" Ross asked.

"Southern Hills Country Club," the mayor said, referring to a swank, segregated establishment.

"I'll go with you," Ross said. The mayor leaned back. "I realize," Ross continued, "all I have to do is wear a red coat and a white cloth over my arm." The tactic was typical of Ross: scare the white people first, then use their fear to get something you want. Indeed, Ross was more of a dealmaker than an ideologue. He and another young black activist, Homer Johnson, played "good cop–bad cop" with politicians. In meetings with the mayor, for example, Johnson would curse and fume over, say, the need to create a human rights or a fair housing commission. Then Ross would apologize. "Homer is very emotional about this issue, but it is a real issue," he would say. He'd then call the mayor for a private meeting. (Both commissions were created.) When Ross later became a state legislator, he used these same tactics to create a race riot commission.

Ross married and started a family. He smoked, drank, maxed out on credit cards, drove shiny new cars, was always good company, and knew how to get what he wanted. When the Oklahoma Eagle's publisher, James Goodwin, who was also a lawyer, tried to raise money for an indigent client, Ross rustled up $500 — but he would not

hand over the cash unless Goodwin participated in a Vietnam protest march. Reluctantly, Goodwin marched. "He's a brilliant guy," he
said. "He disguises it with the sound of his voice and pronunciation
of his words, and you think he's loud and inconsequential, but that's
misleading."

Ironically, the greatest political progress for black Tulsans, reached
through the civil rights gains in the 1960s, coincided with the economic collapse of Greenwood. Its businesses had relied on captive
customers, within walking distance of their stores, but a crosscurrent
of forces — integration, highway construction, and urban renewal
— decimated the district's core. These pressures exacted similar tolls
on black communities around the country, but Greenwood's disinte-
gration produced an eerie parallel to what the city had tried to do after the riot: drive blacks away from downtown Tulsa.

   Through court rulings, federal legislation, and local ordinances,
legal segregation in America ended by the late 1960s. For most black
Tulsans, integration did not mean integrated neighborhoods, but access to the previously restricted movie theaters, restaurants, clothing
stores, pharmacies, grocers, and shopping malls. Black Tulsans could
now buy dresses at Seidenbach's, eat lunch at Coney Island, and
watch movies at drive-in theaters. They voted with their feet and
spent their dollars in the white community, starving Greenwood's
businesses in the process. But even without integration, the district's
core — Deep Greenwood, at the intersection of Greenwood and Archer — was in turmoil.

   Beginning in the late 1950s, seven expressways, funded mostly by
the federal government, were constructed through and around Tulsa
and connected by the Inner Dispersal Loop, which formed a ring
around downtown. The goal was to link Tulsa to interstate highways
and to stimulate new downtown development, but it could only be
achieved by tearing through established neighborhoods. The city
condemned property in West Tulsa, where low-income whites lived,
and in Greenwood, forcing the residents to move. Completed in the
1970s, the northern side of the Inner Dispersal Loop cut a high concrete swath along the southern boundary of Greenwood while the el-
evated Cherokee Expressway ran north through Greenwood. This

created a concrete box canyon that bound the remaining population in Greenwood's core and created dead space under the overpasses and near the exits.

Expressways wiped out neighborhoods all over the country. Between 1957 and 1968, the construction of federal highways destroyed about 330,000 housing units, mostly in black and poor areas. "A 'kill two birds with one stone' mentality prevailed almost everywhere," wrote the urban scholar Raymond A. Mohl. "Cities sought to route interstate highways through slum neighborhoods, thus using federal highway money to reclaim downtown urban real estate. Inner-city slums could be cleared, blacks removed to more distant second-ghetto areas, the central business districts redeveloped, and transportation woes solved all at the same time — and mostly at federal expense."

Greenwood's families and businesses were further dispersed in the 1960s through urban renewal. The federally financed effort tried to rehabilitate blighted areas by condemning property, paying occupants to move, then redeveloping the land. It achieved its first two goals, but most of the blacks who moved never returned, and the promise of redevelopment proved hollow. In time, black Tulsans would call urban renewal "urban removal."

By the early 1970s this initiative had claimed and demolished more than a thousand businesses and homes in Tulsa, many of them in Greenwood, and the blacks moved north, east, and west — but with few exceptions, not south of the railroad tracks. De facto segregation remained. The old Negro business district was primed for the development of a warehouse, commercial, or industrial district, which the city had envisioned after the riot; it never happened. The land's value originally lay in its proximity to the railroads and downtown, but rail transportation had long been eclipsed by car and air travel, and suburban sprawl had diminished downtown's primacy. Greenwood Avenue became a stretch of boarded storefronts, parking meters, winos, and vacant lots. About the only business that remained was the *Oklahoma Eagle.* Mount Zion Baptist Church also held on, though it was now trapped beneath the concrete arm of an expressway.

In November 1971 the Chamber of Commerce magazine, *Tulsa,*

published a story, "Say Goodbye to Greenwood Avenue." "There is no place in the modern city for a Greenwood, where the poor spend their spare time starving," it said. "Much of Greenwood cries for mercy killing. The buildings that remain have sprained attics and broken basements. Signs on the windows advertise ghosts . . . Greenwood, once reborn, is settling into its grave again. A transplant belongs to the next generation."

The 1960s saw America's worst race riots since the years following World War I, and the "red summer" of 1919 seemed to repeat itself in 1967, when violence erupted in 128 cities, killing 83 people, and again in 1968, after Martin Luther King Jr. was assassinated. Unlike the Tulsa riot, these were seen on television, and they captured young blacks battling white police officers and setting fire to their neighborhood. "Watts" and "Newark" entered the vocabulary as synonyms for black rage, yet these conflagrations were far different from those in the first quarter century. Then it was white rage that drove the riot, whites who wanted to send messages to "impudent Negroes," and whites who destroyed black property. Tulsa's riot was not only forgotten, it was antiquated.

Don Ross did what he could to keep Tulsa's riot alive. In 1968 he wrote three consecutive columns about it in the *Oklahoma Eagle*. He placed it in the racial context of the time, suggesting that it was an extension of the government's policy of separatism. He quoted a book, *Confrontation Black & White:* "'The net effect of [this separatism] is to make Negroes quasi-colonials in their native land. White America used the police power to grind them down by law, vigilante action and terror.'"

These stories may have resonated with Ross's readers, but they had no impact on white Tulsans, who didn't read the *Oklahoma Eagle* and were certainly not going to use contemporary disturbances to rediscover their own history. Even the Tulsa County Historical Society refused to acknowledge the riot. In the 1960s its board was integrated by B. C. Franklin's daughter, Mozella Jones. She had pictures of the riot from her father, who died in 1960, and she urged the group to sponsor a commemoration or exhibition about the event. Her plea was rebuffed. Even most blacks saw little to gain by dredging up painful memories while they were seeking public accommodations, fair housing, and other basic rights. But at least one former Tulsan did want to talk about the riot, and the words of John Hope Franklin — Mozella Jones's brother — reshaped Ross's thinking about the possibility of retroactive justice.

By the 1960s Franklin had achieved renown as a historian and civil rights advocate. His landmark book, *From Slavery to Freedom* (1946), became the definitive text of the African American experience; it ultimately sold more than three million copies and was translated into six languages. While Franklin had a formal, understated style, his books were considered radical, specifically those on the antebellum South and Reconstruction. He rejected mainstream historians' benign interpretation of slavery and segregation and described how racist policies had brutalized black Americans. Franklin also did research for the NAACP in its lawsuit that became *Brown v. Board of Education*. He marched with Martin Luther King Jr. in Montgomery, Alabama; he would later assist Nelson Mandela in creating a constitution for the new, democratic South Africa; and he would head President Clinton's advisory board on race.

Arriving in Tulsa four years after the riot, Franklin was aware of it not only from the "half-built churches" he saw but also from his trips to the courthouse with his father. When a probate matter arose for someone who had mysteriously died on or around June 1, 1921, B. C. Franklin would lean over and whisper to his son, "That's a riot case." Franklin's boyhood friends described how they hid in attics as bullets whizzed by, and George Monroe told him about when he hid beneath the bed and his fingers were stepped on by the white raider.

After high school, Franklin left Tulsa for Fisk University in Nashville, Tennessee, earned his doctorate in history at Harvard, taught, wrote, and lectured, traveling throughout the country and the world. But when he returned to Greenwood, particularly in the 1960s, he felt pangs of sadness at its decline. He did not romanticize the Greenwood of his youth — his parents could not afford to buy him a bike and on some Christmases gave him only nuts and fruit — but at least that community had energy. The Greenwood he returned to seemed to be in a trance, and he knew that its malaise was not simply the result of urban renewal or the highways or some other mysterious affliction. It also had to do with its history, with the riot.

Even though Tulsa's black population continued to increase — in 1970 it was 35,277, and it never dropped below 10 percent of the city's total — the riot drove many of Greenwood's most important leaders away and, Franklin believed, deterred future leaders from moving to Tulsa. His father, in fact, was one of Greenwood's few men of prominence who stayed. Franklin also understood the true cost of the riot. It was not just the value of his father's business, his house, and his belongings that was destroyed. It was also the four years that B. C. Franklin lost with his family, who stayed in Rentiesville until conditions in Greenwood stabilized. It was four years that John Hope Franklin lost with his daddy, and that loss — never tabulated in a claim against an insurance company or the city — was greater than anything lost in the fire.

Neither B. C. Franklin nor any other victim was compensated for these losses, but John Hope knew there was a precedent for government reparations to victims of state crimes. In the 1950s West Germany paid more than a billion dollars in reparations to Israel, an acknowledgment of the war crimes committed during World War II and a "moral restoration" of Jews in German history.

Tulsa was not Nazi Germany, but the city's responsibility in the riot was clear. Why shouldn't it be held accountable? On a trip to Tulsa in the 1960s, Franklin discussed the idea of compensation with Don Ross.

"Why not ask for reparations?" Franklin asked him.

"What are reparations?" Ross replied.

"*Money, Negro.*"

Ross had other battles to fight in the '60s, but he now had a way to vindicate the losses of the riot and redeem the history of Greenwood.

It Happened in Tulsa

I F CENTRAL CASTING were looking for the prototypical white Oklahoman, Ed Wheeler would be its man. He was a strapping six feet four and 225 pounds; a police officer's son who became a brigadier general in the U.S. Army and a captain in the Oklahoma National Guard; an expert marksman who collected Civil War rifles and Spanish sabers; a history buff who knew the difference between Confederate and Union bullets; and a college professor who called his students "mister" or "miss" because "it's hard to flunk someone you know on a first-name basis." A conservative Republican who flew the American flag outside his home, he was also a family man whose eyes welled up when he told a stranger about his wife, who had passed away years before.

In 1971, as the riot's fifty-year anniversary neared, he also played a critical role in redefining perceptions of the event among whites.

Wheeler was a gifted storyteller with a baritone voice and a sense of theatrics. In the 1960s and early '70s, he broadcast ten-minute historical dramas on KVOO radio in Tulsa and briefly expanded them into a television show. On the radio, Wheeler did not simply tell the story but provided sound effects; Pickett's charge at Gettysburg, for example, was accompanied by sounds of cannons and rebel yells. An Aztec flute provided the atmosphere for a lesson on Aztec civilization.

In the summer of 1970 Wheeler, then thirty-two, received a call from Larry Silvey, the young white editor of *Tulsa*, the magazine of the Chamber of Commerce. The former newspaper reporter was a liberal gadfly at the stodgy Chamber. His yellow Pinto bore a bumper sticker that read I SUPPORT OPEN HOUSING — hardly a rallying cry among the city's business leaders — and he would occasionally forsake boosterism for tough stories in the magazine. He wrote about the shortcomings of its zoo ("our dirty little menagerie"), the decline of Greenwood, and the barriers blacks faced in moving into white neighborhoods. Silvey also liked to beat Tulsa's two newspapers on stories and generate some buzz as well.

He admired Wheeler's radio dramas and wondered if there was any story he would not do on the air. Wheeler said there was one — the Tulsa race riot. He worried that in recreating the event, listeners would think that an actual riot was occurring — he recalled Orson Welles's "War of the Worlds" broadcast, which convinced millions that Martians were invading — and he feared that Tulsans would take to the streets in search of mayhem. Silvey asked if he would do the story for the magazine, which would coincide with the riot's fiftieth anniversary. He assumed the story would also scoop the *World* and the *Tribune*.

Wheeler accepted. He considered himself an impartial historian whose only agenda was to tell the story accurately. As a captain in the National Guard, he knew his way around the Oklahoma Military Department, and he had friends in the Tulsa Police Department. These contacts could help him find documents. He also had ties to the business community through his work in corporate communications for Oklahoma Natural Gas Company. Meanwhile, many black Tulsans trusted him because they remembered his radio shows on slavery and black history.

He began by looking for the official records on the riot at the state military archives, the police department, and the Tulsa County Sheriff's Office. To his dismay, any records that would have covered the riot were virtually gone, vanished. The police department, for example, had records from 1920 and 1922 but not 1921, and the Oklahoma Military Department showed a nine-month gap in 1921.

Wheeler read the newspaper accounts of the riot and noticed the missing front-page article of the *Tribune.* He also observed that the newspapers' first editions were more objective — reporters describing what happened — while the later editions were more opinionated and politically charged. "Negroes" became "black Bolsheviks," for example, and "whites" became "innocent whites." Wheeler assumed these changes came from editors in the newsroom, whose opinions he did not want. He wanted his story simply to tell what happened.

Wheeler began talking to riot survivors and eventually interviewed sixty people, forty blacks and twenty whites. His meetings with the African Americans drove home the riot's haunting legacy. The survivors would meet him only at night, at various churches in Greenwood, accompanied by their minister. They told him where they were during the riot and what they saw; Wheeler took fast notes, recording the times and street locations of every shooting. Many of the survivors brought yellowing photographs of Mount Zion Baptist Church burning to the ground and blacks marching to internment camps with their hands held high; they also brought the nametags issued to black prisoners and other documents from their scrapbooks, all proof of the tragedy. The blacks allowed Wheeler to take the pictures only if he promised not to reveal their names, and they all spoke only on the condition of anonymity. Though fifty years had passed, they still feared retribution if they spoke out. Some even feared another invasion of Greenwood.

Wheeler also asked the white survivors for specific times and locations of the shootings. They demanded anonymity as well but were less circumspect. Some expressed regret over the destruction, but many others used the same word to describe the event — "exciting." Some whites remained defiant, even hostile. Wheeler interviewed four former Klansmen, one of whom said, "If it hadn't been for the soldiers" — the National Guard — "we would have killed every goddamn nigger in the city." Another white survivor showed him a scar on the bottom of his neck sustained during the fighting. In time, Wheeler came to another realization. It had not been a race riot at all. It had been a race war.

Reconstructing the battle was difficult; selective memory and the passage of time blurred everyone's testimony. Wheeler did not ask people what they heard — just what they saw. He then took a 1921 map of Tulsa and stuck pins at the site of every shooting (where the body fell, where the witness stood). Drawing on his military experience, he wrapped string around the pins; two strings crossing, in his mind, confirmed a shooting. Slowly, the battle unfolded. Using the photographs, he counted the dead bodies and supplemented the count with information from his interviews and the newspapers. He estimated that three hundred were killed.

This research took months, and Wheeler was hard at it in early 1971 when the phone calls began late at night.

"You got better things to do than to write that article." *Click.*

"It might be a good idea if you took a vacation from Tulsa." *Click.*

"By the way, how's that four-year-old son of yours?" *Click.*

One day, a man in gray overalls approached Wheeler near a chili parlor downtown. "Don't write that race riot story," he told him, then walked away. Another morning, Wheeler walked out to his blue Ford sedan and saw a message scrawled in soap across the windshield: "Best look under your hood from now on." Wheeler continued to work on the article, but he moved his wife and son to his mother-in-law's house.

He finally turned in the story, and Silvey planned to package it with a second piece from the Reverend Ben Hill, Tulsa County's first black state representative, on how race relations had progressed in fifty years. The stories and the riot pictures that Wheeler had accumulated would make Silvey's magazine the talk of Tulsa.

But his coup was aborted by his own supervisors. Silvey had lived in Tulsa for only three years and did not understand the silence and denial that had surrounded the riot for five decades. According to Silvey, several days before the magazine was to come out, the head of the Chamber, Clyde Cole, held an afternoon meeting with the Chamber's attorney, several board members, and other Chamber executives. When the meeting was over, the administrative vice president walked into Silvey's office and told him the riot package had been killed. It was "possibly inflammatory," he said. Silvey, crushed, left his office and consoled himself by drinking Heineken, alone, at a nearby tavern.

When he told Wheeler the news the following day, the man who had put his life on the line for the story was furious. He went to the Chamber and, as he recounts it, got a meeting with Cole.

"What's going on?" he asked. "I didn't put in all this effort to have you shoot it down."

"We can't publish the story," Cole said. "It will cause a race riot." *

Wheeler then took the issue up with the all-white Chamber board, but its members rejected his request to print the story. During the meeting, it occurred to Wheeler that some of the directors — men in their late sixties and seventies — would have been the age of the rioters fifty years earlier.

Wheeler still didn't give up. He took his story to an editor he knew at the *Tulsa World*, who read it, praised it, and rejected it. "It's a wonderful story," he told Wheeler, "but the *World* won't touch it with an eleven-foot pole."

As the anniversary date approached, it appeared that the article was dead. Then Wheeler heard that a new black magazine in Tulsa, *Impact*, might be interested in the story. Its editor was Don Ross.

Like Silvey, Ross assumed that Tulsa's white newspapers would ignore the anniversary, and he wanted a story that would break the news. While his riot columns reflected the oral history of Greenwood and his own politics, he now wanted a thorough independent account. He asked two white *Tribune* reporters to write the story, but he rejected it because their overtly liberal views compromised the content. "It was too 'woe is me,'" Ross said. Wheeler's account was exactly what he was looking for.

It was published in June 1971 with the subhead "It Happened in Tulsa" and a direct, flat style. "This is a story of a race riot," it began. "It is not a pretty story, and it is not told for its shock value or to reopen old wounds. It is presented because it happened fifty years ago."

Wheeler wrote that lower-class Negroes were blamed for starting the riot, which became the official civic position. "But this is hogwash," he wrote. "Prejudice, suspicion, ignorance and hate caused the riot. Intolerance, anger, rumormongering and fear fanned its flames." He described the elevator incident, the "misleading" *Tribune*

---

* Cole, in an interview, said he did not recall the riot story and denied ever censoring the magazine.

article, the courthouse confrontation, and the armed white mob yelling "Get the niggers." He also described the blacks as a "negro mob." It was, he wrote, a "virtual war." Only at the end of the twelve-page story did Wheeler's sense of outrage surface. After the riot, he wrote, "The negroes moved back in their 'ghetto' with its disease, illiteracy and narcotics problem of epidemic proportions. The whites settled back to whisper in their cocktail parties about the 'coloreds,' making profound public pronouncements for political purposes in election campaigns about helping 'those less fortunate' and then continued to maintain the status quo."

The magazine sold out in Greenwood; Ross had his scoop. "We broke the race riot story," he said. Some whites in town called Wheeler a "nigger lover" (although not to his face), but the threats against him stopped. Wheeler also made one more discovery after the article was published. He received a call from the commander of the Tulsa Police Academy, Bill Wilbanks, who wanted to meet with him. He was about to retire and, in cleaning out his files, had discovered something of interest. He handed Wheeler six brittle sheets of paper that had been clipped together. The paper clip had all but rusted away, but the typewritten words were still legible. Each page listed two columns of people identified by their sex and race, their approximate age, and their cause of death. There was no date on the pages, but Wheeler realized what it was — the casualty list of the riot — and it seemed to confirm his theory of three hundred dead.

"I'd sure like a copy of this," he told Wilbanks.

He believed that the list, carefully studied, would reveal not only the number killed but also how they died and the injuries they suffered. It also represented something tangible from the police department about the riot. But Wilbanks said he couldn't give Wheeler a copy because it was "an official document," and he didn't want to jeopardize his pension. Wheeler left empty-handed, and the papers never surfaced again. Wilbanks, reached by telephone thirty years later, declined to comment.

Wheeler's story made few ripples because most white Tulsans never saw it, but he still helped to shape the public's understanding of the event. In the 1980s and '90s, he appeared on several television news shows and documentaries about the riot, and his commanding presence, precise recall, and polished delivery made him an effective presence. As interest in the riot grew, dozens of newspaper and magazine reporters also sought him out; his picture appeared in a *New York Times Magazine* piece on the riot. He liked the spotlight, and his story resonated not only for what he said — a story of official coverups, unrepentant Klansmen, and carnage — but also for who he was: a white patriot who had no affection for Afrocentric history but whose interpretation of the riot essentially affirmed the "black" version of the event.

One other publication acknowledged the riot's fiftieth anniversary.

On June 2, 1971, the *Tulsa Tribune* published an article on page 7. "For 50 years," it read, "the Tribune did not rehash the story, but the week of the 50th anniversary seems a natural time to relate just what did happen when a city got out of hand." It was the first substantive story about the riot in either of Tulsa's two main newspapers since 1921. The article, which did not carry a byline, recounted the elevator incident, gave casualty estimates, and described the shootings, the fires, and martial law. It did not blame the whites or the blacks and was nonjudgmental about all the participants. It did, however, find one hero — Richard Lloyd Jones.

Jones had died in 1963 at the age of ninety; his son, Jenkin Lloyd Jones, succeeded him as editor and carried on his father's bristling conservative voice. The anniversary article did not mention the *Tribune*'s own role in the riot, nor did it cite the editorials that blamed the violence on the "bad niggers." Instead it quoted a front-page editorial from June 1, 1921, that condemned lynch law and urged peace. "Richard Lloyd Jones," the article said, "did much to calm the stricken city. [His] editorial hit home, as a timely and courageous piece by a young man who had only recently purchased the newspaper. There was no further violence on either side." In this version of history, Richard Lloyd Jones was a voice of reason and a civic savior. He was neither, nor — at forty-eight — was he even "a young man."

It took almost a decade for more information on the riot to emerge, but the fiftieth anniversary did deliver an important message for many whites as well as blacks: it happened in Tulsa.

Bridging the Racial Divide

DON ROSS'S OBSESSION with the riot was born of personal experience in a community he loved. Like Ross, Scott Ellsworth turned the riot into a personal mission, but there the similarities ended between the two men.

Ellsworth was a white Tulsan who could have been a poster boy for middle-class heartland values. Born in 1954, he belonged to the Boy Scouts, delivered newspapers, played baseball, and lived in a comfortable brick house with a swing set and basketball hoop. His family never locked its front doors (until the movie *In Cold Blood* was released in 1967). His parents gave Scott a sense of duty and social justice. During World War II, when his father, Elmer, was in his thirties, he initially did not join the war effort because he was responsible for taking care of his mother. After she died, he went into the army and was part of the occupation of Japan. He had a quaint but abiding code: duty to God, duty to family, duty to country. After the war, he moved to Tulsa to work as a petroleum engineer, and his formal bearing — he would show up at Little League games wearing a coat, tie, and hat — was an endearing sign of respect that his son would adopt. Scott Ellsworth, as an adult, would go to the dentist wearing a tie.

His mother, Helen, was the daughter of Norwegian immigrants who raised four girls on a factory worker's wages. She was the first woman in her family to receive a college degree, and her strong liberal politics — she was an FDR Democrat, but she probably liked Eleanor even more — conveyed the importance of social justice to her three children.

But young Scott was no radical. To him, Tulsa was a clean, beautiful city whose oil interests made it one of the country's most important towns. He was certain that if the Russians ever bombed America, Tulsa would be one of the first five cities hit. He read history books, played war games, and celebrated the centennial of the Civil War by reenacting the Battle of Fredericksburg, one of the Union's worst defeats. In a neighborhood where one woman flew the Stars and Bars, Scott and his friends usually sided with the rebel states. As a freshman in high school in 1968, he went to Oklahoma City with the Tulsa chapter of Youth for Nixon and listened to speeches by Wilt Chamberlain and Clint Eastwood. During the Democratic Convention in Chicago, he rooted for the cops in their clashes with the hippies.

Before high school, blacks were almost nonexistent in his world; neither his family nor his neighbors could afford maids or yardmen, the kinds of jobs that exposed many white Tulsans to African Americans. Scott's grade school and junior high were almost all white, but at least one racial incident left an early mark. As a twelve-year-old, he worked as a stockboy at a lighting store, and one day a well-dressed black couple entered. After they left, Scott was instructed to vacuum the floor where "the niggers" had walked.

He was more aware of race by the time he went to high school. As the city was beginning to integrate its public schools, many of Scott's friends stayed in a white environment by attending Holland Hall, a private preparatory school. The alternative was the racially mixed Central High School downtown. Scott applied to Holland Hall, wore a jacket and tie to his interview, and was admitted, even receiving a scholarship. But he rejected the offer. He decided it was time to experience a new environment; besides, his father didn't particularly want him "going to school with a bunch of wealthy white kids." Scott entered Central High, where he encountered rich kids, poor kids, black kids, hippies, jocks, rednecks, Native Americans — the whole spectrum of Tulsa class conflicts and racial tensions.

In his sophomore year, a race riot broke out. There was a stabbing on a bus, then fistfights in the hall, reporters at the front door, policemen, and rumors that the Ku Klux Klan would show up. The sporadic fighting went on for three days. Ellsworth, who stayed out of harm's way, was troubled by the actions of the adults, not the students. During swim practice, his coach stood in front of the all-white team and said, "Boys, I don't want you to go looking for trouble, but if it comes your way, I don't want you to be backing off." The message, to Ellsworth, was clear: defend the honor of your race. Later, sitting in geometry class, he listened to the principal announce over the intercom that the school would hold student meetings to defuse the racial tensions. The black students, male and female, would convene in the cramped north auditorium, while the white students — male only — would gather in the carpeted, spacious south auditorium. All the white female students would stay in class.

The meetings, Ellsworth realized, were emblematic of the school and perhaps the community: blacks and whites didn't talk to each other, and racial tensions were to be resolved, somehow, by keeping them apart. He also understood the prejudice behind this arrangement. The principal assumed that the black girls were involved in the fighting and that the white girls were innocent.

Though the Tulsa race riot was glossed over in school, Scott had heard about it by the sixth or seventh grade and even went to the downtown library to read about it. When he worked as a busboy at IHOP, a black cook told him stories about corpses in the Arkansas River and machine guns on hotel roofs. It wasn't clear who had won or lost the battle, but he knew the riot was a big thing and that most adults didn't want to talk about it.

His knowledge of Greenwood became much more personal after his freshman year at Reed College, in Portland, Oregon. He returned to Tulsa for the summer and found a job in the black district, at 319 North Boulder, cleaning stoves with spray acids for the Tulsa Stove Hospital. The job's one saving grace was a co-worker named Bill Skillern, an old black preacher who talked about history, the civil rights movement, and Greenwood. He was not a riot survivor — he was a Texan who had moved to Tulsa — but his remarks impressed

on Ellsworth that the black community had been destroyed long before and had never truly recovered.

Ellsworth studied history in college and by his junior year was
searching for a subject for his thesis. Besides his family, there was,
perhaps, nothing he loved more than the city of Tulsa, but was there
anything historic about it? He remembered the riot. He looked for
books on the subject and, not finding any, figured he could make a
real contribution by writing about it.

He returned to Tulsa in the summer of 1975 to do his research. By
then, the battle had become an even more elusive memory, for the
wrecking ball had knocked out not only much of Greenwood but
also downtown Tulsa. The courthouse was vacated in 1955, torn
down in 1960, and eventually replaced by an office building. The Hotel Tulsa, shut in 1962, was also bulldozed. So too were old theaters,
bank buildings, and the city's library. The 1970s saw an attempt to
revive downtown through the Williams Center Complex. Where
blacks and whites had once raced through the streets shooting at
each other now stood the state's largest office tower, which included
a shopping gallery with elegant restaurants, specialty shops, a movie
theater, and a fine clothing store, all overlooking an ice skating rink.*

When Ellsworth finished high school, his parents moved to San
Francisco, so that summer he lived in a garage apartment that had
once been a servant's quarters. He needed a job to pay the bills, so he
worked the graveyard shift at an industrial yard, cutting and stamping iron used for power lines. The backbreaking work toughened
him as he witnessed bloody fights (and got into one himself) among
the crew of winos, Vietnam vets, and ex-cons, and it gave him the
thick skin he needed to do his research.

In asking about the third rail of Tulsa history, he encountered a
city he never knew. The Tulsa County Historical Society rebuffed his
requests for information. A friend's mother casually talked about
"the nigger riot," and former neighbors and friends expressed re-
morse about his new interest. When he visited his old neighborhood,

---

* Urban renewal was no more successful in downtown Tulsa than it had been in Greenwood. The shopping gallery struggled for years and was eventually closed.

he bumped into George Norvell, a Tulsa mayor in the 1950s who later lived across the street from the Ellsworths.

"Oh, Scotty, how you doing?" he asked.

"I'm back in town this summer," he said, "and I'm going to write my thesis on Tulsa history."

"Oh, that's great. What are you going to write about?"

"The Tulsa race riot."

Norvell blanched and muttered, "Oh, no."

Ellsworth spent time in the library, the courthouse, and city and county offices and made some progress. He found old city directories and figured out that the letter *C* denoted a colored person, but his research was difficult. Whites either denied any knowledge of the riot or said that no one really knew how it happened, and he didn't know any black riot survivors personally. The whole project might have collapsed had he not tracked down Ruth Avery Sigler, a white woman who had gone to the same church as his mother's best friend. Sigler was seven at the time of the riot and had spent years gathering information in an effort to write a book. She gave Ellsworth a copy of Ed Wheeler's article, which had useful information but lacked footnotes, sources, or even the names of witnesses. But with it was an interview with W. D. Williams, the teacher who first told Don Ross about the riot. Ellsworth finally had a name.

He called Williams on the phone, and the teacher invited him over. It was the first time Ellsworth had ever been in a black person's house, and he was struck by the similarities to his old house in Tulsa — the green Formica counters, the 1950s kitchen, the comfortable but weathered sofas. Williams, a small, slender man, was clearly pleased, and probably a bit surprised, that this white kid had appeared out of nowhere, eager to hear the story of his life. Sitting at the kitchen table, he spoke in a low, patient voice, and his words were a revelation to Ellsworth. The riot was not an inexplicable act of nature, as some whites suggested, but was triggered by the blacks' intent to stop a lynching. Williams told him about the *Tribune* editorial "To Lynch a Negro Tonight," about the chaos at the courthouse, and about the invasion of Greenwood. Ellsworth had read about some of it, but hearing the words made the events more authentic. Williams also brought the old Greenwood district to life. Ellsworth asked about specific places he'd found in the musty city directories, and Williams described them as if they were still in business. As the afternoon wore on, the riot was no longer a blur of anonymous figures but a tragedy that took the lives of actual people and destroyed a real community. Williams did for Ellsworth what he had done for Ross — convinced him of the importance of the story and inspired him to keep it alive.

Ellsworth returned to Reed and wrote his thesis, then went on to graduate school at Duke University. The traditional history students were primarily white, but an oral history program had recently been created, mostly attracting black students — and Scott Ellsworth. Its premise was that the history books were often misleading because they relied on traditional sources of information, such as newspapers, government documents, and court records, which reflected the biases of the institutions that produced them. These sources also marginalized the voices of minorities, outsiders, and the poor. Oral history, on the other hand, sought to remove these filters and to discover what really happened through the participants' own words.

The riot seemed to fit this paradigm perfectly. The official history had been preserved in Tulsa's white newspapers and government reports, but the black history had been handed down through stories told on Greenwood's porches. Ellsworth wanted to record those narratives on tape and use them to turn his thesis into a book.

It was an ambitious idea for a twenty-four-year-old who had not published so much as a newspaper article, but it would fill a huge vacuum. The first book on the riot had been written in the late 1920s by a young black riot survivor named Mary E. Jones Parrish. She interviewed black Tulsans, recorded their stories, and added them to her own recollections in *Events of the Tulsa Disaster*. Few copies, however, were published. In 1946 a white World War II veteran, Loren Gill, wrote his master's thesis on the riot, interviewing more than a dozen local officials (including Tulsa's mayor and police commissioner in 1921) as well as several black riot survivors. But the thesis, never published, was buried in the library stacks of the University of Tulsa.

Scholars gave the riot more attention in the 1970s, when black

studies programs were being set up at universities, millions of view-
ers were watching *Roots*, and historians were digging more deeply
into the African American experience. The Tulsa riot was discussed
in Kay M. Teall's *Black History in Oklahoma* and in Arthur Tolson's
Black Oklahomans: A History 1541–1972, both published in the early
1970s. In 1972, Rudia Halliburton Jr., a history professor at North-
eastern State University in Oklahoma, wrote an article on the subject
in the *Journal of Black Studies*, which he then adapted into a book.
Published by a small academic press in California, it included excellent photographs, many of which he had collected from his students,
but the narrative was brief and received little attention outside aca-
demia.

Ellsworth wanted to put the riot on the literary map, so in the
summer of 1978 he returned to Tulsa, this time with a tape recorder
and money from Duke to work full-time on his research. The former
Eagle Scout and Nixon supporter now sported a mustache, smoked
cigarettes, and told his subjects that his goal was to "rewrite history."
He interviewed W. D. Williams again and sought out other black
survivors. Mabel Little wouldn't talk to him because he was white,
but he met with Robert Fairchild, Seymour Williams, and Mozella
Jones, who later introduced him to her brother, John Hope Franklin.
Many of the survivors were now in their sixties and seventies —
about the same age as Ellsworth's father, who was forty-seven when
Scott was born. His father, older than those of his friends, had increased his respect for his elders, an attitude that helped him forge
close ties with the aging survivors.

Interviewing whites, however, was still difficult. He found the
names of Tulsa's police officers in 1921 and checked the directory to
see if they were still alive. After discovering that none of them would
meet with him once he mentioned the riot, he resorted to subterfuge. He would say he was writing about the early days of the police
department and, if he got the interview, ask about the riot at the end.
One retired police officer, I. S. Pitman, showed him his riot pictures
but would not let them be used in the book. He did, however, tell
Ellsworth about his Klan participation, saying, "It was a nice order
. . . If somebody got out of line, they put him back in line. That's
what the public didn't like."

Ellsworth spent three years writing the book while doing other research, and in 1982 *Death in a Promised Land* was published by Louisiana State University Press. A relatively slim volume — the paperback edition had 111 pages, excluding footnotes, appendices, and source material — it never sold well. Neither the *Tulsa Tribune* nor the *Tulsa World* reviewed it, although the *World* wrote a flattering profile of the author. Ellsworth earned less than $10,000 from the book.

While the book itself relied on black interviews and testimony, it was not a "black oral history" but an evenhanded, heavily documented account of events. It was also a milestone. The most comprehensive and thoroughly documented narrative of the riot, it represented the first account widely accessible in Tulsa and available in libraries across the country. And it identified individual blacks and whites (such as W. D. Williams's father and Richard Lloyd Jones) and the roles they played. Yet one of the story's most intriguing characters was the author himself.

Ellsworth had an abiding, almost sentimental, attachment to Tulsa. At his wedding in 1993, the first song was "Take Me Back to Tulsa." (His wife, Betsy, was from New Jersey. They married in Washington, D.C., and settled in Portland.) When he took Betsy to visit his hometown, he proudly drove her past his old house and schools and revealed a deep connection to those buildings and what they stood for: family, neighborhood, community. Yet his book laid bare the racist underbelly of the Magic City and made Ellsworth, in some corners, a traitor. Friends asked why he wanted to "stir up trouble," and the former president of the Tulsa County Historical Society, Beryl Ford, kept a dog-eared copy of the book in his office, having underlined what he considered the most scurrilous attacks on the city.

Ellsworth saw no contradiction in his love for Tulsa and his indictment of it. On the contrary, the book was his gift to the city. It may not have been a pretty gift, but it could help the community understand itself. His father had given him a rigid sense of right and wrong, and if he offended a few white people along the way, that was a small price to pay for, in his words, "tossing a dagger at the heart of white supremacy."

What Ellsworth did not anticipate was that he would offend some blacks as well. Certainly most were appreciative. John Hope Franklin wrote a glowing introduction for the book. Mozella Jones sponsored a book signing, and even Mabel Little attended. Ellsworth had described as heroes those blacks who came to the courthouse and tried to defend Greenwood. But he didn't support the more radical black assessment that the riot was a planned conspiracy by the white elite, nor did he endorse the oft-repeated stories that the authorities had wantonly disposed of black bodies. He wrote that a death toll of seventy-five was "probably the most accurate" — well below the top estimate of three hundred — and devoted only three paragraphs to the airplanes. He noted that the planes, according to black witnesses and news accounts, had been used for offensive purposes — a position long held by many black Tulsans. But Ellsworth did not validate that claim. He used oral history not to create the history but to inform it — which kept him one step removed from the black narrative of the riot.

When he gave a speech about the riot at the University of Tulsa in 1989, it was that rare event that drew both blacks and whites. At the end of the speech, a group of middle-aged blacks gathered outside and expressed their disappointment. "They thought they would hear stories about blacks being burned alive and buried in cellars, hundreds of people killed and thrown into the Arkansas River," said the Oklahoma historian Danney Goble, who attended the lecture. "Scott didn't say any of that."

Ellsworth assumed his research had ended with the publication of the book, but events would bring him back to Tulsa to launch another investigation. He would once again try to straddle the racial divide, but this time the stakes would be much higher, the complaints much sharper, and the gulf much wider.

Death in a Promised Land caught the attention of Sister Sylvia Schmidt, another white Tulsan who tried to forge common ground between blacks and whites.

Sister Sylvia arrived in Tulsa in 1967 to head the religion department of a Catholic high school. Her experience growing up in a small Texas town deeply divided between whites and Hispanics made her sensitive to racial issues, and she encouraged her students, black and white, to discuss race in class. But she did not learn about the riot until 1982, when Ellsworth's book was published. "I was shocked," she recalled. "I said, 'What riot?'" She was mortified not only by the destruction but also by the lack of any public discussion or even acknowledgment of the incident. Her students didn't know about the most important racial event in the city's history because their parents, teachers, pastors, and politicians had been silent.

In 1982 she accepted a job as associate director of the Tulsa Metropolitan Ministry, an interfaith group that promotes religious and racial tolerance. Sister Sylvia believed the organization, which drew its members from black and white churches as well as temples, should sponsor the city's first riot observance. The sixty-fifth anniversary, in 1986, would be an appropriate time. "We have to help people in Tulsa admit there was a Holocaust," she told the ministry. To her dismay, whites and blacks alike told her she was making a mistake. "It will just make our children angry," one said. "It will stir up bad emotions," said another. A black pastor who had agreed to co-chair the event had to resign because his church would not accept his involvement.

Sister Sylvia was still determined to mark the event, so on May 31, 1986, the ministry sponsored Greenwood Era Day at Mount Zion Baptist Church. The ministry could sponsor an event; it simply could not say the word "riot." A racially mixed crowd of about two hundred fifty attended, and Juanita Hopkins, a teacher in Greenwood for many years, gave a speech about the resilience of the black community. She referred to the riot only in the context of rebuilding Greenwood.

Recalling that night, Sister Sylvia said, "I saw the fear in people. The blacks feared that their children would learn about the riot and want to retaliate. They knew that anger could destroy you, and they didn't want that anger to destroy their children."

A Commemoration

Eᴀʀʟʏ ᴏɴ ᴛʜᴇ ᴍᴏʀɴɪɴɢ of April 19, 1995, a Ryder rental truck packed with ammonium nitrate fertilizer drove through the quiet streets of Oklahoma City. It parked in front of the Alfred P. Murrah Federal Building and, at 9:02 ᴀ.ᴍ., exploded. The 7,000-pound bomb crushed the north face of the nine-story concrete building, killing 168 people, ruining lives, and shocking a nation. Timothy McVeigh, the army veteran convicted of the crime, later said that the 19 children killed were "collateral damage." Press reports decried the incident as the "deadliest terrorist attack ever on U.S. soil" and the "worst urban disaster in American history."

Don Ross, watching the news in Tulsa, was outraged but also incensed by these descriptions. While the tragedy was heartbreaking, it was not, in his view, the country's deadliest terrorist attack or worst urban disaster. Those designations belonged to the Tulsa race riot, and he was now in a position to do more than write a column about it.

He still wrote for the *Oklahoma Eagle*, a column called "Urban Shades," but he was no longer the humorist tweaking the political establishment — he was the political establishment. Since 1982 he had served in the state house of representatives, representing North Tulsa. In a legislature controlled by white rural interests, this black liberal firebrand was the ultimate outsider. The day he was sworn in, Ross was approached by a fellow Democrat, John Monks, a Republican whose racially insensitive comments would occasionally get him in trouble. (He once referred to the Chinese as "chinks.") On this occasion, Monks introduced himself, and, according to Ross, asked him a question.

"What do you call a condominium that's half black?" Ross knew the punch line, and waited.

"A coon-dominium!" Monks cried. Ross looked at him, smiled, and walked out of the building. (Monks later apologized.)

Ross became an effective legislator. He led the drive to remove the Confederate flag from the capitol; he wrote the Martin Luther King holiday bill; he was the first African American in Oklahoma's history to head a state budget committee; and he built the state's black caucus into an important political organization. He was known for his stem-winding speeches, flamboyant persona, and snappy one-liners. "I've made a profession of being black," he would say. But he reached deftly beyond his core constituency. He wore a *chai* necklace, the Jewish symbol for life, which helped him with Jewish supporters. After a bitter debate on the floor of the house, he would give his white adversary a big hug and kiss, which would be captured by photographers and splashed across newspapers throughout Oklahoma. He called middle-aged women "baby," and he once said to Susan Savage, Tulsa's mayor, "I've tried really hard not to like you, Susan, but I do." He was an advocate for the poor, although he was no longer among their ranks (he also ran a public relations firm). He drove around town in his red Lincoln Town Car, wore a fur coat, frequented the city's finest restaurants, and savored the power and respect that his job conferred. When presented with the bill at a posh Chinese restaurant, he handed it to his dinner companion and said, "I never pay."

Time and tragedy had taken their toll. His black Lincoln was torched in the dead of night after he moved into a white neighborhood. His marriage ended in divorce, and in 1992 his son Curtis died at twenty-three from a massive infection of his foot, complicated by diabetes. (He and his former wife had six children.) His petulance alienated some of his friends of both races, but he reveled in his stridency, bullying, and rhetorical excess.

When a white interviewer suggested that race relations had improved since the 1950s, he leaned forward and glared. "How in the hell can you tell me that?" he demanded. "You know, you talk about privilege and entitlement. The biggest entitlement white folks have is the entitlement of being white. Break that for me . . . I mean, it don't make sense to me, the white folks' attitude, that somehow I ought to be appreciative that you don't hate me as much. That's the progress. Once you would physically kill me, and I have evidence of that, and now you just choke me to death economically and politically and socially, and you want me to say that's progress from dying! 'Because you sonofabitch you, we coulda killed your black ass,' that's what you're telling me. But now we let you live, and I'm proud of that progress. White folks let me live. Until I get the same entitlement irrespective of skin color, fuck you . . . But I love you."

In 1995 Don Ross was fifty-four, and he had not forgotten the riot. The following year would be its seventy-fifth anniversary, and he wanted to break the city's silence and organize a public commemoration. Just ten years earlier, the Tulsa Metropolitan Ministry had tried the same thing but could not even use the *R* word in its sparsely attended observance. Were Tulsans now ready to talk about it? As national print and radio journalists and network television anchors streamed into Oklahoma City to cover the bombing, Ross told anyone who would listen about the Tulsa disaster of 1921, the "conspiracy of silence" that followed, and the anniversary coming up. If Tulsans were not going to talk about the riot, maybe outsiders would.

Ross was not a detail man or an organizer. He needed help to carry out a commemoration, and he got it from a young white Jewish lawyer named Ken Levit. Born in Tulsa in 1965, Levit believed the city needed not only to acknowledge the riot but also to establish a memorial so that it would never be forgotten. He had grown up like a lot of white kids, never going north of the railroad tracks except on a dare. He attended a private high school and had a vague sense that a riot had once occurred in Greenwood. After college he worked in

Washington, D.C., for Senator David Boren of Oklahoma, whose wife suggested he read *Death in a Promised Land*. It came as a stark and troubling revelation to him. He went on to Yale Law School, where he became interested in the issues of memory, history, and reconciliation. He took a course on Holocaust memory and got involved in a project on Argentina's "dirty war" of the late 1970s, when more than 10,000 people "disappeared." Levit went to Buenos Aires and watched the Mothers of the Plazo de Mayo marching in front of the presidential palace. They were dressed in black, with the names of their missing children printed on white handkerchiefs wrapped around their heads. It occurred to Levit that there was no permanent monument for either the children or any of the other "disappeared." It also occurred to him that Tulsa shared a similar history, if on a smaller scale.

After law school, Levit returned to Tulsa and was struck by how much the city had changed since his childhood. He had lived about a mile and a half south of Greenwood, near the city's first shopping mall, at Utica Square, where he rarely saw an African American except those waiting for a bus to North Tulsa. By 1996 the city was still largely segregated, but at least he saw blacks in his old neighborhood in restaurants, movie theaters, and shopping malls. A school desegregation program that was started in the 1970s had chipped away at the racial boundaries. It turned Booker T. Washington into a magnet school, which attracted students of both races, while black students were bused to traditionally white schools.

North Tulsa was still depressed, but part of the old Greenwood business district had received a facelift with the construction of the $3 million Greenwood Cultural Center. It housed the Oklahoma Jazz Hall of Fame and had classrooms, offices, an auditorium, a bookstore, and beautiful gardens. Next to the center was the campus of Rogers University, a consortium of four state universities that brought students, white and black, to Greenwood. (The school's name was later changed to Oklahoma State University–Tulsa.)

To Levit, these signs of progress all augured well for a riot observance. He went to the cultural center in the summer of 1995 and met Don Ross. Ross saw Levit as a godsend: young, idealistic, and energetic, with ideas about a commemoration and a monument, all of which Ross himself had been imagining. (In addition, some black junior high school students had written to him about the need for a memorial.) Levit also had ties to the city's legal and Jewish communities, which would be vital in raising money for a monument. Tax dollars are commonly used to fund memorials, but no one believed that the city of Tulsa or the state of Oklahoma, whose leaders never even talked about the riot, would finance this project.

Ross had been impressed by the Vietnam Veterans Memorial, with the victims' names engraved on black marble walls, and thought something like that would be fitting for the riot monument. But it would need a catchy name, something that would summon the greatness of the old Greenwood so that the public would appreciate the extent of its losses. It would also need the right setting. Do you put it in Greenwood, to honor the community that was destroyed, or in downtown Tulsa, where whites as well as blacks would actually see it?

As the anniversary approached, the project overwhelmed Ken Levit. He thought he had developed a persuasive pitch to potential donors, emphasizing that a monument would be a reminder of what hatred and division can do, and the commemoration itself would be a time for Tulsans to come together. But the contributions, while steady, did not keep pace with the costs of the architect, contractors, landscapers, and materials. At one point, the contractors stopped work because they had not been paid, and Levit and Ross had to scramble for more money. Another setback occurred when a nine-foot-long, five-hundred-pound beam, part of the Mount Zion Baptist Church destroyed in the riot, was stolen. The beam was to have been the memorial's centerpiece.

The monument was to be dedicated on Saturday, June 1, but three months before, work had stalled, the beam was gone, and Levit feared that there would be nothing to dedicate. What would that say about remembrance and reconciliation? He also figured he'd have to return the thousands of dollars he had raised, some from his parents' friends.

As Levit made daily calls to the architect and he and Ross looked for corporate donors, another Tulsan with a stake in the riot joined the effort — Scott Ellsworth. Since writing his book, he had earned a doctorate in history at Duke and continued his interest in race relations. He became the first white to teach African American history at the historically black Howard University, and he later wrote an article about a clandestine basketball game in 1944, in violation of Jim Crow laws, between Duke and a black team from the North Carolina College for Negroes. Living in Portland, he learned of the commemoration when the Tulsa Historical Society asked him to write a letter about its meaning. He did more than that. He flew to Tulsa, grabbed an office in the Greenwood Cultural Center, and began a media campaign, contacting the *New York Times,* the *Dallas Morning News,* the *Los Angeles Times,* National Public Radio, and other outlets.

Joining the effort as well was Sister Sylvia Schmidt of the Tulsa Metropolitan Ministry, whose work toward an observance ten years earlier had failed. This time she was determined to win broader acceptance by making the event less threatening. The specter of dead bodies and torched businesses would be replaced by messages of hope and reconciliation. The commemoration would begin Unity Week, also called Seven Days of Harmony, a series of interracial, interfaith activities (dances, concerts, lectures, picnics) that would show how far Tulsa had progressed since 1921. The riot would be a catalyst for a feel-good celebration — "People tend to let their guards down while they're eating and socializing," said the chairman of the Family Festival Day Committee — and the merrymaking neutralized the fear that a riot observance could trigger some unknown danger.

Inclusiveness was emphasized at every turn. Though the commemoration would take place at Mount Zion Baptist Church, the sponsors wanted the invocation and benediction to be nondenominational. Hearing this request, the Reverend L. L. Tisdale said, "I'll try, but if the spirit moves me, the spirit moves me." The spirit moved him, but no one objected.

The memorial was completed by June 1. It was placed in front of the Greenwood Cultural Center to honor the riot's black victims, although most white Tulsans would never see it. Slabs of black granite created a modest ten-foot-high wall. One side was engraved with the names of businesses destroyed; the other side had a three-paragraph summary of the incident ("as many as 300 black citizens died") above Don Ross's name. A gas eternal flame, attached to a top corner, symbolized the torching of Greenwood. Built into the other side was a water fountain representing the rebirth and resilience of the area. Brick benches circled the monument to represent the ruined houses.

Levit was grateful, despite the monument's evident shortcomings. He had hoped for one solid piece of black marble, but instead at least a half-dozen granite blocks had been cobbled together. The actual water fountain was not completed on time, so a more modest sprinkler head was installed. And the eternal flame had a short life. It had not been fitted with an "electronic igniter," so strong gusts of wind would blow it out. Lighting it by hand was laborious, and in time the flame went out for good. About $80,000 had been raised, but Levit later estimated that they would have needed about $350,000 to build a first-class structure.

Don Ross named the structure the Black Wall Street Memorial, a brilliant if historically questionable designation from a man who could always turn a phrase. An early reference to Greenwood as "the Negro Wall Street" appeared in Mary E. Jones Parrish's book in the 1920s, but it was clearly not commonly used in 1921. After the riot, Greenwood was the subject of hundreds of articles in the white and black press, and not one referred to it as the Negro Wall Street; nor did the *Tulsa Star* before it was destroyed in the riot. As John Hope Franklin said: "For this to be transformed into a 'Black Wall Street,' or any kind of 'Wall Street,' is pretty extreme. These businesses were modest places, but now they've been glorified and romanticized."

But the name had its purpose. In 1996, when the real Wall Street connoted prestige and wealth, journalists covering the riot for the first time had a compelling shorthand description of Greenwood, and the Black Wall Street name stuck. It rightfully distinguished Greenwood from the hardscrabble ghettos that many people associate with black neighborhoods, but it also misrepresented the actual economic conditions of the community, which were good for some, precarious for most. In effect, Greenwood had completely reversed its persona. In the days following the riot, the newspapers mitigated the destruction of "Little Africa" by describing it as a cesspool of blight and disorder. Now, Greenwood's gilded image made its devastation seem all the more unspeakable.

The effort to drum up national publicity for the anniversary produced substantial stories in the *New York Times* and the *Washington Post* (whose newswires carried them across the country) and on NPR and the *Today* show. This coverage satisfied a major goal of the event by shattering the silence that had prevailed. The *Tulsa World* used the anniversary as an opportunity to write a six-part series, "Divided We Stand," on the status of black Tulsans. The *Tulsa Tribune* had folded in 1992, ending its role in the riot legacy.

On the eve of the anniversary, the First Presbyterian Church sponsored An Evening of Remembrance, and a racially mixed crowd of about two hundred people gathered in the church basement. Guests saw how white mobs razed and looted Greenwood in newspaper clippings mounted on boards and spread on tables. The lights dimmed, and clips from a documentary silenced the room with pictures of hundreds of black survivors living, months later, in tents on charred lots where their houses had once stood. Then a white congregant who had witnessed the riot, Betty Payne, shared sketchy childhood memories of how her parents feared not only for the blacks in Greenwood but also for the whites who could get caught in the violence. "These were worry times for all of us," she said.

It rained hard late that evening and the next morning as well, but by the time the service began at 1:30 P.M., it was a hot spring day with the sun shining through the church's stained glass windows. A flag hung in the balcony, video cameras were set up to record the event, and congregants used their programs as fans to cool themselves. The turnout exceeded all expectations. Twelve hundred guests filled the pews, including those in the balcony, and seven hundred more sat in an adjacent auditorium and watched the ceremony on a large screen.

The organizers did not shy away from the *R* word for the historic day. It was called March Against Hate, 75th Anniversary of the 1921

Race Riot, with Don Ross presiding. "He was fearful that no one would show up or that no blacks would show up," recalled his son Kavin. "But I saw that sense of pride in him. He knew what he had done. When he's in his prime, he's like a peacock in love who spreads his feathers out."

Mayor Savage was one of the first speakers. She had grown up in Tulsa, married her childhood sweetheart, and worked on a citizens' crime commission. Elected in 1992 at the age of forty, she was the city's first female mayor and, after two successful reelection bids, served in that post longer than anyone else in the city's history. A moderate Democrat who emphasized neighborhoods, infrastructure, and citizen participation, she led a city long dominated by business interests and old-boy networks. She also stressed diversity, placing the first blacks on authorities that managed the utilities, the airport, and housing, and she even discussed the riot when addressing black audiences. But her commemoration speech would be before a large and diverse audience, video cameras, and the press, so she had to choose her words carefully.

"This gathering has a great purpose, one that was made especially clear to me this morning," she said in her opening remarks. "A longtime family friend of mine who has lived in Tulsa only two years now posed the question to me earlier today. 'Why should such a tragic event be commemorated with a celebration? Why should we recall a past event that cast a shadow on Tulsa's history? What value is there in this event today?' The answer seemed so obvious to me."

She said she didn't know about "Tulsa's past" until she was an adult and that Tulsans "have an obligation to seek tolerance, understanding, mutual respect, and dignity, a responsibility that is greater in Tulsa than in other communities because of the events of seventy-five years ago."

Her remarks befit the healing theme of the day, but some blacks would remember the mayor for what she did not say. Despite the city's role in the melee, she did not apologize for what had happened; nor, for that matter, did she ever use the word "riot." Savage later said she assumed she had apologized or at least had expressed regret for the incident, but the politics of the riot had already shifted from acknowledging that the battle took place to finding words that would appease the aggrieved parties.

Don Ross soon followed, and he warmed up the crowd with his opening line: "My pastor knows me well, and he gave me some instructions as I walked up here. Be brief and be gone." He thanked several journalists for calling attention to the riot. "People will not only see this as a national story, but I got a call from Paris at six o'clock this morning. This makes it an international story."

He recognized Scott Ellsworth with a jibe — "Many of us met [him] twenty years ago and frankly got sick of him" — but he acknowledged the importance of his book. The history of the riot, he said, was lost in "a conspiracy of silence, and if not for the stories in our oral history told over and over and over again by the survivors, we wouldn't be here." He then asked the half-dozen survivors in the audience to rise, which led to a prolonged standing ovation.

Ross then wrapped up his remarks: "I've been told by my grandma that no public apology has ever been made by a public official. Well, I am a public official." Laughter and applause rippled through the crowd. "And from my good office I'll offer an official apology to the African American community for the events of the Tulsa disaster, and I ask you for your kindness and forgiveness . . . on behalf of the state of Oklahoma and the city of Tulsa. Dr. McCutchen, I be gone."

Ross's brief, self-effacing comments were in tune with the spirit of the day, and his public "apology" was a personal and political triumph. The service lasted for several hours, as a long roster of speakers, civic and religious, tapped into the soothing themes of healing and perseverance. The service was climaxed by a rousing speech from Benjamin Hooks, the former president of the NAACP, whose booming voice carried religious exultations, inspiring narratives of black history, and whimsical asides. "If nothing else," he said, "I want to teach the white folks today how to say 'A-men!'"

He described a climactic moment in the play 1776, when General Washington sent a letter to the Continental Congress and, noting the ravages of war, asked, "Is anybody listening? Does anybody care?" Those same questions, Hooks said, "must have been on the minds of the black citizens of Tulsa, Oklahoma, on June 1, 1921. According to the historical record, fires were set, an unknown number were killed, thirty-six square blocks were destroyed, twenty-three churches were burned, and later more than 6,000 African American citizens were marched to temporary jails. Gray smoke arose from smoking ruins, clouded the skies, and hid the sun of hope." Hooks then identified the fear that still hung over some black Tulsans. "Today we've gathered at Mount Zion Church, one of the churches that was destroyed, not to celebrate but to observe and commemorate that occasion; but more than to observe and commemorate, to ensure that it [will] never ever happen again!"

"A-men!" yelled the crowd.

The crowd then embarked on its "march against hate," walking a block under the blue sky to dedicate the Black Wall Street Memorial. The late afternoon was still warm, but onlookers gathered around and read the names of the lost businesses. Benches were set up beneath a tent and a tree was planted in Pioneer Garden. The Reverend John Wolfe, who is white, a former pastor of All Souls Unitarian Church, stood before the group. "It is time," he said, "for the white community to repent of what happened and to acknowledge the role that it played." Black attendees later thanked him for saying what they had never heard any white person say before.

Listening calmly was Robert Fairchild, the black riot survivor whose account had been doubted by college students fifty years earlier. At ninety-two, he had white hair, small fragile bones, and poor hearing, but no one stood larger in Greenwood. Fairchild had had a long career in the city's park department, pushing for recreational facilities in public housing and other improvements affecting black Tulsans; he ran a North Tulsa Meals on Wheels program and taught an adult literacy course. For almost thirty years he ran the "teen canteen" that Don Ross had frequented as a teenager, spinning records and keeping youths off the street, and he took home countless kids who needed a meal, feeding them his wife's meatloaf. Ross once wrote that Fairchild had "generation after generation of children, hundreds of kids — they were all legitimate and his." He had always been a man of faith — as a homesick student at the University of Nebraska, he sang church songs to ease his lonely nights — and in recent years he had relied on that faith to help him overcome cancer, a stroke, and arthritis. "I don't have a whole lot of money," he said, "but Lord knows I have a whole lot of will."

Like most survivors, Fairchild rarely talked of the tragedy unless someone asked about it. Mayor Savage had known him for ten years but was shocked to see him at the commemoration. She had no idea he had been in the riot. His kindness for white people, she thought, was particularly remarkable given what he had endured. She approached him at the dedication and gave him a hug.

"Why didn't you say anything about this?" she asked. "Why didn't I know?"

"Honey, if you're going to live this life, you're going to have to live it with the good as well as the bad," he told her. "If you allow people's anger and hatred to consume you, it will."

To dedicate the memorial, Fairchild and two other survivors raised a torch high above their heads and lighted the flame. All was quiet as the fire shot up in the air, creating, in the words of one observer, "a reverent moment, a sense of living in that era for just a brief instant. It was all so real."

And for Robert Fairchild, a poignant closure. Nine weeks later he died, ending a life that had touched four generations of Tulsans and silencing the most humane of witnesses to a heartless tragedy.

By nightfall the commemoration was over, and Ross had returned to his house, pleased at the day's success and grateful it was over. But he suddenly had an urge to see the memorial's flame at night. He was exhausted, but he got back in his car, drove to the cultural center, and pulled into the parking lot. Ken Levit was also at home, pondering what a magical day it had been. After his wife fell asleep, he too wanted one more taste of the day's remarkable proceedings, and he returned to the monument. There, the two men most responsible for its construction startled each other with their spontaneous visits, and they hugged beneath the fire. The rasping orange swirls were whipping in the wind; pedestrians in the neighborhood for a concert had come by to read the inscription, feel the cool water, and marvel at the flame.

For Ken Levit, the luminous tableau was the perfect conclusion to an emotional day, but for Don Ross it was not enough. Today had been about healing and reconciliation, but he wanted more than that. He wanted justice. He wanted accountability. He wanted reparations for what whites had done to his community.

Money, Negro.

The Last Man Vindicated

O N THE MORNING OF May 31, 1996, Cornelius E. Toole turned on the television in Chicago and was stunned. He watched Bryant Gumbel on the *Today* show introduce a piece about the Tulsa race riot and describe the activities surrounding the seventy-fifth anniversary. Toole knew the riot well. As a great-grandson of J. B. Stradford, he had long resented the white Tulsans who had destroyed the Stradford Hotel, driven its owner from his city, and smeared his reputation.

After the show, Toole excitedly called the Greenwood Cultural Center and Mayor Savage's office. He thought the Stradford family should be part of any riot commemoration. Unfortunately, no one at the center or in the mayor's office had ever heard of J. B. Stradford, and Toole's messages were not returned. Three weeks later he wrote an angry letter to the mayor, recounting his great-grandfather's remarkable story. He also declared that his family was contemplating "appropriate legal proceedings in Oklahoma to vitiate [J. B. Stradford's] arrest, requesting a declaration as to his innocence."

The threat seemed serious from a man with Toole's credentials. He was a former lawyer for the NAACP who had become a circuit court judge in Cook County, Illinois, and he had wanted to clear his great-grandfather's name for many years.

Toole was only two years old when Stradford died in 1935, but his grandmother Anna — Stradford's only daughter — told him of J.B.'s accomplishments, losses, and resilience. Anna, who had a distinguished career as a concert pianist, inherited her father's 480-page memoir, and she used it to create a mythic family figure of strength, independence, and heroism, a warrior who survived slavery, segregation, and discrimination only to see his beloved hotel destroyed by bombs hurled from an airplane owned by the governor of Oklahoma. Even if the details of his life were sometimes embroidered, the message had a powerful effect on his heirs. They were told how his son, Cornelius, raced to Independence, Kansas, rescued his father from the lynch mob from Oklahoma, and spirited him away to safety in Chicago. Cornelius's daughter Jewel often heard that story from J.B. himself at the dinner table. It made her believe that that's what lawyers did — they saved other people — and it inspired her as well as Cornelius Toole to become lawyers.

Toole had learned about his great-grandfather from sources outside his family as well. He sought out former patrons of the Stradford Hotel, who described the opulent chandeliers, fine dining, and first-class service offered there. He also admired the self-sufficiency of the old Greenwood district, which was unlike black communities today, where "money leaves forty seconds after it gets there."

Toole's most prized possession was the memoir he had inherited from his grandmother. He kept the fragile typewritten pages, inscribed with biblical flourishes and impassioned commentaries, in his office among ancestral portraits and other memorabilia. The judge did not simply read the words but tried to transport himself to Greenwood before the riot, next to his great-grandfather. "I can see him believing good things were going to happen to him," he said. "I can see him planning the hotel, ordering the furniture, seeing people dance in his dance hall. I can see it all coming to fruition — like a painting. Then someone takes a match to it. I don't think he ever got over it."

Neither did Toole. "I get bitter," he said. "I can visualize the airplane dropping the bomb."

By the time Judge Toole saw the *Today* show he was sixty-three years old and longed for vindication. In past years, he had written to the Tulsa district attorney for information on Stradford's case. He had also read about riot victims in other states suing for reparations.

Toole's letter to the mayor had also been sent to Don Ross, who agreed that the charges against Stradford should be dismissed. He took the matter to a black judge in Tulsa, who could act only on the direction of the Tulsa DA, Bill LaFortune, the youthful scion of a prominent, philanthropic family. Born in 1957, he had grown up in Tulsa, graduated from the University of Tulsa Law School, and was the nephew of a former mayor, yet he had never heard of the riot until a few years before. When the judge told him about Stradford, he had been DA for only a year. If he accepted the case, his task would be to examine a strict legal question — did the evidence support the charge that J. B. Stradford incited the riot?

It was not an easy call. After seventy-five years, how could a prosecutor accurately determine the actions and whereabouts of a single man? LaFortune's office would have to launch an investigation, but when the DA raised the subject with his staff, he was met with resistance. "I wouldn't touch that," said one assistant DA. "We have enough to prosecute the criminals we've got here," said another. The question of liability arose. If the indictment were dismissed, could Stradford's heirs sue the city for wrongful prosecution? Could the city be held responsible for his losses in the riot?

But LaFortune did not back down. His family had deep roots in the city — his grandfather had come to Tulsa in the late 1920s — and it troubled him that he never knew of the riot until adulthood. He did not believe there had been an official cover-up; rather, Tulsans simply preferred to keep the matter "hush-hush." He thought those days should end and that J. B. Stradford deserved his day in court. He assigned Nancy Little to the case.

At sixty-five, Little was old enough to be Bill LaFortune's mother, but she had been a lawyer for only four years. After raising five children, she went to law school and found a job in the DA's office, where she worked in the Bogus Check Department. She was now asked to investigate the charge against Stradford and, in the process, confront the myths of her own youth. She had grown up in Tulsa and was told about the riot by her father (he was fifteen at the time but couldn't participate because his mother locked him in his room). He said it began after a black man raped a white woman, which caused the whites to burn Niggertown — what everyone around Nancy called Greenwood. Afterward, her father said, if a white person was walking down the street, a black person, out of fear, would move to the other side. He said something else about the riot: "The Arkansas ran red."

Growing up in a segregated society taught Nancy the true meaning of separate and unequal. The restrooms in the department store were supposed to be segregated; but if the facility for whites was broken, they could use those for the "coloreds." The blacks, however, could never enter the white restroom, even if their own was out of order. When she and her friends rode the city buses as teenagers, they liked to sit in the back and socialize. They were supposed to give up those seats for black riders, who weren't allowed to sit in front, but sometimes they wouldn't. On those days an African American would board the bus, look at the girls in back, look at the empty seats up front, then silently stand in the aisle, while Nancy and her friends talked and laughed together.

Little knew these practices were wrong, but she had never questioned them because no one ever questioned them. No one ever questioned the riot stories either. But by the time she was assigned to investigate Stradford's indictment — seventy-five years later — she was ready to challenge not only the merits of the case but also the official history of the riot. She looked back at property records and found the deeds on Stradford's half-dozen buildings. She unearthed the indictment against Stradford: with fifty-three other black Tulsans, he was accused of murder, robbery, and arson. (For allegedly starting the riot, they were also responsible for its outcome.) She discovered that the indictments against all the black defendants (including Dick Roland) were eventually dismissed except for one: J. B. Stradford. He remained the one man still accused of starting the riot, a designation that probably reflected his well-publicized "escape" from the law.

Other surprises awaited Little. Reading through the Tulsa County Sheriff's records on microfilm, she found that handwritten records had been kept from 1911 straight through until May 30, 1921. Suddenly there was a two-week gap. She scrolled the film back and forth but could find no explanation, and she suspected the records had been purged to protect the names of whites who had been arrested. She also noticed the appointment of Wash Hudson, a Klansman, as Dick Rowland's lawyer and speculated that that might have been to ensure Rowland's guilt had the case gone to trial.

The most disturbing discovery by far occurred when a woman from the cultural center, alerted to Little's work, sent over Mary E. Jones Parrish's book, *Events of the Tulsa Disaster*. Only a handful of copies had survived the original printing, and its pages were so brittle that the lawyer worried that merely touching one would destroy it. (The book was reprinted in 1998.) So she carefully wrapped the book in plastic and took it home. Reading it was a revelation, as the author unveiled a history that Little had never known. "There was a great shadow in the sky," Parrish wrote of what she saw and heard on the morning of the riot,

> and, upon a second look, we discerned that this cloud was caused by fast approaching aeroplanes. It then dawned upon us that the enemy had organized in the night and was invading our district, the same as the Germans invaded France and Belgium. The firing of guns was renewed in quick succession. People were seen to flee from their burning homes, some with babes in their arms and leading crying and excited children by the hand . . . I walked as one in a horrible dream. By this time my little girl was up and dressed, but I made her lie down on the [sofa] in order that the bullets must penetrate it before reaching her. By this time a machine gun had been installed in the granary and was raining bullets down on our section. Looking out of the back door, I saw people still fleeing and the enemy fast approaching. I heard a man groan; I looked up just in time to see him fall and be pulled into the house.

Other personal accounts rounded out the searing images of innocent black families under ruthless attack. These descriptions contradicted everything Nancy Little had ever heard about the riot, but they were so precise, vivid, and abundant that she was convinced they could not have been fabricated. "It was the most moving book I've read in my life," she recalled. "It was just such a shock. This is my city that I grew up in, and I just couldn't believe it. It just seemed like such a wrong."

When she tried to share her epiphany with her white friends, they refused to accept this new version of history. She gave the book to one friend, who returned it after a time with some other items and never said a word about it. When she went to her fiftieth high school reunion, she told a man sitting next to her that her research on the riot had been one of the most interesting things she had done as a lawyer and that she had been amazed at the mistreatment of innocent blacks during the incident. The man angrily responded that this view "was a pack of lies" and that he was gathering evidence to show that none of the things the blacks said happened to them actually occurred.

Little, of course, knew better, but she understood why he felt that way. "Would you want to believe the white part of town had done something that terrible?" she said. "Nobody wants to believe their own people behaved like that." Little herself no longer believed it was a riot. It was a war followed by an armed invasion.

Little had only three weeks to investigate the Stradford indictment. She concluded that Stradford had gone to the courthouse carrying a gun, which was illegal. He also violated the law by jumping bail in Kansas and by flouting the extradition order. But she did not believe there was any evidence suggesting that Stradford incited the riot, and his subsequent defiance of the legal orders seemed understandable.

When she finished the investigation, LaFortune asked one question: "Do you think he's an innocent man?"

"I think he did what any of us would have done at the time," she said.

LaFortune dismissed the charges.

On October 18, 1996, J. B. Stradford was formally vindicated in a ceremony at the cultural center, across the street from the site of his hotel. Attending the event were Judge Toole and twenty other members of the Stradford clan. Spanning four generations, they traveled from Texas, Illinois, Ohio, and New York. It was the first time since their patriarch had fled that any Stradford had set foot in Oklahoma.

When LaFortune presented the motion to dismiss the charge, Judge Jesse Harris accepted it. "With each new hour comes new chances," Harris said. "This hour begins a chance to right an injustice." At the request of the family, Stradford's name was added posthumously to the list of those allowed to practice law in Oklahoma.

Governor Frank Keating, a Tulsan, granted an honorary executive pardon at the ceremony. "It is regrettable that we have to come together to recognize an embarrassment, a historic event that never should have happened," he said. "Our tragedy as Oklahomans is that [the Stradfords] are not [living] here."

That loss was significant. Stradford's son, Cornelius, became a prominent labor lawyer and a founding member of the National Bar Association; he argued the winning side of *Hansberry v. Lee,* a crucial civil rights case concerning restrictive covenants, before the U.S. Supreme Court. His daughter, Jewel Lafontant-Mankarious, became a prominent trial lawyer as well as a U.S. ambassador and a deputy solicitor general; during the 1950s she was the first black woman to be an assistant U.S. attorney. Her son, John Rogers Jr., was founder and president of Ariel Capital Investment in Chicago and in 1994 was named by *Time* magazine as one of the country's most promising leaders under the age of forty. Another Stradford granddaughter, Letitia Toole, became a stage and film actress and a member of the American Negro Theater, acting with Ossie Davis and Sidney Poitier. Also in the audience were a cardiologist, a tennis professional, a sculptor, a ballet dancer, and a movie director.

These successes bore out the legacy of J. B. Stradford, who believed blacks could flourish by working within the system. Though his country betrayed him many times, his faith in America made his an "American story," Cornelius Toole said. But the return of his descendants was also a reminder that the true cost of the riot was not simply the lost lives and property. It was also the lost contributions of the blacks who fled and of their heirs who never returned. Tulsa needed their leadership, their energy, and their skills to save Greenwood from economic blight in the same way that it had needed Stradford and other black pioneers to create Greenwood in the first place. The black district's shortcomings were particularly poignant on the night of his vindication. The Stradford Hotel had been built precisely for people like Stradford's descendants — smart, successful, cosmopolitan African Americans. Now, there was no Greenwood. The hotels, good restaurants, movie theaters, playhouses, fashionable stores, and supermarkets had been gone for some thirty years. The Stradfords stayed at the Adams-Mark in downtown Tulsa.

Stradford's exoneration repudiated one false story of the riot, but his heirs found little reason for celebration. Emma Monroe, eighty-five and a Stradford granddaughter, said, "We're glad, but seventy-five years to free someone who didn't do anything in the first place is too much." Judge Toole appreciated Governor Keating's "forceful apology," but it hardly compensated for his great-grandfather's suffering. "There is a feeling of closure," he said. "However, the pain is still there. The pain and loss will go on forever. He was on his way to building a dynasty, but he did not get a chance."

The Disappeared of Tulsa

D ON ROSS HAD REASON to believe that the state of Oklahoma would consider compensating black riot survivors. In 1994 Florida had approved reparations to African Americans victimized in a long-forgotten riot. The two events had numerous similarities — black communities were wiped out in both — and Ross believed Florida had created a model for retroactive justice that Oklahoma could follow.

The Florida incident, in 1923, centered on the hamlet of Rosewood, near the Gulf coast. After a black man allegedly assaulted a white woman, a posse was formed, with bloodhounds, and within a day or two it lynched an African American who supposedly helped the assailant flee. Over the next few days, the tensions escalated into an all-out attack by whites on Rosewood. At least five more blacks and two whites were killed, and the community's churches, stores, and eighteen homes were torched.

After decades of silence, a state commission confirmed that the county sheriff and other law enforcement authorities ignored their responsibility to protect lives and property; the report also cast doubt on the original assault claim. The riot's few remaining black victims and their allies demanded restitution from the state, setting off an emotional debate in the legislature. Opponents said that payment would encourage anyone who had ever been injured by state or local government to sue. But the state's nineteen black legislators made reparations their top priority and won support through bluster and threats. At one point during the debate, the entire black delegation stalked off the house floor, and the group, all Democrats, threatened to side with Republicans on health care legislation if whites from their own party did not vote for the Rosewood bill. The cause was further helped by Florida's Democratic governor, Lawton Chiles, who publicly supported reparations and lobbied conservative Democrats. The state's largest newspapers also backed the measure, and Florida's biggest law firm, Holland & Knight, represented Rosewood's victims pro bono. The lawyers steered them away from legal claims, which seemed impractical, toward a legislative solution modeled after the reparations act passed by Congress in 1988 to compensate Japanese Americans interned during World War II.

In the end, Florida lawmakers passed a reparations "claims bill"; it paid up to $150,000 for each survivor (fewer than ten were known to be alive), established a $500,000 fund to compensate families for property loss, and created scholarships for needy students, giving preference to Rosewood descendants. The total cost was limited to $2.1 million. These payments were believed to be the first ever made to American blacks who had suffered white mob violence, and the move stimulated talk about payments to similar victims, including reparations to descendants of slaves. The fear that the Rosewood legislation would spur a wave of reparations claims against Florida was also proved unfounded, as the state did not have to compensate any other victims for injuries incurred in the past.

Ross believed that Greenwood's riot victims deserved the same consideration as Rosewood's. In January 1997 he submitted a joint resolution to the Oklahoma legislature calling for $6 million in compensation for riot survivors, for the descendants of victims, and for children's programs in North Tulsa. State senator Maxine Horner, a black Democrat who represented North Tulsa, cosponsored the resolution. The similarities between the two riots — the trumped-up assault charge, the torching of a black community, the failure of authorities to protect the citizenry — buoyed the hopes of reparations advocates, but the optimism glossed over the different political cultures of the two states. Florida was far more urban, liberal, affluent, and multicultural than Oklahoma, whose five black state representatives had little leverage in a legislature dominated by conservative rural interests. In Oklahoma, reparations didn't have the support of the state's governor or legislature or its major newspapers or its biggest law firms or any other constituency save African Americans, who made up less than 8 percent of the population.

By 1997 Ross had been a lawmaker for fifteen years, long enough to know his bill was dead on arrival. But it drew attention to his cause. "Money is a magnificent healer," he told the *Tulsa World*. The seventy-fifth commemoration, he said, was not enough. "You know [whites] mean forgiveness when they are willing to pay. I don't need white people to make a speech about how sorry they are. That's almost an insult."

This disparaging remark elicited a justifiable backlash of criticism, and Ross quickly issued a public apology. But he did not retreat from his demand for reparations, and that too prompted quick and visceral opposition. In the *World's* "Call the Editor" column, one reader phoned in this response: "Taxpayers have in effect been paying reparations to blacks for many years in the form of welfare and various government subsidies. Latest statistics show that over 44 percent of blacks receive some form of assistance compared to 12 percent of whites. Horner and Ross should preach hard work and self-reliance to their constituents, not more government handouts."

Reparations, in this view, were not about justice for victims. They were just another transfer payment to an already dependent, lazy class of citizens.

While reparations had negligible political support, Ross's bill served its purpose. Anytime the state confronted a controversial issue, it set up a fact-finding commission. So Ross proposed that the state create a commission to investigate the Tulsa race riot. In theory, such an inquiry could uncover evidence that would undermine the political opposition to reparations. Even if that failed, it would shine a light on this hidden corner of Oklahoma history, identify those responsible, and — not least — keep the story alive in the media.

To other lawmakers, a commission seemed harmless enough. Oklahoma created many commissions and published countless reports, most of which were ignored. As a sop to Don Ross and to sidestep a potentially divisive issue, the legislature passed a bill creating the Tulsa Race Riot Commission. Its eleven members were charged with identifying survivors, establishing a historical account of the event, and making recommendations for reparations.

The task seemed manageable; many government commissions have been created to render an accurate account of a riot. The Chicago Commission on Race Relations wrote a 670-page report on that city's riot in 1919. The Kerner Commission, empaneled by President Johnson in 1967, was probably the most historic; it blamed the urban "disorders" on the hostility between police and "ghetto communities," but it became famous for its account of the underlying social chasm between white and black America. Riot commissions have often cited systemic social problems, such as inadequate housing, education, and jobs for blacks, but they have also routinely blamed police abuse. After the 1935 Harlem riot, for example, a mayoral commission revealed long-standing police discrimination against African Americans.

The Oklahoma commission followed this tradition. That the riot occurred more than seventy-five years earlier handicapped the effort and meant that some information would never be recovered, but a time gap did not prevent Florida's riot commission from evaluating the Rosewood "massacre," faulting law enforcement officials, and producing a report accepted by all parties.

But Tulsa's riot was different, not simply because it was the worst racial conflict of the century. It had also produced two sharply conflicting histories, which were recorded (in newspapers, memoirs, and letters), remembered, and quietly passed down in pockets of both communities. These interpretations reflected the different self-images of the two communities: blacks courageously preventing a lynching and defending their homes; whites repelling a Negro uprising and magnanimously providing shelter and comfort to the victims. Many Tulsans still had a stake in these narratives because the accounts defined their city, their country, or their race. Now a state commission was asked to sort through these competing claims. Unlike the assessments of academics or journalists, the commission's version would bear the state's imprimatur and would be considered

THE DISAPPEARED OF TULSA

the official history. It would try to validate remembrances, discredit myths, expose lies, anoint heroes, and identify culprits. The battle over the memory of the riot would be almost as fierce as the riot itself.

The commission's six black members and several whites were sympathetic to civil rights issues, giving it a liberal tilt that hardly represented the state. Eight of the eleven members favored government payments to survivors. The commission, by law, included two state officials (from the historical society and the human rights commission), while Governor Keating or Mayor Savage appointed the other members. They included activists, academics, businesspeople, and one survivor. Don Ross was not an official member but took an active part in the process.

The first chairman of the commission was Bob Blackburn, the deputy director of the Oklahoma Historical Society. A scholarly bureaucrat who had written twelve books on Oklahoma history and had edited the quarterly *Chronicles of Oklahoma,* he advocated "public history" — making the past accessible to the general public through exhibitions, museums, publications, and symposiums. He also tried to nudge the historical society away from its "white ethnocentric" view of the world. (Blackburn is part Cherokee.) He oversaw exhibitions, for example, on slavery in Oklahoma and on the state's black towns, and he tried to blend what he called "academic" with "grassroots" history, such as oral accounts, in ways that met traditional standards of accuracy while enriching the average person's understanding of an event.

The riot dovetailed with his own interests. Like most of the commissioners, he believed the group's work could be a vehicle for achieving both reconciliation and reparations, but it would be critical to take the "shared memory" of both blacks and whites and remove, or discredit, the extreme positions of both. "We've had two radical opinions about the riot," Blackburn said in an interview. "The black perspective was, 'Whiteys wanted to destroy us. They tried to keep us from rebuilding, and it was a conspiracy.' Radical whites say, 'Niggers got what they had coming because they came to our part of town and confronted our white boys.' The question was, what could we do to bring those two sides closer together?" If that were achieved, a consensus would emerge around one historical narrative, which could help to educate the public and build support for compensation or other forms of justice.

The problem was the polarizing nature of reparations. For both whites and blacks, they represented an acknowledgment of responsibility more than payment for past losses, and few white Oklahomans were willing to claim that responsibility, particularly if it involved tax dollars. Even private reparations were anathema to many whites. Yet to many blacks, they were the only acceptable form of justice: public money conceded public responsibility. Blackburn faced a dilemma. If reparations were the path to redemption, such payment would only anger whites and harden their opposition to a conciliatory "shared memory." But to forge a consensus, he would have to sacrifice black demands for restitution. Somehow he had to strike a balance between the communal need for healing and the moral imperative of justice.

Even Blackburn didn't anticipate how deeply reparations would divide Tulsa. For John Ehrling, a conservative radio talk show host, the topic always triggered a barrage of calls. "I can bring that topic any day, and I can have a war," he said. "It's the most polarizing thing we have in the community." Reparations set off highly charged emotions, he said, because they confirmed the worst stereotypes whites had of blacks. "This is where the South begins, and there's a lot of prejudice here," he said. "Face it, a lot of whites think blacks are looking for handouts anyway, and the thought that we should just give them money for sitting around and doing nothing upsets people."

Those sentiments were frequently reflected in the "Call to the Editor" column of the *Tulsa World*. One man said his car was hit by a black driver who did not have insurance, forcing him to pay the deductible. He asked, "Is there any chance of me getting reparations from the state for this? As I see it, it is the same difference." Another person said: "I am 43 years old, and I have nothing to do with the Tulsa race riot. I'll be damned if my money pays for anybody's reparations. You're going to start another riot." Said still another: "I am

American Indian, and my ancestors' villages were burned, their land was stolen, and they were murdered. Where do I sign up for reparations?" The column occasionally ran items supporting compensation, but more typical were comments that reexamining this history was a pointless, even dangerous, exercise. "Tulsa's love of tragedy has started again — 1921 revisited," a caller said. "Just what we need to do — bring up more trouble."

Blackburn's first job was finding a consultant to study the incident and draft a report explaining what had happened. He hired Scott Ellsworth. Blackburn liked *Death in a Promised Land* and figured Ellsworth was the most qualified person to handle the investigation. The state had allocated $55,000 for the project, which could be used for Ellsworth's time and expenses.

More than fifteen years had passed since Ellsworth had done his research, and, living in Portland as a freelance writer, he now had to commute to Tulsa. But he was eager for the assignment. His interest initially had nothing to do with reparations — his own book never mentioned them — but reflected his belief that this could be the last opportunity to record oral histories of the riot. The youngest survivors with any memory of the event were now more than eighty years old, and their testimony could help solve the riot's single largest mystery: the death count. To get a more accurate tally, Ellsworth wanted to find the rumored mass graves; he envisioned exhuming black victims and burying them again with a memorial service, giving them the funeral they were first denied.

His search for bodies was part of a sprawling investigation involving commission members, the staff of the historical society, and independent scholars. The inquiry would ultimately amass more than 10,000 pages of riot documentation, including court records, property records, newspaper clips, letters, and memoirs; more than fifty taped interviews with survivors and witnesses were also recorded. A Web site requesting information was created, and the historical society even placed a classified ad in the *Tulsa World* offering an unspecified cash reward for anyone with a copy of the *Tribune* editorial "To Lynch a Negro Tonight." (It was never found.)

But the entire archive was secondary to the mass graves. By itself, the discovery of a burial site would reveal nothing about the underlying causes of the riot, the government's responsibility, or the best attempt at justice and reconciliation. It wouldn't even establish a definitive body count, but it could repudiate the official death toll of thirty-six, prove that the authorities had literally buried their most important evidence, and support the charge of an official cover-up. It would, in short, obliterate the official narrative of the riot. Moreover, it would have a shocking emotional impact. The chilling image of rows of skulls among piled bones and clothing fragments and chipped jewelry, would be displayed across the country and the world. More tangible than an old photograph, more dramatic than a personal account, the bones would silence those who tried to deny the enormity of the event, build sympathy for the survivors, and generate support for reparations.

No court record, no personal testimony, no government document, individually or collectively, could achieve that. But it all hinged on finding the graves.

Ellsworth began his work in February 1998, but he needed help. (Consulting for the commission was John Hope Franklin, who lent his moral authority but did not do any of the research.) On a visit to the Tulsa Historical Society, Ellsworth met Dick Warner, an easygoing sixty-seven-year-old Tulsa native who had retired years earlier after selling his forklift dealership. A bibliophile, he liked history, true crime stories, and archaeology, and belonged to a Sherlock Holmes club. He loved a good mystery, and when Ellsworth said he was looking for volunteers to help find bodies from the riot, maybe even a mass grave, Warner happily signed on.

Their first task was to assemble a list of the known dead and to determine where they were buried; remarkably, an official record had either never been made or never been disclosed. While funerals had been banned after the riot, the mortuaries still processed victims, so their records would show names and cemeteries.

Warner had a partial list of the victims from newspaper accounts, so he went to the only funeral home from 1921 still in business, Stanley & McCune. But he couldn't find any of the victims in its records. He felt confident that, as one of the larger homes, it would have handled many of the bodies, but where were the names? (The city's two black funeral homes were destroyed in the riot; white homes hired black morticians to handle African American bodies.) Riffling through the records, Warner opened the *T* file to find, en masse, twenty of the riot dead. The victims, most of them black, were classified by the agency that paid for their funerals — Tulsa County. These and other funeral records essentially confirmed the official death count of thirty-six and indicated that most of bodies had been buried in Oaklawn Cemetery, south of downtown, which includes an old potter's field for white and black paupers. This mostly bare, sloping plot marked the final indignity for the riot's African American victims — to be interred by strangers in graves among the destitute, without ceremony or even a headstone for survivors to adorn.

In the course of Warner's research, a promising lead surfaced about a mass grave at the former Booker T. Washington Cemetery, about twelve miles southeast of downtown, in what had been a mostly agricultural area in 1921. The cemetery, long used by the city's blacks, had recently been sold and its name changed to Rolling Oaks Memorial Park, and the new owner needed a better record of burials and plot locations. Over Memorial Day weekend in 1997, when many families came to decorate graves, the cemetery assigned employees to ask visitors for the names and burial sites of their relatives. About five or six African American women told the employees that race riot victims were buried on the south side of the cemetery, even though, according to employees, no graves were supposed to be there.

Ellsworth and Warner interviewed the cemetery's maintenance chief, who said that an old black woman with a blue cane had asked him to take her to an alleged mass grave site in a golf cart. Pointing to a spot, she told him that after the riot, her father and grandfather had brought several truckloads of bodies there and laid them in a long trench; the dead were all black, wrapped in sheets and tarpaulins. She said she had seen this herself. The man didn't know her name, but he believed she would return this Memorial Day weekend.

When the holiday arrived, Rolling Oaks employees once again interviewed visitors. But this time Ellsworth and Warner set up a table

with a pastel cloth under a green awning and hung a sign: NORTH
TULSA HISTORICAL SOCIETY. They set out several books about
Greenwood and filled a cut-glass bowl with pink carnations, which
they gave to the women and young girls passing by. Another banner read: PLEASE SIGN THE BOOKER T. WASHINGTON HERITAGE
CEMETERY BOOK. They were setting a "trap" for the lady with the
blue cane.

They got some help from the cemetery workers. Whenever an
employee saw an older black woman, or even a man, he alerted
Ellsworth by walkie-talkie. The device crackled and a voice came on:
"Scott, I've got a real old guy in Section 8B." Ellsworth jumped into a
golf cart and raced to the spot with his heritage cemetery book. He
then approached his subject and made his pitch.

"Hi, my name is Scott Ellsworth, and I'm helping the Tulsa Race
Riot Commision!" he said. He explained his task. "We heard there
were stories that some riot victims were buried here in unmarked
graves. Do you know anything about it?"

For three long hot days, he chased elderly blacks from one end of
the cemetery to the other, desperately seeking clues. Near the end of
the weekend, he approached a petite figure, barely five feet tall, wearing a pink shirt, yellow undershirt, white pants, and diamond earrings.

"I'm Elwood Lett," he said. He was eighty-four years old, remembered the riot clearly, and knew all about a mass grave. He boarded
the golf cart and pointed Ellsworth up a hill. They made their way to
a wooded area near a ridge that led to a creek. Lett said that after the
riot, his family was fleeing town in a wagon when his grandfather
was shot and killed. After living elsewhere for several years, Lett returned to Tulsa, and one day when he was playing in the creek that
rolled past the cemetery, his uncle yelled at him, "Don't you play
there. That's where they buried the race riot victims." He pointed to
the ground that his uncle had identified.

"How do you know that's the site?" Ellsworth asked.

"Because it's next to the ridge."

Ellsworth interviewed one hundred fifty people in addition to
Lett. About fifteen of them said they had heard something about a
mass burial; eight others had more specific information on sites.

Ellsworth never found the lady with the blue cane, but he was confident a mass grave lay somewhere in the cemetery.

Dick Warner had a lead on buried skulls at another site. He heard that a man named Jack Britton told the story of how he, as a teenager in the late 1940s, was walking through Newblock Park when he noticed some workmen digging a large hole. He first thought it was a swimming pool. He watched for a long time and finally noticed skulls in piles of dirt. He returned with a friend after the workers had left, shoved some skulls into a bag, and fled. He then sold them as souvenirs.

Warner and Ellsworth had other reasons to look for a mass grave in the park, which is west of downtown along the Arkansas River; in 1921 it was the site of a city landfill and incinerator. (The park is named after H. F. Newblock, a mayor in the 1920s who was also a member of the Ku Klux Klan.) Several men had told Ed Wheeler in 1970 that they had seen bodies on a sandbar near Newblock. One man said he counted sixty-seven bodies being guarded by uniformed men. Three days later, the corpses were gone. Perhaps the sandbar was a staging area for a mass burial, which Britton stumbled on almost thirty years later.

Warner needed to find the exact location of the skulls, but Britton was now dead, as was his wife; their friends did not know where their two sons had gone. Warner found Britton's obituary, which led him to a relative who would only talk in exchange for money. Warner, uncertain about the value of the information, declined. He then began knocking on the doors of Britton's former neighbors and found a woman who said that one son, Jeff, lived in the Glenn Pool area. Warner and Ellsworth met him in a cafeteria. Jeff Britton said that driving past Newblock Park, his father would always say, "That's where I found them bones."

Warner tried to learn more about the park. He visited the Tulsa Water and Sewer Department, interviewed the older employees, and pored over maps of the grounds. He discovered that a "sewage lift station," which pumped up sewage so it could flow down to its final destination, was built in the late 1940s with a large well beneath it, about thirty by twenty feet. *Bingo.* That must have been the "swimming pool" Jack Britton saw. The station had since been razed, but Warner inspected old aerial photographs of the structure (from a Kansas City engineering firm) and calculated its location using nearby trees as reference points. He found other maps that disclosed that there were no utility lines beneath the site, which he needed to know in case it was excavated. Completing his work, he felt confident that only the abandoned sewage line — and maybe skulls — were underground.

The most useful excavation requires mechanical equipment, such as a backhoe and a hydraulic coring rig, but without a precise location, such an effort can be inefficient and costly. Beginning in the 1940s, archaeologists began using less invasive methods to study the subsurface by sending "physical impulses," such as electrical currents and radar signals, into the ground. These souped-up metal detectors can show unusual particles in the soil and even sketch out shapes of buried objects, such as houses, fireplaces, or graves. But they can also produce misleading signals and prompt futile excavations. Only by digging can one truly know what's below.

Ellsworth found several experts to help him literally unearth the evidence of the riot and then interpret the bones once they were found. He began by calling a chain-smoking, slump-shouldered, white septuagenarian named Clyde Snow, a world-renowned forensic anthropologist who identified human skeletal remains for a living. He was also an Oklahoman, living in Norman. His obsessions were macabre but, for him, comforting. On his desk at home sat two human skulls. "They're always smiling," Snow said, "and they cheer the place up."

Snow had examined the bones of victims and persecutors alike all over the world. He identified the remains of the infamous Nazi doctor Josef Mengele in Brazil. He exhumed massacre victims in El Salvador and dug up the scarred bones of civilians from Ethiopia to Guatemala, Sri Lanka to Bosnia. He had also spent years searching for the *desaparecidos,* the disappeared, from Argentina's "dirty war" of the late 1970s.

Snow agreed to help Ellsworth. Studying the riot, he believed that

historians and commission members had completely mischaracter-
ized it. It was not a riot or a massacre or a war. It was homicide, and
the Tulsa Police Department bore clear responsibility because it had
deputized white marauders. To Snow, no crime was more profound
than a government attacking its own people, and the Tulsa tragedy
was both a mass murder and a human rights violation.

He believed that exhuming a mass grave would bring about an entirely new understanding of the incident. The bones could disclose
the age, sex, height, and race of the victims and indicate whether
they were killed by a bullet, knife, blunt object, or fire. They could
also divulge the circumstances of death; a gunshot wound to the
back of the head, for example, might mean the victim was fleeing
when killed. Sophisticated DNA analysis could also yield health and
nutrition characteristics of the victims and shed light on the social
habits of Greenwood.

To find the bones themselves, Ellsworth called Robert Brooks, director of the Oklahoma Archeological Survey at the University of
Oklahoma. A white man with a graying beard and almost thirty
years of archaeological experience, he typically spent his time
searching for Indian houses and buffalo bones. He was outraged by
the riot but, like Clyde Snow, believed "riot" misrepresented the
event. To him, the door-to-door eviction of innocent blacks was ethnic cleansing. He also believed that the official death count was out-
rageously low. In 1921 he estimated that Tulsa had 11,000 blacks,
which meant the official death count of twenty-six blacks meant
a mortality rate of 0.2 percent. That struck Brooks as impossibly
low. The sporadic but often furious combat spanned almost sixteen
hours. He thought there would have been at least one hundred fifty
deaths, a black casualty rate of only slightly more than 1 percent.
Those bodies, he believed, had been buried, hidden, and forgotten; it
was now up to him to find them.

For two days in July 1998, with temperatures reaching 106 degrees,
Brooks led a small team through Newblock Park, Rolling Oaks Memorial Park, and Oaklawn Cemetery, using ground-penetrating radar to search for the "disturbed soil" associated with bones or

coffins. While the commissioners were kept apprised of the work, reporters had stopped coming to meetings, so the public knew nothing
of the search. The radar sweep showed positive results, confirming
soil anomalies at both Rolling Oaks and Newblock. The latter occurred on the very site where Jack Britton supposedly picked up the
skulls.

Before excavating the area, Brooks wanted to gather more data by
penetrating the ground with three-inch cores mounted to a truck,
then reeling them up like fish lines in the hope of catching bone fragments. These probes could confirm the presence of a grave before
more disruptive digs took place. After spending several months finding additional maps of buried utility lines, Brooks's crew drove out
to Newblock Park on a cold sunny morning in December.

There, in a quiet lowland surrounded by gray oaks and cotton-
woods, Warner had sprayed orange Xs on a patch of yellowing grass.
A white pickup driven by one of Brooks's assistants pulled up next to
the site, and the driver activated a long steel arm mounted to the vehicle. As a low whine filled the air, the arm thrust a hollow tube into
the soil. After a few seconds, he reversed the gears and slowly began
to crank the core out of the earth.

Wearing gloves and a heavy coat, Ellsworth anxiously watched the
digging. No one wanted to see those bones more than he, but he suddenly felt unnerved. The loud hydraulic machine — called a truck-
mounted bull probe — driving a hard object six feet into the earth
in search of remains seemed . . . disrespectful. The radar had not disturbed a weed, but if they were now standing on top of a mass grave,
the thrust of the bull probe could crack a pelvis or shatter a jaw.

With the small motor droning, the driver pulled up the first hollow tube of moist red soil. With Ellsworth peering over his shoulder,
Brooks shaved the dirt off the tube's open face and examined its con-
tents: brick fragments, concrete, and broken glass. "Nothing here,"
he said. A second core contained cinders, shards of white pipe, rubble, silt, and sand, but no bones.

More cores yielded the same result. Three men, pulling up one
hundred years of urban debris, but finding no human remnants. At
one point, a policeman noticed the large white truck and pulled over.

"What are you doing here?" he asked.

Ellsworth explained the situation and said that their "historical digging" had been cleared by the police department's chief homicide investigator. "We've heard rumors that there might be some race riot victims here," he said.

The cop soon left, convinced that nothing untoward could happen with three white guys pulling dirt out of the ground, and the cold morning wore on in the otherwise lifeless park. More cores were pulled up, yielding nothing, further diminishing any hope of success. Finally — *crack!*

The metal tube slammed into something hard underground, and the chain that pulled the core snapped. The motor stopped. The core had struck a solid block of concrete, probably from the basement of the water pump station. The bull probe was disabled, and the search ended with a broken chain, three frustrated men, and ten spools of worthless Oklahoma clay.

Later the crew used manually operated rods to pull up dirt at the Rolling Oaks cemetery. This meant they could find soil "inconsistencies" but not actual bones. The electronic scan had indicated potential bone fragments on the cemetery's sloping southern edge, where the lady with the blue cane had pointed. But the cores did not produce any soil that suggested any kind of grave.

The failures did not preclude mass burials at these sites; they may have existed, but the investigators had not found them. "We learned that the world gets very big," Ellsworth said, "if you don't know exactly where you're looking."

In January 1999 Ellsworth told the *Tulsa World* that anyone with information about the riot should call the commission; several numbers were given at the bottom of the story. He did not anticipate much but figured he had nothing to lose.

The calls poured in, and out flowed riot memories from Tulsans who seemed to have been waiting all their lives to tell their stories. Many were grisly. ("One hundred and twenty-three blacks were clubbed and shot to death in the basement of Convention Hall." "My mother told me they could smell the burning flesh all way to their house." "My great-uncle shot blacks with a shotgun and watched the bodies jump when they were hit.") Some were absurd. (One caller said she saw Gene Autry in an ice wagon haul bodies to the fairgrounds.) But most had to do with bodies — bodies put on flatbed trucks, bodies thrown into incinerators, bodies floating under bridges, bodies dug up decades later when a highway was expanded. Ellsworth and Warner received 107 calls; these recollections, however accurate, were reminders of the harrowing memories that had been passed down through generations of Tulsans. They also convinced Dick Warner, a self-described right-winger, that the official death count was egregiously low. "You hear enough stories about bodies stacked like cordwood on flatbed trucks, you begin to believe them," he said.

More important, the calls yielded their most promising lead about a mass grave. A man named Clyde Eddy called and said that he had seen a large burial at Oaklawn Cemetery. If true, Ellsworth would finally have an actual witness. He drove Eddy to the cemetery and was gratified by what he saw and heard. Eddy was a tall, lanky white man whose coat, tie, and hat gave him a dignified presence. He was ten years old in 1921, and he said that after the riot, he and his cousin Ben were cutting through the cemetery. "There were six, maybe eight, men there, dressed in overalls and digging a large hole," he said. "Near them were about a half dozen large wood crates." At first the two kids watched through a wrought-iron fence, then ventured through the gate for a closer look. "We went over to one of the crates, lifted the lid, and saw the bodies of three black men inside. The stench was terrible. Then we walked over to another one and looked in it and saw four more bodies. Then one of the workers yelled out, 'You boys get out of here! You've got no business here!' I never will forget it. Just like a picture. Just as plain today as it was at that time."

When he told his parents what he had seen, they were shocked. "After that night, I never said anything more about it, until years later, when I tried to explain the whole sad affair to my children."

Eddy showed Ellsworth the spot in the cemetery, in the white section of the potter's field, where he had seen the trench. Bob Brooks returned with radar equipment to examine the "Clyde Eddy Area," as it became known, and found soil anomalies that bore the characteristics of a trench with vertical walls and an unidentified object within. This data, combined with Eddy's testimony, led Brooks to conclude in November of 1999 that there were "compelling arguments" for the presence of a mass grave. He began plans to excavate a fifteen-square-foot patch with trowels or shovels. Real digging, for the first time, was about to begin.

By now, however, the entire dynamic of the search had changed. Early in the year, an AP reporter noticed that the commission was looking for dead bodies. When the wire service published its story — in Ellsworth's words — "the land rush was on." Journalists from all over the world swarmed into Tulsa to report on the riot, and the search for mass graves was usually the lead. As Brooks and Ellsworth walked through cemeteries, they were followed by camera crews or reporters from *60 Minutes II*, the BBC, the *New York Times*, the *Philadelphia Inquirer*, and the *Tulsa World*. CNN called the mayor's office to ask if it could film the possible digging from a helicopter; an assistant for the mayor discovered the cemetery was outside the "airport zone," and CNN or anyone else could fly over the site.

Nightline broadcast a show, "The Dirty Little Secret: The Tulsa Race Riot." HBO aired a documentary, *The Tulsa Lynching of 1921: A Hidden Story*. (The subtitle had been *Holocaust in the Heartland*.) A *60 Minutes II* producer asked Mayor Savage if she would state on the air that the city had engaged in a cover-up. She would not. *NBC Nightly News*, NPR, the *Washington Post*, the *Los Angeles Times*, and the *Dallas Morning News*, among many others, all ran stories about the horrors of 1921. Web sites posted riot stories claiming that 3,000 people had been killed. Al Gore, in a presidential campaign debate at the Apollo Theater in Harlem, would say in February 2000 that reparations for riot victims in Tulsa was a "definite possibility."

For a city that had always relied on its shining image to recruit business and attract families, the coverage was devastating. Tulsans viewed themselves, not without reason, as more educated and cosmopolitan than other Oklahomans. They still bristled at *The Grapes of Wrath*, whose famed "Okies" were driven off their parched farmland during the Depression and depicted as "dirty and miserable" simpletons. The riot stories mocked Tulsa's sophisticated aspirations and confirmed the worst stereotypes of redneck Oklahomans. The possible discovery of a mass grave, with cameras beaming the ghastly smiles of skulls to an international audience, would be a proud city's greatest disgrace.

As Brooks prepared for the Oaklawn dig in January 2000, an attorney in Mayor Savage's office announced that he had found records indicating that one Ed Baker was buried in the very spot that the excavation was to take place. To dig, Brooks would now need permission from Baker's survivors, and if the survivors were not found, a court order would be necessary as well as a permit from the County Health Department. Brooks had already become uneasy with the media circus and feared that the press was now driving the search for bodies. The state official was also uncomfortable with criticism. The *Daily Oklahoman,* the state's largest newspaper and published in the capital, was an influential conservative voice. It condemned the dig for disturbing sacred ground, an act that would be "worthy of criminal prosecution" if done on a recent gravesite. Brooks decided to delay the excavation to sort out the burial records and allow passions to cool.

Five months later, the commission reversed its previous authorization and unanimously voted to halt any digging. It was an embarrassing decision, negating countless hours of work begun two and a half years earlier by its consultant, state employees, and volunteers. Moreover, the move ensured that the commission could not wield its potentially most valuable weapon — certification of a mass grave — in its appeal for reparations. But the continued search, in the commission's view, had become risky. Just as finding one would reveal the lies of the riot, *not* finding one could be seen as confirming the event's official history, including the body count. The commission wanted to discredit that history, but the highly publicized quest for burial sites — if never found — could now undermine its work. No one understood that better than Don Ross, who had initially encouraged Ellsworth to search for graves but now recommended that the excavation be stopped. Eddie Faye Gates, a black commissioner, agreed that the panel's credibility would be hurt if a grave were not found.

This reversal was a bitter disappointment to the researchers, particularly to Clyde Snow. His examination of riot death certificates would later yield important insights, but he never was able to study the *desaparecidos* of Tulsa. "There are more bodies than whites would like, but there may not be as many as blacks would like, so we're caught in the middle," he said. "Perhaps the commission can pass a resolution on what is the politically correct number of bodies to be found in a race riot."

The Age of Reparations

To VIVIAN CLARK-ADAMS, the black men who marched on the Tulsa courthouse to stop a lynching were not just defending an innocent prisoner. They were war veterans who had risked their lives abroad for freedoms denied them at home. They were heroes, they were freedom fighters, and they were American patriots.

Clark-Adams was a black member of the commission, a tall, broad-shouldered activist whose credentials — a master's degree in history, a doctorate in education administration — added credibility to her revisionist interpretation of American history. In her view, African Americans had long had their voices shunted aside, their achievements discredited, and their courage discounted, all of which coalesced in the distorted history of the riot. The official version found in white newspapers, court records, and public pronouncements ignored black Tulsans. Even Ellsworth's book, Clark-Adams believed, understated the duplicity of the city's elite and downplayed the heroism of Greenwood's defenders. While others on the commission and in the community held these views as well, Clark-Adams was their most articulate and unwavering proponent, and she believed the evidence supported her position. Moreover, she had had a lifetime of experience to buttress her convictions.

She moved to Tulsa in 1961 when she was eleven from the relatively tolerant city of Washington, D.C. Her father, Major Clark, a retired army lieutenant colonel, tried to shield Vivian from the degradation of Jim Crow. He forbade her to ride on the bus so she would not have to sit in the back, and he rarely allowed her to go to restaurants or movie theaters — even black ones — so that she would not learn to accept segregation. Vivian understood only that she was proscribed from doing the things she had done in Washington, so she hated her new city. She lived in a racially mixed "transition neighborhood" north of Greenwood, and her anger only deepened when she helped integrate McLain High School. As one of 12 blacks in a class of about 455, she excelled academically but was ostracized, called "nigger," and not recognized as the class salutatorian. Her temper flared. When a boy wiped his chalkboard eraser on the back of her blouse, she turned around and yelled, "I'm going to rearrange your face!" (She didn't; he didn't bother her again.)

In high school she saw her heroes assassinated (Malcolm X, Bobby Kennedy, Martin Luther King Jr.), and when she graduated in 1968, her parents sent her to a historically black college because they feared she was too "belligerent" to attend a white school. After her mother's death in 1981, she returned to Tulsa to be close to her father, holding various teaching and administrative posts. When she learned about the riot in the 1980s, the story resonated with her. The black men who went to the courthouse had marched there in military formation, and an unknown number had fought in World War I. Yet these soldiers were blamed for starting the battle. Such disrespect — their valor discredited, their motives impugned — typified the experiences of black servicemen, a lesson she had learned from her father.

Major Clark was known as "the godfather" of African American soldiers, a veteran of two wars who had spent much of his life studying black military history. He enlisted in the army in 1940, fought in Italy as an artillery officer — disproving the myth that blacks lacked the math skills for the job — and received the Bronze Star. He was later decorated by both the South Korean Army and the U.S. Army for his service in Korea. But his own medals did not mollify his feelings about the army's treatment of black soldiers. Segregation (first de jure, then de facto) was only part of his grievance. The army's official World War II record and other history books either neglected the accomplishments of the black 92nd Division or wrongly reported that the black soldiers had performed badly. In addition, no black serviceman received the Medal of Honor, the nation's highest military decoration. This oversight outraged Clark, who believed that black soldiers fought on the front lines with less military support than white soldiers because their lives were not as highly valued. He tried to correct the war record, leading an effort that finally compelled the army to acknowledge its failure to recognize the black soldiers' bravery. In 1997, at a special White House ceremony, President Clinton awarded the Medal of Honor to seven African Americans, one of whom, First Lieutenant Vernon J. Baker, was still living. Clark refused his invitation to the event. "He turned it down because he was tired of a system that took fifty years to acknowledge the black vets," Clark-Adams said. "It was part of his protest."

Clark-Adams adored her father (he died in 1999), and her affection for him intensified her sympathy for the black soldiers at the Tulsa courthouse. Their redemption became her passion. "I knew how hard it was for the black vet. I knew how hard it was for my father and our family," she said. When he was stationed in the South, for example, his son could not attend public school but had to take classes on the army base. "My mom said, 'They didn't care what color blood you spilled in World War II, but now you can't get an education.'"

Clark-Adams was chair of the liberal arts division at Tulsa Community College, and her interests led state Senator Horner to recommend her to the commission. (Governor Keating appointed her.) While Ellsworth assembled a team of scholars, including a law professor (for reparations), an anthropologist (for burial remains), and a historian (for Greenwood property valuations), as well as Clyde Snow and Bob Brooks, Clark-Adams led another group. It assumed what some called the Afrocentric view of the riot, emphasizing the primacy of black sources — old black newspapers and journals, the NAACP files at the Library of Congress, interviews with elderly blacks in Tulsa, Muskogee, and elsewhere.

They tried to build a case that the riot was not a spontaneous outbreak, triggered by a newspaper article about a fictitious assault charge, but a carefully planned conspiracy among Tulsa's elite to rob blacks of their land. If proven, it would lend credence to their view that blacks have long faced the organized hostility of powerful whites, and it would fortify demands for reparations against local and state government as well as businesses.

The conspiracy claim was not new. It arose from a series of stories published immediately after the riot — in the *New York Times,* but mostly in black or socialist newspapers — claiming that printed warnings had appeared in newspapers in Oklahoma three weeks before the incident, warning Negroes to leave Tulsa by June 1. Another version was that "riot warnings had been pinned to the homes of colored people threatening death and arson unless they moved away from the oil properties or sold them at speculators' prices." According to reports, five to eight Oklahoma "refugees" had heeded the advice and gone to the NAACP offices in New York, where they accused white oilmen of trying to wrest valuable land from black Tulsans. The *New York Evening World* reported that these newspaper warnings "appeared on three successive days, and the five were among the thousands who left panic-stricken immediately afterward."

The events after the riot seemed to support the conspiracy theory. The city did try to drive its blacks out of Greenwood with the illegal fire ordinance. That the riot could have been planned was reinforced by Maurice Willows of the Red Cross, in his memoir. "This was NOT a RIOT, as some of the out of town papers called it in their screaming headlines of the next day," he wrote. "It was a well-planned, diabolical ouster of the innocent negroes from their stamping grounds. The planners were key persons in both races . . . reaching into officialdom in the city hall."

But to prove the riot was planned, Adams-Clark and her allies needed something more than hearsay. Maybe such evidence wasn't necessary, however. Maybe the airplanes were proof enough.

Many black witnesses said that planes dropped explosives or "rained fire" on Greenwood. Mary E. Jones Parrish's book, J. B. Stradford's memoirs, A. J. Smitherman's poem — all provided firsthand testimony of the bombing or strafing, as did black newspapers like the *Chicago Defender.* "At the signal of a whistle, more than a dozen aeroplanes went up and began to drop turpentine balls upon the negro residences, while 5,000 Whites, with machine guns and other deadly weapons, began firing in all directions," a black witness told Parrish. But there were no photographs or film footage of the planes (unlike the implosion of Mount Zion Baptist Church, which was captured on film), and it was never mentioned by Tulsa's newspapers, the grand jury, the mayor, or any other official.

On one level, the planes hardly seemed important. With or without them, the result was the same: Greenwood's liquidation. But to the conspiracy theorists the planes meant everything. They meant that Greenwood's destruction was abetted by Tulsa's business and political leaders — not lawless, drunken ruffians who didn't own or have access to airplanes. But rich oilmen did. Policemen did. So did military men and maybe even politicians. Once again, the black press offered tantalizing clues.

In October 1921, the Associated Negro Press ran an article about Van B. Hurley, a former Tulsa policeman. Hurley claimed that he attended a meeting with city officials who carefully planned the attack on Greenwood by instructing local aviators to drop nitroglycerin on buildings. Hurley, who was white, had signed a twenty-page affidavit, or "confession," for a black attorney representing Greenwood's residents. If that affidavit could be found, maybe it would lay bare the conspiracy. But even if the commission only confirmed the bombings, that too would incriminate Tulsa's elite, strengthen the claims for reparations, and enshrine Greenwood as the first target of an aerial assault on U.S. soil. Confirming their use also bolstered the view that blacks would have won the riot if whites hadn't taken extraordinary measures. "I know of no other riot where they had to resort to aerial assault and machine guns," Clark-Adams said.

Linking the Ku Klux Klan to the riot was another priority. Again, it seemed to make little difference whether members of the mob wore white hoods — the racial hostility was the same — but Clark-Adams believed that the Klan's involvement further supported the position that the rioters were the city's leaders. A Tulsa Klan registry from 1928 to 1931, discovered in the mid-1990s, showed that the secret order had attracted Tulsa's top officials. According to this theory, if the Klan were shown to be riot instigators, then one could infer that the top officials were implicated. It required a leap of faith, and the press (black and white) made few references to Klan rioters, but Clark-Adams was determined to find a connection.

In her view, the various histories of the riot also omitted the role of an obscure militant black group called the African Blood Brotherhood. On June 3, 1921, the *New York Times* wrote that the "authorities" had evidence that members of the ABB, who were "highly aggressive in character," were leaders of the black "mob" at the courthouse and had "fomented unrest among the Negroes." Founded in 1919, the ABB rejected W.E.B. Du Bois's views as accommodationist and urged the overthrow of capitalism. Its leader, Cyril Briggs, from the West Indies, was the first black man to join the American Communist Party, and he used the Tulsa riot to further the revolution. "Better a thousand race riots," he wrote, "than a single lynching."

Even though Briggs denied that the ABB "fomented" the riot, Clark-Adams believed the group helped black Tulsans organize its defense. She read the ABB's monthly publication, the *Crusader*, from July 1921, in which its Tulsa "commander" described in detail how the city's Negroes, fighting like trained soldiers, resisted the white mob.

> The Negro fighters early took up good positions inside and behind railroad cars, and in hastily dug trenches . . . and were under cover most of the time. The whites, on the contrary, were attacking in the open and in idiotic mass formation until the little steel bullets tripping on their errand of death by determined Negro hands [convinced] them killing Negroes wasn't such a pleasant and easy job after all . . . Especially in the attack on the Negro church held by a handful of ex-soldiers — fifty to be exact — were [whites] badly mauled and punished. Five times they came against it in mass formation, and five times were they repelled with deadly force. However, what they had not valor enough to accomplish by force, they treacherously achieved.

The whites, wrote the *Crusader*, crushed Greenwood only by dropping "incendiary bombs" from airplanes.

Eddie Faye Gates, a black commissioner and a close ally of Clark-Adams's, found support for this account in an interview she conducted with an elderly black man. He said that he was in Greenwood during the riot and saw ABB members prepare for battle by unloading ammunition in Mount Zion Baptist Church.

These accounts, Clark-Adams said, confirmed the black Tulsans' bravery and sacrifice while upholding the event's oral history in Greenwood. "This was not a one-sided massacre," she said. "This showed that black Americans would not be walked over by white mobs." She wanted mainstream historians, including those working with the commission, to take the ABB seriously. "It was a militant organization with communist affiliations, and we tend to dismiss groups like this," she said. "If you're fighting against the establishment, traditional historians label you as agitators and militants and undesirables. But in my view, they were freedom fighters."

But to prove that the riot was a planned land grab engineered by the Klan and repelled by the ABB, documentation, not hearsay, was needed. Clark-Adams and her allies, for example, searched for a copy of a newspaper ad or signs warning blacks to leave Tulsa by June 1, 1921. They did find a printed warning for blacks to leave an Oklahoma town, but the date was for Saturday, August 19, in the town of Caddo. In 1921, August 19 fell on a Friday. Wrong town, wrong date, wrong year.

They never did find a printed warning or a sign or anything else that could undermine the most heavily documented and plausible account of the riot: namely, that the initial outburst was spontaneous but that business leaders who coveted the land may have organized Greenwood's invasion. The evidence that the ABB played a role in the upheaval was also thin. There appear to be no reports of the ABB ever doing anything in Tulsa besides the riot. Robert Hill, a history professor at UCLA who has studied Cyril Briggs, suspects that Briggs exploited a false report that the ABB was in Tulsa to generate publicity for the organization, thus creating the "Tulsa Post" to send dispatches about the violence. "The ABB did not spread beyond the East Coast," Hill told the *Tulsa World*. "The likelihood, geographically, of its reaching Tulsa is not very great." But the memory of the ABB's role in the riot was important. "Was that the actual ABB? I doubt it," Hill said. "But that doesn't lessen its importance in folk memory. The ABB became a scapegoat for the authorities. The scapegoat takes on a reality for people who were victims. There is a sort of valorization, of being able to say, 'Yes, we stood up and defended ourselves.'"

Eddie Faye Gates was the most visible commissioner, a retired high school teacher who lectured at black churches about the riot, traveled to other cities to talk about reparations, gave many media interviews, and wrote columns for the *Oklahoma Eagle*. She could be aggravating: she rarely missed an opportunity to promote her autobiography and a collection of oral histories she had assembled, and editors at the *Tulsa World* grew weary of her lengthy polemics on race. But her compassion for the black riot survivors was real. Even before her appointment to the commission, she had taped interviews with several survivors as part of an oral history project for the Oklahoma Historical Society, and she continued those interviews with the commission. She saw herself as their advocate, specifically on reparations. "I will not compromise on the survivors," she said.

Born in 1934, she spent much of the civil rights movement in England, where her husband was stationed with the military, and she regretted not playing a role in that historic drama. But now she had her own civil rights battle, and she was in the vanguard of what she called the Age of Reparations.

"You did it for Japanese Americans," she said. "You did it for Native Americans. The German people are doing it for Holocaust survivors. I don't know why this brings up so much controversy when it's for people of color. We didn't get forty acres and a mule either."

Like Clark-Adams, she resolutely believed that the riot had been planned and involved the Ku Klux Klan and Tulsa's white leaders, and she made bold assumptions to support her position. That Walter White, the NAACP journalist, was in Tulsa on the evening of May 31 was evidence to Gates that blacks knew the riot was coming. On several occasions, she said the death toll was at least three hundred blacks and one hundred whites, and she homed in on seemingly trivial issues as metaphors for the government's indifference to black suffering. In 1931 *Scribner's Magazine* published a riot story belittling the white authorities, claiming, among other things, that the National Guard promptly ate breakfast after arriving by train in Tulsa at

8 A.M.* "People were being robbed and killed while they were getting ready to have their coffee," the story said. This outraged Gates, even though she was told by military experts, including her husband, that the guard could not legally rush into Greenwood until the civilian authorities had transferred power. "Forget breakfast," Gates said. "People are dying and burning up, and the planes are in the sky and they're eating breakfast."

She also believed that the failure of the city's white leaders to acknowledge their own culpability was almost as shameful as Greenwood's demolition.

"Tulsa wants to keep this Magic City image," she said "It was, 'Come to this promised land, and everybody will be better off.' [Tulsans] want that and they want their leaders to be impeccable, but [the leaders] weren't, and people don't want this conspiracy out." Government reparations were the only appropriate measure because they would symbolize the responsibility long denied by public officials. "If you're not held accountable, what keeps you from doing the wrong thing?" Gates said. She rejected the argument that today's taxpayers should not have to pay for an old injustice. Her reasoning was that unlike private debts, which are not passed down to heirs, government debts should always be redeemed to maintain — or in this case, rebuild — confidence in public institutions. The city and state owed the riot survivors something for assisting the white mob and failing to protect lives and property. Asked if such payments would cause a greater problem in race relations by generating resentment among whites, Gates bristled.

"Why should everything be done for your comfort?" she said. "Whites say that all the time, but this is a government issue. This is a justice issue. This is a God issue, I believe, and there are some things that transcend your comfort level."

Currie Ballard grew up in Los Angeles in the 1960s but was fascinated by the stories of the Choctaw freedmen who were his ancestors in Oklahoma. These former slaves and their descendants owned homes, restaurants, and a small "juke joint" in foreign-sounding cit-

---

* The Guard's defenders said the story included fictitious anecdotes.

ies like Wapanucka, Muskogee, and Tulsa. Despite one grisly story —
an ancestor was lynched in 1916 — the collective tales lured Ballard
to Oklahoma. After fourteen years in management at a General
Motors plant, he took a buyout and was hired as a "historian in
residence" at Langston University — in a town, he said, that had
"more cows than people." But the articulate, telegenic Ballard found
many outlets for his strong views on history, race, and politics, including a monthly radio show. He was also an anomaly in Oklahoma
— a black Republican — but that was not a liability, as Governor
Keating, a Republican, appointed him to three state commissions:
human rights, the pardon and parole board, and finally the race riot.

Although most Oklahoma Republicans vehemently opposed reparations, Ballard was an exception. His advocacy was based not on
how city or state officials conducted themselves during the riot but
on the system of racial discrimination that local and state governments had already adopted, codified, and practiced. Culpability, to
him, was not a legal issue, to be proved in a court of law, but a moral
one, and Oklahoma's culpability began long before May 31, 1921.

"It's not easy to say that you had a state born into racism," said
Ballard, sitting in his office at Langston University. "It was a state that
held such opportunity for African Americans. They flocked here by
the dozens because they knew opportunity is what made America
different." Oklahoma's constitution, ratified by the voters in 1907, included little Jim Crow language to ensure the approval of President
Theodore Roosevelt, but it did not take long for lawmakers to pass
the bill that segregated Oklahoma's public facilities. "It wasn't the
eighth law, it wasn't the seventh law, it was the first law put on the
books," Ballard said, pointing to a copy of Senate Bill One on his
desk. "We went from a land of promise and hope to a legislature
filled with damn Klansmen." And "Alfalfa Bill" Murray, he added,
"doesn't even justify interment."

Ballard saw a skein of corruption leading from Senate Bill One, in
1907, to Greenwood, in 1921. "It's all related when the first law on the
damn books is this" — he picked up the bill and slapped it — "and
it's all related when you have lynchings and you have public officials
who don't make a stand and say, 'We don't condone it.' Every society
must have a footstool to place their feet on, and black people have

traditionally been the footstool in America, particularly under Jim Crow. It didn't matter how poor and white and backwards and ignorant and uneducated you were, you were still better than the most educated black, the wealthiest black, the most honest, God-fearing black. And once it's all right to treat blacks as subservient to white folks, then, well, let's carry that a little bit further. It's all right for them not to receive the same millage that we receive in the school system so they can't get the proper textbooks and equipment and fix the damn leaking roofs. Then carry that a little bit further and it never stops."

The riot, he said, was planned, although not by the participants. "It was planned as far as lack of leadership in the state. It was planned in terms of separate streetcar compartments, then separate water fountains, then separate phone books, then separate colleges. Then one black was lynched and nothing much was said. In terms of condoning wrong, it was planned."

He hoped the commission would convince white Oklahomans that the riot had not been caused by "a bunch of redneck, tobacco-chewing, ignorant farmboys who drove through Greenwood and burned it up" but was effectively sanctioned by the state's highest officials. Ballard led a subcommittee on reparations, and he believed he had proof of the state's culpability right there on his desk.

"This law on the damn books says that the state of Oklahoma is culpable," he said. "The National Guard didn't sign it, but the house, the senate, and the damn governor signed off. When your first law on the books is to put blacks in their place, hell, you're culpable."

Reparations also had some ardent if idiosyncratic white advocates who marshaled evidence for compensation claims against government agencies and businesses. Jim Lloyd, another member of the commission, was a lawyer in Sand Springs who had represented clients against insurance companies, and he believed the riot could give him another chance to challenge insurers. He was serious about his mission: he hired a court reporter to attend commission meetings and interrogated certain witnesses as if they were in a courtroom. But he had unconventional ideas about other matters as well as the riot. He had his own beehives, for example, and used bee venom and bee stings to heal injuries. He was also a fan of *Think and Grow Rich*, Napoleon Hill's self-help bible from the 1930s, which used imaginary advisers for guidance, such as Abraham Lincoln, Charles Darwin, and Napoleon. Inspired by such tactics, Lloyd would gather with friends and seek guidance on the riot from his own imaginary adviser, J. Edgar Hoover. "I consider him a pretty good supersnoop," Lloyd explained. Specifically, he wanted Hoover to help him find the lawsuits that black Tulsans had filed against insurance companies and the city, records that Lloyd thought could build his own case for a lawsuit.

"These historians had told me that the records were destroyed, so I'd go to J. Edgar Hoover and say, 'What about it, did they destroy these records?'

"And he told me, 'No, they're not destroyed.'

"'You mean, I can find them?'

"'Yes, you can find them.'

"'Where can I find them?'

"His answer was, 'Just keep looking.'"

In fact, Lloyd did find the lawsuits in a dusty annex in Tulsa, although his discovery may have had more to do with his understanding of Tulsa County's archaic filing system. The lawsuits documented the losses of almost two hundred households and businesses, offering a glimpse into the comfortable life that a select few enjoyed (Hamilton watches, Havelin china, pianos, mahogany Chippendale bookcases). The documents also helped the commission confirm previous estimates of the riot's toll: between $1.5 and $1.8 million in property, equivalent to more than $14 million today.

Seeking further investigative help, Lloyd wrote to President Clinton in Washington, D.C., and The Hague in the Netherlands and asked NASA for copies of LandStat (satellite) images of mass burial sites, which could help them identify similar sites in Tulsa. While these efforts were unsuccessful, he felt he had enough material to sue, although once again he raised eyebrows with his choice of possible targets. He wanted to sue unnamed insurance companies and the descendants of Richard Lloyd Jones as well as the Ku Klux Klan, proposing to unearth FBI records under the Freedom of Information Act to identify the leaders of the hooded order. He also expressed interest in Hollywood's making a movie about the riot, which could also raise money for reparations. His actions suggested to some that he was mainly interested in making money for himself by representing the survivors in some capacity, but he insisted that his goal was justice.

"I bought every newspaper on the riot from the morgue of the *Tulsa World,* and I stayed up late at night and I recreated it like the movie *Platoon,*" he said. "I put myself there, heard the crackling of the fire, I heard the gunfire, and I heard the screams, saw the blacks, and felt the terror. It moves you to tears."

The case for reparations was put on firmer legal ground by Alfred Brophy, a white law professor who specialized in race and property law in antebellum America. A consummate eastern liberal, Brophy had been raised in Philadelphia and educated at Harvard and Columbia; he was fascinated by jazz and liked to quote Ralph Ellison. In 1994 he accepted a job at Oklahoma City University School of Law and suddenly found himself a political outcast. Three years later he received partial deliverance when he read about the commission's work. He volunteered his services and gladly joined the reparations crusade, which he felt Oklahoma would embrace. "This is a way to purchase absolution very cheaply," he said. He believed all African Americans deserved compensation for slavery and wanted Tulsa to be the opening salvo in that battle. He could romanticize the black experience — he referred to black newspapers like the sensational *Chicago Defender* as "vehicles of the renaissance" — and he brought a missionary zeal to his work. He would tell writers researching the riot, "You're doing God's work."

Brophy himself burrowed into the riot archives, plastered his office walls with news articles, sponsored symposiums, and gave speeches accompanied by slides. He even evoked the era by listening to jazz from the early 1920s, including "The Tulsa Blues" by Bennie Moten's Kansas City Orchestra. "It's so haunting, it's unbelievable," he said.

Brophy drafted a legal argument for reparations, citing four "limiting principles" that applied specifically to Tulsa: the state was directly involved in arming white rioters; black victims were still alive; the harm had been concentrated in time and location; and the city had promised to rebuild but failed to deliver. This established a framework for the debate, and Brophy's wide-ranging paper, capping more than two years of work, included references to jazz and opium dens as well as the law and established him as the legal expert on the Tulsa race riot. As his secretary told him, "This is why God put you in Oklahoma."

The commission held its first meeting on reparations on November 22, 1999, at city hall. After consulting with Vivian Clark-Adams, Eddie Faye Gates, and Commissioner Jimmie White, a black history professor, Currie Ballard presented his recommendations to the group. To display the state's racial climate before the riot, he showed a heart-rending picture of a lynching in Okemah, Oklahoma — a mother and son, hanging from two ropes on a bridge, while men in neckties and women holding umbrellas looked on. He showed photographs of black-hooded "knights" from an Oklahoma high school and a burned black man from the southeastern part of the state; the latter had been turned into a postcard with the caption "Coon Cooking." Race relations, Ballard said, "were a time bomb waiting to explode."

Then he dropped his own bomb. He recommended that the state or local government allocate $26 million in scholarships (half for Langston University and half for other Oklahoma universities); $20,000 for each survivor (with sixty-four known survivors, it would equal $1.3 million); $5 million for an interactive museum in Greenwood; $1 million for a gallery of African American history at the Oklahoma Historical Society; and $250,000 to expand the M. B. Tolson Black Heritage Center at Langston University. The grand total: $33.6 million. Ballard also proposed that a memorial be built on Standpipe Hill and improvements made in North Tulsa's schools.

Ballard thought Oklahoma could finance these proposals with money it was receiving for tobacco lawsuits; still, the amount was staggering. It was also not lost on anyone that the proposal would disproportionately benefit Ballard's own institution, Langston. While the commissioners did not vote on the proposal, it served as a gambit in the debate over restitution. The group's two state legislators, Senator Robert Milacek, a Republican, and Representative Abe Deutschendorf, a Democrat, both said the state would never agree to such payments. They also rejected the position that Oklahoma's racial atmosphere implicated the state, and they believed that the National Guard, with or without its breakfast, behaved properly. Milacek said, "People are going to say, 'If we do this for Tulsa, where does it stop?' What about the Mennonites whose homes were burned during World War I? And the American Indians. We could go on forever."

The *Daily Oklahoman* editorialized that if the riot victims were compensated, so too should the "Wichita Indians," who had been displaced not by European settlers but by the Osage, Apaches, and Comanches. Calling reparations "ridiculous," the newspaper wrote: "What this is about is the transfer of wealth, just as the tobacco lawsuits were and just as so many civil rights actions are. The state is seen as a source of money which somebody wants. The request will be couched in terms of 'justice' and 'closure,' but it is based on little more than greed."

By 2000 the riot commissioners had been wrestling with reparations for three years, but their work began to assume a greater importance as a national push to compensate blacks for slavery moved into high gear. These demands were nothing new, but they had typically been made by radical scholars and had never gained much attention. Every year since 1989, Congressman John Conyers Jr. of Michigan had sponsored a bill to establish a commission to study reparations for slavery, and every year the bill had died. But the dynamic of the debate changed in the early months of 2000 with the publication of *The Debt: What America Owes to Blacks,* by Randall Robinson, an urbane, self-assured black intellectual. He had already led previous crusades to correct racial injustices, including an American boycott of South Africa during apartheid. *The Debt* argued that the economic gap between white and black America reflected the legacy of slavery as well as years of subsequent discrimination, and that the federal government was obliged to narrow that gap with a massive infusion of funds. "Let me try to drive the point home here," Robinson wrote.

> Through keloids of suffering, through coarse veils of damaged self-belief, lost direction, misplaced compass, shit-faced resignation, racial transmutation, black people worked long, hard, killing days, years, centuries — and they were never paid. The value of their labor went into others' pockets — plantation owners, northern entrepreneurs, state treasuries, the United States government.
> Where was the money?
> Where is the money?
> There is a debt here.

The Debt was that rare book that changed the conversation of America. It sold well in black bookstores and received extensive media coverage, and Robinson made his pitch — firm but not shrill — on talk shows and in newspaper and magazine stories. The following year saw the creation of the Reparations Coordinating Committee, which attracted the country's leading black lawyers and intellectuals, including the Harvard Law School professor Charles Ogletree, the attorney Johnnie Cochran, and Harvard professors Henry Louis Gates Jr. and Cornel West. The committee said it planned to file lawsuits against public and private defendants for their role in the slave trade. Conservatives peppered editorial pages opposing reparations, claiming, among other things, that the debt to blacks had been paid with the blood of white soldiers during the Civil War. Even many white liberals and black scholars (including John Hope Franklin) believed that reparations for slavery were too impractical and too amorphous (Who should receive the money? How would it be distributed?) to be pursued as public policy.

But emotions ran high. A conservative white activist named David Horowitz began placing ads against reparations in campus newspapers. Several university papers (at Columbia, Harvard, the University of Massachusetts–Amherst) rejected the ad; those that printed it (at Brown and the University of Wisconsin) faced student protesters who stole or destroyed the remaining copies or demanded the editor's resignation. Talk shows, newspaper columnists, and academics all weighed in on slavery, the First Amendment, and "restorative justice," as some called it.

In fact, Robinson's proposal was far less radical than it was depicted in the press. He did not advocate that the federal government cut checks to the descendants of slaves; he argued that it should create a large trust fund to fuel economic and educational opportunities for African Americans. He recast the traditional argument for government intervention by focusing on the most appalling, the most deplorable, the most shocking violation blacks have ever faced — slavery. At a time that affirmative action programs were in retreat in corporate America and under assault in the courts, reparations became the new battle cry.

Indeed, the distinctive evil of slavery could shame companies, if not the federal government, into expressions of public contrition. The Aetna Insurance Company of Hartford, after discovering that it had insured slaveowners against the loss of their human chattel, apologized for its actions in March 2000. Three months later the *Hartford Courant*, which had run a front-page story on Aetna's apology, offered its own page 1 mea culpa for publishing ads for the sale and capture of slaves. A new California law required that every insurance company licensed in the state research its past business, and that of its predecessor companies, and report to the state if it ever sold policies insuring slaveowners against the loss of their slaves, and if so, to whom. Civil rights lawyers began investigating companies that had profited from the slave trade, in preparation for possible lawsuits or just to embarrass the firms publicly. When the *Philadelphia Inquirer* published two full-page editorials in May 2001 urging the creation of a national reparations commission, this issue was clearly no longer the preserve of black radicals.

Tulsa was now seen as a case study of whether blacks could reasonably expect to receive compensation for past injustices. The opponents of reparations for slavery repeated a common refrain: the victims were long dead. But that could not be said for Tulsa: the victims lived! The money would not go into some ill-defined pool for government programs but to those whose homes had been destroyed, whose businesses had been torched, whose families had been killed. The money would go to George Monroe and Mabel Little and Veneice Sims and Otis Clark and all the others who had overcome their losses. Who could oppose justice for them? Reparations for slavery would be a Herculean challenge, but reparations in Tulsa were comparatively easy. Once the case was made, it would add momentum to the national movement, giving it a legal and moral framework for broader claims of restitution.

By February 2000 the commission, having neglected to give a deadline, had not received its reports from Scott Ellsworth and the other consultants. Under the law, its charter was to expire at the end of the month. Fearing that the state would not renew it, on February 4 the group convened to vote on reparations. While all eleven commissioners except the two state legislators and Bob Blackburn supported paying victims with state funds, disputes flared over other types of compensation. If justice and reconciliation could be quantified, what produced the most of each? A riot memorial or a scholarship fund? Tax incentives for economic development in Greenwood or cash payments to the descendants of victims?

After several votes and numerous appeals, the commission approved a list of priorities:

1) Compensation to survivors.
2) Compensation to the descendants of victims.
3) Scholarships to students in North Tulsa.
4) Tax incentives for Greenwood.
5) A memorial.

To avoid alienating legislators and the public, the commission did not put a dollar amount on its recommendations. The vote was front-page news in the *New York Times,* and it again thrust the commissioners onto talk shows and television news programs. The recommendation seemed to capture the emerging Zeitgeist for retroactive justice, but was it realistic in Oklahoma? Don Ross believed it was.

"They told me I couldn't take down the Confederate flag over the capitol, but the legislature changed its attitude," he said after the meeting. "They told me I couldn't pass a Martin Luther King holiday, but the legislature changed its attitude. I can't help but believe that if a compelling document is delivered that the attitude of the legislature will change again.

"There is no statute of limitations," he added, "on a moral obligation."

The Last Pioneer

To BERYL FORD, the black men at the courthouse were not noble war veterans who stopped a lynching but armed thugs who had driven through white Tulsa, looking for trouble. They were two hundred strong, with thirty-man units stationed between the courthouse and Greenwood as "fall-back protection," and they had come downtown to break out the black prisoner. The whites who met them were not part of an angry mob but were curiosity-seekers who had heard that Negro vigilantes were coming to storm the jail. "I've got several photos here of the courthouse scene, and if you call that a torchlight mob, I'll kiss your rear," said Ford, who is white. "They were just dancing for the cameraman and cutting up."

Indeed, Ford did have pictures of well-dressed men and women strolling to the courthouse in the early evening of May 31, 1921; but even without the images he knew perfectly well who was responsible for the riot, and it wasn't white Tulsa. Ford himself had not been there — he was born five years later — but he had heard the story of the riot many times. He revered the men and women who transformed this piece of grassland into a great city, and he was outraged by the attacks on their reputation. Yes, the riot was awful, but it certainly didn't happen the way the "coloreds" and their white allies would have you believe today. If the reporters and television cameras and the commissioners would just sit down with him, he would tell them what really happened.

While Beryl Ford carried the prejudices of his day, he was also a respected curmudgeon, a structural engineer and building inspector who often testified as an expert witness in relevant lawsuits. He also knew more about Tulsa than any person alive. His was not a historian's grasp of the sweeping forces that shaped the city but an enthusiast's passion for the ordinary details of its past. Give him a photograph of downtown Tulsa, and he could tell you the approximate year by the style of car on the street, by the coat of paint on a building, by the chips in the curb, or by crosschecking the businesses with his old city directories. He had spent almost fifty years amassing a collection of Tulsa memorabilia — tens of thousands of items piled in a dusty warehouse: street signs, license plates, and newspapers stacked to the ceiling, the walls covered with panoramas of the city skyline. The most prodigious collection ever assembled of Tulsa history, it existed because Ford wanted to preserve the community that he loved. He proudly displayed his loyalties with his two vanity license plates. One read TULSAN; the other, TULSANS. When he inadvertently failed to renew TULSAN, some guy with a Harley grabbed it, and it took Ford five years to get it back. "I consider it a badge of honor," he said.

His views on the riot reflected how the incident had been understood for decades among the city's older white residents. As a teenager, Ford attended the annual picnic of the Tulsa Pioneers Association (founded, coincidently, in 1921). It was a proud, exclusive club, with admission granted only to Tulsans who had lived in the city since 1907 or were descended from that group. On the second Friday of each May, they assembled for a celebration replete with Indian dancers, historical speeches, and fried chicken. There Ford heard the stories of the riot from the men who had been part of it. The same stories were told year after year, decade after decade, until the participants died, and now it was left to Beryl Ford to tell their stories, to defend their honor, and to protect their good name. Ford was as committed to those pioneers as he was to his own family, and each year he hauled old oil lamps, school bells, and saddles to the picnics, evoking the city's rugged frontier days and paying tribute to the sacrifice of their forebears. As president of the association for six years, in the 1990s, he wore a ribbon on his shirt designating the honor. But by the end of the decade, dwindling numbers forced the group to stop meeting. The pioneers had died, and their heirs had lost touch with their past. The association was now recognized by a granite memorial at Owen's Park engraved with the names of the presidents. The last name was Beryl Ford's.

His affection for Tulsa did not come from its material comforts. Beryl grew up in a four-room house during the Depression, the son of a stonemason whose seasonal work produced lean winters. On weekends, he and his younger brother, Charlie, explored downtown Tulsa, sneaking into the back of abandoned buildings, roaming the alleys, going to the movie palaces, eating at the chili parlor, and prowling through the pawnshops, where the smell of leather and the sight of guns and pocketknives conjured up images of the great frontier. Beryl was a small (five-foot-six) but cocky teenager who liked fast cars (he was among the first kids in the neighborhood to own one, a Plymouth convertible) and dreamed of becoming a pilot. He graduated from high school and later became an army air corps pilot trainee. He never saw combat, but he did learn about death during World War II — in Wichita, Kansas, where he worked in a mortuary, shaving and embalming bodies. He later used that experience to impugn riot witnesses who claimed that hundreds had been killed but never discussed the stench. "I learned the smell of death," he said. "It gets stuck in your nostrils and won't go away for three days."

Ford had a dark pompadour and bore a slight resemblance to Bing Crosby. He saw himself as a scientist whose judgments were shaped by data, not emotions, and his insistence on precision surfaced in times of personal tragedy. After the war, at twenty-one, he eloped with a young woman from Tulsa, speeding out of town in a 1933 Ford coupe. Thirteen months later his wife died from kidney poisoning, and the cosmetologist who prepared her body gave her an ungainly pompadour and garish deep red nail polish. Ford corrected the flaws himself, combing her hair with a side part and repainting her nails. "She preferred light red," he said. She was seventeen.

Saddled with $20,000 in hospital and funeral bills, Ford left college and found a job as a structural engineer. He remarried, started a family that in time produced six children, and became involved in civic affairs. In addition to his years with the Pioneers Association, he was president of the Young Republicans in the 1950s and of the Tulsa County Historical Society in the 1960s; he was also a founder of the Tulsa Air and Space Museum in the 1990s. But he was best known as the city's number one scavenger.

He began his collection in the middle 1950s by picking up old postcards, then began gathering anything associated with Tulsa or IT (Indian Territory) — a meal ticket to the old Brady Hotel, a brick engraved with PLEASE DON'T SPIT ON THE SIDEWALK, a 1905 Commercial Club Booster button, maps, souvenir pencils, an Indian head nickel the size of a satellite dish. Alleys were his favorite source, but condemned buildings were also rich depositories of old cityscapes (banks were the best). The wrecking ball of urban renewal was a boon, allowing him to sift through the rubble for black-and-white images of a movie theater showing *Mrs. Miniver* to raise war bonds, of the skyline in dozens of incarnations, of nondescript streets and buildings and people whose only import was that they were part of Tulsa. Ford rummaged through attics, digging through layers of history — old checkbooks, yellowed business cards, invitations to "hen fights" — left by successive homeowners. He walked into decrepit buildings, pulled up the linoleum, and rescued old newspapers. He went to yard sales, auctions, and pawnshops, amassing nine hundred pounds of vintage newspapers, seven hundred pounds of silver-plated flatware from the Hotel Tulsa, pieces of a *Tulsa World* printing press, and a watch from Tulsa's first jeweler. Nothing interfered with his obsession. Driving to dinner with his wife, Lydia, he would spot something promising, like a trash can or an abandoned building, slam on the brakes, whip the car around, and pursue his treasure.

Ford did not limit his search to Tulsa. A plumber doing work for him once mentioned that he thought he saw a photograph of Tulsa at a shop in Rogers, Arkansas, 115 miles away. The following day Beryl told Lydia they were going for a ride.

"Where are we going?" she asked.

"Rogers, Arkansas."

They found the photograph.

"It needs to be home in Tulsa," Beryl told her.

Lydia vacillated between resignation and exasperation over her husband's obsession. "He would go out and get so engrossed in searching for something, he wouldn't notice it was dark outside and he'd forget that it's ten o'clock," she said. "You don't know how many times I've thrown up my hands and said, 'Do you want a family or do you want that darn history?' "

That "darn history" was now under assault in newspapers, television programs, and documentaries, fueled, according to Ford, by reckless comments from riot survivors and the commissioners. Ford attended many commission meetings and voiced his opposing views in a meeting with the chairman, Bob Blackburn. The matter eventually went to the Oklahoma legislature, where Ford had the ear of at least one senator — his brother, Charlie, who by 2000 had been a state lawmaker for thirty-four years. As the commission was preparing its final report, Beryl was undergoing radiation and chemotherapy for rectal and colon cancer. He wore two hearing aids, he couldn't eat solids, and he was suffering from radiation burns, swollen lips, exhaustion, and other side effects. But he still took anyone interested to his muggy warehouse, where Tulsa's sprawling, glorious history came alive in mounted panoramas of the skyline or in banner headlines declaring the end of World War II. With a loud fan humming nearby, Ford sat next to a stack of newspapers with riot stories designated by pink markers. Forty-four years of smoking had made his voice coarse and gravelly, but the cancer had not mellowed his temper.

"Blacks say they pass their heritage down at the knees of their grandparents," he said. "Well, what if you don't have very smart grandparents?" He occasionally made other disparaging remarks, but he said his anger was not rooted in racism but in his belief that blacks were distorting history for personal publicity and aggrandizement and that his city had been unfairly maligned.

As Ford saw it, the first misconception about the riot was how it began. He didn't believe that the notorious *Tribune* editorial was ever written. It wasn't there now, and it had never been reprinted by other journalists. "If somebody read it," he said, "surely they would have given a synopsis." And if the editorial existed, why didn't anyone know what it said? "All they can say is, 'There's going to be a hanging of a nigger tonight,' or something like that. That's all they can come up with. Well, hell, if they can read, they'd remember." The second misconception was that blacks came to the courthouse to prevent a lynching from a white mob. According to his sources, the blacks reached Fifteenth Street and without provocation fired their weapons. "The whites weren't a mob," Ford said. "They came because they heard the coloreds were going to storm the courthouse."

After several forays by car, he said, a group of two hundred blacks marched from the railroad station toward the courthouse, but thirty-member detachments would fall out and hold positions as protection. "Some of the coloreds had been in the service and knew what military action meant," Ford said. "They were protecting their rear. If they started out with two hundred, they arrived with eighty or ninety at the courthouse, so if a fight started, they could go back through their own lines, and the rear guard could slow [the whites] down so that everybody could make it back to Greenwood."

He did not believe three hundred people could possibly have been killed, and he used his own experience killing chickens to make the point. "I used to try to catch chickens, and they're hard to catch," he said. "You got to take a hand ax and kill it, let it flop around and die. Well, [the blacks] were not lined up ready to be killed, eager to be slaughtered. You'd have to chase someone to kill him, and it would take you a while to do that. Then you would have to get all those bodies together and load them up on some sort of trucking vehicle . . . It would probably take forty trucks to get them all out of here, and there weren't that many damn trucks available."

He could also explain the many reports of crates, or wooden boxes, that were used as coffins to transport bodies on flatbed trucks.

At the time of the riot, construction had begun on a sewer line along the edge of a cemetery, and wooden boxes were used to carry materials to the site. Witnesses assumed they were being used for bodies. Similarly, huge holes that were being dug for the construction could have been seen as a mass grave. Ford also ridiculed claims that bodies were eliminated by fire ("you can't burn a body in a fire; you need a crematorium") or by drowning. (Bodies would have either floated downstream or at least been visible on the water, but such reports were never made.)

What most infuriated Ford was the claim that planes were used to drop explosives on Greenwood. It was the ultimate slander — not against Tulsa's elite but against the aviators Ford had admired as a youth, sought to emulate in World War II, and promoted his entire life as part of Tulsa's rich heritage. The open-cockpit aircraft flown in the early 1920s, called Jennies, were made of wood and thick canvas, with flammable paint, and no pilot would have lighted an explosive in such a craft. The aviators "were like teenagers with their first damn automobile. They wouldn't abuse it," he said. The planes "were so fragile they had to keep them in hangars and barns because the wind would sometimes damage them. Even some rain would. They pampered those things. Why the hell would they take a chance of setting them on fire with a cigar or cigarette in their mouth throwing dynamite out the window or the side."

He believed the logistics of such an attack could not work. "How in the hell are you going to light a stick of dynamite in an aircraft that's got a windstream? You can't even light a cigarette." Given the positioning of the wings and the cockpit, he thought it would have been almost impossible to hurl an explosive without hitting the tail of the aircraft. What's more, Ford said as a structural engineer he had done thousands of inspections both before and after blastings, as well as fire analyses, and the pictures of Greenwood after the riot lacked the signature marks of an air raid. An explosive would have left a crater in the ground, radiating "seismic vibrations" in all directions, with debris tilting away from the center. "If you light a firecracker on the grass, you'll see a small crater and blades falling like spokes from the wheel," he said.

But that pattern was not visible in the pictures. Rows of houses were toppled while rickety outhouses stood nearby undisturbed. "If you dropped a bomb, as fragile as [the outhouses] are, they'd be the first to go," Ford said. The debris and ashes also did not appear to be blown out from any "ground zero" but instead just fell in — "normal debris fall from a fire." Ford also noted that witnesses never described the feeling of a bombing — what he called "air concussions" or the sound of a blast — only the sight of the explosives. This omission supported his view that the bombing story was "induced in [blacks] by hand-me-down hearsay" to exaggerate what actually happened. He believed he knew where the story of the air raid originated. When the Ku Klux Klan marched in Tulsa on April 1, 1922, an airplane flew about the crowd with lights stretched across the bottom in the shape of a cross, and a newspaper published an evocative headline. Ford pulled the paper out of his own archive and triumphantly pointed to the top of the page: "Fire in the sky," Ford said. "That's what the paper wrote about the plane, and that was used for the riot description."

Blacks, he said, have completely reversed the purpose of the airplanes. They were mobilized after the riot to save blacks, not assault them. As scores of blacks fled to the countryside and began searching for food, white farmers saw them on their property and sometimes shot at them. When city authorities discovered this, they ordered three planes for reconnaissance and dispatched a posse of men on horses, the goal being to bring the black refugees home safely. Ford envisioned a scenario in which a group of fearful blacks saw "this flying machine" coming at them, then saw the posse, then panicked as both plane and horses tried to hem them in. As that incident was told over and over among blacks, an effort to offer protection transmuted into an aerial assault. "If I was a colored person, I'd be fearful too," he said.

Ford did not defend the destruction of Greenwood, although he did note that there were "lawless people on both sides. But now it's every black is a saint, and only the whites are devils."

He scoffed at the notion that blacks were mistreated after the riot. In his view, they were not incarcerated at detention camps — let alone "concentration camps," as some blacks contended — and they did not suffer at the hands of the police or the National Guard.

Rather, they were given protection, food, clothes, and medicine and were offered jobs. The city was faced with a massive logistical problem — what to do with more than 6,000 homeless Negroes — and its response reflected the resourcefulness of its people and the generosity of its institutions.

The black refugees, Ford said, were well treated at McNulty ballpark. "There were bleachers behind first base and third base, and underneath one was the home team's facilities, with lockers, shower, and toilets; and beneath the other was the visitors' facilities. So they had sanitary facilities and they had shelter. The infield was like a lawn, and the outfield was a little bit rougher but good. It was in the summertime, and they had green grass and a good place to set up tents and they had room to wander around. Plus, there was a ten-foot fence around the park to protect against anybody who would want to snipe at them or holler at them or cause a disturbance. Sure, they were concentrated, but they were catered three times a day for meals by ladies from the church, and the clothes were brought by other humanitarian groups. This place had all these attributes, but [blacks today] don't recognize it as anything but a Goddamn concentration camp."

Refugees had also been taken to the city fairgrounds, where a large barn was converted into a homeless shelter. Called the Kafircorn Palace, it had been built for the International Dry Farming Congress, a major convention. "It was just a barn, but a good barn, and in 1921 it wasn't even ten years old," Ford said. "It had a concrete slab floor, and in one wing prize cattle were shown. There were concave platforms where you could groom cows, and there were locker rooms and toilet facilities."

The green cards given to the blacks who left the fairgrounds in the custody of an employer were not stigmas but badges of honor. "If [the blacks] had jobs, they would tell [the authorities] who they were working for, and if they were a trusted employee and were not about to get fired the day before the riot, the employer would come and get them and sign them out with a green card," Ford said. "They could come and go between seven in the morning and seven in the evening.

"Where the meanness came in," he continued, "is that there were a lot of coloreds who were unemployed, dope dealers, and gamblers, and nobody could vouch for them. So they stayed in detention and were made to work. They were made to pick up papers and clean the area and do chores. And they got madder than hell. They were big shots. 'I got a diamond in my teeth and a big watch, and now I'm being asked to pick up papers.'"

To many refugees, Ford said, detention was a blessing because they were treated by doctors. "They were checking for general health, particularly for venereal disease. There were fifteen hundred cases, including two hundred twenty cases of syphilis, and several cases of tuberculosis and several cases of chicken pox. They were trying to administer them." Most of the blacks, he said, "were appreciative that they had a place to sit down, to rest, to lay back, and to ask questions and get answers." Even the notorious fire ordinance, to Ford, had a benevolent purpose: the city had allowed black Tulsans to construct homes and businesses without adhering to the building code, but now Greenwood could rebuild a better and safer community if it did follow the code, including the fire ordinance. By resisting it, blacks "built back the rattiest bunch of crap you ever saw," Ford said.

He had ongoing personal feuds with both Don Ross ("We've been arguing about this for thirty-five years, and he hasn't learned a damn thing") and Scott Ellsworth, who met Ford when he was doing research for his book. But Ford seemed most outraged by the "pitiful" black survivors whose word had become gospel. "We've got these one hundred twenty-five alleged survivors, and the memory of a seven-year-old on his eightieth or ninetieth birthday is pretty thin," he said. "But we're disrespecting them if we don't accept what they say as carte blanche. Well, I'm not disrespecting their story, but they're just mistaken."

The riot fabrications, he said, were part of a plan to humiliate Tulsa so badly that only by compensating the victims would the smear campaign end. He called it an "airtight myth" to get reparations.

While the commissioners may have seen Beryl Ford as a cantankerous voice of dissent, he represented the mainstream views of white

Oklahomans of his era and perhaps later times as well. He also had energetic allies. The most strident was Bill O'Brien, whose Tulsa of the 1940s was a place of outdoor cotillions at Southern Hills Country Club, the Hotel Tulsa, and the Renaissance Garden of the Philbrook Museum. "These were the things money built," he said. "We'd have a major orchestra, and the men wore tuxedos and the women wore long dresses. The white roses were blooming, the moon was above, and my God, you could be in France or Venice."

O'Brien, who served in the Marine Corps, had a personal tie to the riot: his father, a decorated war veteran, had participated as a member of the American Legion. "They saved the damn city from militant blacks," O'Brien said. The riot was a Negro uprising, perhaps supported by blacks from other cities, and now the whites who risked their own lives to protect Tulsa — including his father — were being ridiculed and dishonored.

Bob Norris did not need to vindicate his father, but he did want to redeem the white race in general and the National Guard in particular. A lawyer by training, he was a military buff and rare book dealer whose obsession with the riot was perhaps unmatched by anyone else's. He attended virtually every commission meeting, notebook in hand, and he spent months searching libraries and government archives in Tulsa and Oklahoma City for riot data. He also swamped the commissioners, researchers, and reporters with riot calls and faxes at all hours of the night; a commission consultant bought a caller identification device just to alert him to Norris's calls.

His interest was not only in Tulsa's riot but also in mob psychology and the history of military actions in race riots. His principal aim in the Tulsa riot was to exonerate the National Guard, a group that represented martial spirit, discipline, and the rule of law. He gave a lengthy presentation on the Guard to the commission and shared his research with the members. He found materials that no one else had, including a 1987 audiotape of a guardsman, who recounted what had happened during the riot, and Norris would drive around town in his old white Toyota, listening to the memories of gun battles. (A bullet skinned the guardsman's neck, which was "just as hot as any poker you felt.")

But the Guard was not Norris's only interest. He frequently used racist language, denigrating blacks, Jews, and other minorities. In the armrest of his car Norris carried a small loaded pistol.

"It's for small blacks, small Indians, and small Mexicans," he explained to an observer.

He was more pitiful than dangerous, a short, plumpish man in his middle fifties who stuttered noticeably, lived by himself, and ate alone on his birthday. But his view of the riot was revealing. He resented the commission's work, telling a reporter that it was "therapy for neurotic Negroes." What he resented most, however, was the "myth" of black supremacy.

"In the past few years," Norris said, "you've had this myth that 'we would have won the race riot except for the National Guard and the airplanes.' People live by myths and they're made up of whole cloth. No, you weren't winning. You were outnumbered ten to one."

This misrepresentation, he said, was now being used to claim justice. "They want an apology from everybody, they want reparations, and they want a myth — a state-certified myth," he said. "It's unhealthy, and it bothers me the most because it perpetuates the idea that [blacks] are never going to get a break, that all whites are against us, that life is an ongoing race war. At some point, you have to take responsibility. You have to say 'Wait a minute, some members of our tribe ain't acting responsibly and it's hurting us all.'"

Beryl Ford, Bill O'Brien, and Bob Norris all found evidence to support some of their positions. Ford, for example, raised legitimate doubts about an aerial bombing, and Norris made a reasonable case that the National Guard didn't have the manpower to protect Greenwood. But they constantly undermined their own credibility by failing to acknowledge fully the crimes committed against black Tulsans. O'Brien's insistence that blacks fired the first shot, even if true, might justify retribution against those individuals, but it did not excuse the wholesale looting and burning of Greenwood. Norris's view that the National Guard rescued blacks is hardly consistent with the photographs of blacks marching like prisoners with their hands above their heads (black witnesses gave conflicting accounts of the Guard's role), and the soldiers' own riot reports, describing gun battles in the Negro "settlement," suggest that the state militia at times joined the mob against African Americans. And Ford's description of the detention centers as comfortable ignores that the innocent refugees were detained against their will and were temporary wards of the state.

But over a two-year period, Ford, O'Brien, and Norris wrote their own history of the riot in lengthy reports, with maps, charts, and footnotes. Just as the commission tried to find evidence that incriminated government officials, proved a planned conspiracy, or disclosed a mass grave, these men tried to demonstrate that the riot was a Negro uprising that elicited justifiable police action followed by humanitarian aid.

In the end, these two histories — the same parallel narratives that had existed for eighty years — would be submitted to the state lawmakers. Through legislation they would judge whose history was fact, whose was myth, and what resolution would be just.

The Survivors

THE ESCALATING RHETORIC between the blacks who wanted revenge and the whites who disavowed responsibility focused even more attention on the survivors. They had lived in obscurity for almost eight decades, but now they were interviewed by reporters, featured on television, photographed by national magazines, and sought out by church groups and civic or social organizations. Some relished the attention while others shunned it, but the exaltation represented a bizarre twist for a group whose lives had previously generated scant attention. Suddenly these men and women, their faces lined, their shoulders hunched, their hair white, were being celebrated as heroes, yet their acclaim was not for anything they had said or done. They had survived, and that was good enough. Most seemed appreciative, if bewildered; surviving the race war was the least of their accomplishments. It was the next eighty years that had been difficult. They had all moved on from the riot long before, but they all had their own ideas on how justice should be served.

George Monroe was probably the riot's the most famous survivor, an endearing octogenarian who became the self-effacing ambassador of Greenwood. He was a close friend of Scott Ellsworth's, who steered reporters from the United States as well as Germany, France, and England to his front door. Monroe would meet them on his sagging porch, give them a penny that had been charred in the riot, and show them a picture of the ten dimes left in his family's mailbox that had been seared together by the fires. His story of how his fingers were stepped on by white thugs, how his sister covered his mouth to muffle his scream, how the flames inspired the question "Is the world on fire?" — all captured the horror of the event through the eyes of a five-year-old, and the anecdote became a defining moment in the rediscovery of the riot.

His presence lent a saintly endorsement to events in North Tulsa. On a warm summer evening in 2000 he was invited to the Rudisill Regional Library, where a fringe group dedicated to African spirituality had convened. As three black women in white headdresses danced barefoot in a circle, he sat quietly in a dark blue suit, starched white shirt, and straw hat. Monroe didn't really know why he was there amid the din of thumping drums, high-pitched cackles, and exuberant chants. The group's message that blacks could flourish only by rediscovering their African roots held no appeal for him, but he'd accepted the invitation anyway.

"Today we have a survivor!" a man wearing gold beads bellowed into a microphone to the sounds of applause and drumbeating. "We have George Monroe here today!"

The guest of honor walked gingerly to the front and kept his eyes down as he spoke into the microphone. "I was in the race riot," he said slowly. "I was five years old, but it's a memory I carry with me these eighty years, and right now everybody is trying to make me a celebrity. Do I look like a celebrity to you?" The crowd laughed and cheered. Monroe paid tribute to his father, who raised four children by himself, and said he was proud that so many had come to a meeting of any kind in North Tulsa. "It's good to see everybody, and I thank you very much."

Above the ovation, a stranger yelled, "Mr. Monroe, you're my hero!"

He lived in a small one-story house with frayed red carpet, worn furniture, and framed photographs of his four sons hanging on cracked walls in unkempt rooms. He had buried two wives, three siblings, and two sons, including one, a lawyer, who had been killed by a stray bullet as he sat in a Chicago restaurant. He lived with a mutt named Toy. "She's my little heart," he said. "We get along fine." He could be found most days in a long-sleeve work shirt trimming hedges in his large yard, tending his flower garden, and rocking on his front porch. "I can be a bit of a tramp," he explained.

A college graduate, Monroe made history in 1939 when he became Coca-Cola's first black salesman in Tulsa. His route, of course, was limited to Greenwood and other black areas, but he proudly drove the company truck, wore the company uniform, and posed for many photographers. He was also popular because he received the company's permission to hand out free sodas at high school baseball games when Greenwood's team hit a home run. After serving in World War II in a gas supply company, he returned home and worked for the county sanitation department. For many years he also ran a popular nightclub, The Pink House, where civil rights activists in the 1960s convened to plot strategy beneath low pink ceilings; Monroe himself played the drums in a band.

Despite his modest lifestyle, Monroe was financially secure. He had been employed for most of his life, was frugal with his money, and had received more than $100,000 from a life insurance policy after his sister died. But he also believed, on principle rather than need, that he was owed reparations. The riot had destroyed his family's house and business, a skating rink, and afterward his father could find a job only as a janitor earning $14 a week. Osborne Monroe had filed lawsuits against the city of Tulsa and the Northern Assurance Company Limited of London, claming losses of $18,182.26. But the suits had been dismissed and his losses never restored.

George Monroe was not a reparations activist, but he helped to create one in Scott Ellsworth. When he began looking into the riot, Ellsworth adopted several black old-timers, including Monroe, who lived on their own. He drove to their homes with food, CDs, prescription drugs, and other necessities; he repaired their stereos, organized birthday parties, and simply talked to them. The old men were grateful. When Betsy Ellsworth accompanied her husband on one visit, Monroe prepared a big card in his dusty living room that said, "Welcome Mrs. Ellsworth." A long-stemmed rose lay at its side.

Scott Ellsworth's interest in the riot had long been historical, not political, and he had never advocated reparations or any form of retroactive justice. Now others were making the case, but even if he agreed with them, he didn't know how to calculate the losses fairly to make the victims whole. George Monroe had a different idea. He did not see reparations as a process of sifting through legal claims, determining liability, and restoring losses. They were, instead, a symbolic gesture that acknowledged the pain and suffering of the victims. "You know, just a little something," he told Ellsworth. "Just a little something would be good."

Ellsworth knew Monroe didn't need the money, but, he recalled, "I realized that even a token amount of a thousand or two thousand dollars had an important meaning for him, because it was about honoring his family and what they had lost. And I decided, 'That's okay.'"

Monroe, like most survivors, doubted he would ever receive payment, real or symbolic; he had other worries. His appetite was weak, some days he was too tired to answer the phone, and his habit of losing his wallet made him fear Alzheimer's disease. "I fight it real hard," he said from his cluttered living room, "but I'm half the person I used to be." Nonetheless, his celebrity had given his life unexpected meaning — "I got a call from England; that makes me international" — and he would keep telling his story as long as people would listen.

"You're on the face of this earth and there's only so much you can do, but every so often a little light will shine," he said. "Well, doggone it, if it's a light, let's turn it up! Because it's the only chance you're going to get of being somebody. So hell, I say turn it and let it shine."

When Veneice Sims laid out her blue silk dress and pearl necklace on the evening of May 31, 1921, she saw herself gliding across the dance floor of the ballroom in the Stradford Hotel. The riot canceled her first prom, forcing her instead to watch Greenwood's devastation from a friend's hillside porch. Her family moved to Oklahoma City — her father did not want them living in a tent — and Veneice always regretted that she did not graduate from Booker T. Washington. After high school, she married a forty-year-old man, but eight years later she returned to Tulsa alone. "I just got tired of him," she said. She lived in Greenwood for the rest of her life, working mostly as a

domestic for white families but also as a riveter at the Douglas Aircraft bomber plant during World War II. She never remarried.

Few riot victims evoked more sympathy. In 1921 her father was a
well-paid mechanic; the family lived in a house with three bedrooms, a kitchen, a breakfast room, and luxuries like a Victrola and a
good well. All was lost in the riot; not a single house was left standing
on her block. Now she lived in a tired frame house covered with
chipped green paint. The rug and drapes had holes; light bulbs were
missing from fixtures; couch pillows slumped from the weight of
time. A cracked mirror hung on a wall. Wearing a housecoat, she was
thin and wan but still smiled when she recalled playing high school
basketball in her black bloomers or going to the Dreamland Theatre
on crowded Greenwood Avenue. A road map of veins spread across
her bronze hands, and a tear would sometimes run down her cheek
from a rheumy eye.

Most survivors favored reparations, but to Sims the whole question seemed out of context. Who could place a value on her home
and family belongings? How did one calculate the loss of missing a
first prom? What is the price of a senior year in high school, of a
neighborhood, of innocence, all of which Sims lost in the riot? Compensating her now seemed a peculiar gesture. "Most of the people
who deserve it are gone," she said ruefully. She thought the whole
premise of reparations was wrong: money could never restore her
losses, so she did not want some token payment to flatter the vanity
of whites who would believe that justice had been done. "Nothing
could cover what happened, so to tell you the truth I just rather they
keep it," she said.

Fortunately, her new celebrity paid an unexpected dividend. After learning about her aborted prom night, students at the now
integrated Booker T. Washington High School invited Sims to attend their Junior-Senior Prom on April 20, 2000. Sims accepted; she
wanted to wear the same color dress she had had in 1921. A dress
shop agreed to donate an outfit — something that did not show too
much shoulder — and she found a long midnight blue dress with a
black satin jacket and rhinestone buttons, accented by a gold necklace and earrings. On a clear velvety night, she was picked up in a
black stretch limousine and driven to the Greenwood Cultural Cen-

ter, where the auditorium had been transformed into a Roman palace for the prom's theme of Millennium Magic. An entrance featured faux columns draped in sheer white cloth and an archway of blue and silver balloons. Small round tables had mirrored covers with blue or silver skirts; a fish bowl sat on top with a floating candle and crystal marbles inside.

Escorted by her nephew, Sims entered the room and, according to one witness, "the people just parted." The president of the junior class introduced himself and accompanied Sims to her table. The boys, some with spiked hair, wore tuxedoes, and the girls wore formal gowns, although some preferred more revealing numbers — what Sims called "shorty-shorts." One by one, the students approached her, held her hand, and expressed their regrets that she hadn't been able to attend her prom. "We wanted you to have this night," one boy said. "We're so sorry people couldn't get along then." Another girl in a tight dress asked, "Do you recall your high school days?"

"In my days, honey, I wasn't allowed to go to dances like *that*," she said. "My daddy was strict!"

The disk jockey played hip-hop and rhythm-and-blues, and Sims enjoyed watching the boys "throw them girls around" on the dance floor. During a break, a student escorted Sims to the front of the room, where a throne covered in blue and silver crepe paper sat on a wooden platform. Sims, smiling and close to tears, sat on the throne and was crowned with a jeweled tiara as the prom's honorary queen. The students cheered, and a young man with a microphone sang a ballad. Sims beamed for pictures and softly voiced her appreciation: "Thank you so much. I love you all."

She mingled briefly and nibbled on some cake, then said she had to leave because "my daddy never let me stay out past ten." A small crowd followed her to the door; she left wearing her crown.

Standing outside Jackson's Funeral Home on the morning of the riot, eighteen-year-old Otis Clark saw a sniper's bullet crash into an attendant's hand, blood spurting on impact. With his home destroyed and his bulldog missing, he fled from Tulsa, boarding a freight train to Milwaukee in search of his father. At one stop, the youth approached a dairy farm run by an Italian American family and was invited for breakfast. Everyone at the table, including three children who were "fat and fine," received a tall glass of wine. "I wasn't used to that," Clark recalled. "It made me feel kind of funny."

He did not find his father in Milwaukee but on returning to Tulsa was told he was living in Hollywood. So Clark rode freight trains through the desert, drinking the water that leaked from a refrigerated car. He knew he had arrived in California when "miles and miles of orange groves" unfolded before his eyes in San Bernardino County. Finding his father, he stayed in Los Angeles and began what he called his years "on the wild side" and in the "sportin' life." He found odd jobs on studio sets while he lived in a hotel and bootlegged whiskey, keeping pint and half-pint jars under his bathtub. He was eventually arrested for violating the prohibition laws and sentenced to twenty days in jail. It wasn't a long stay, but it was enough to spur a life change in Clark. Each Sunday the Salvation Army sent two preachers to the jail for prayer meetings, and Clark, angered that his "sportin'" friends had not visited, attended one. He was not without a religious background — his grandfather had been a Baptist preacher — and he listened carefully to the ministers' appeal that he "get on the Lord's side." Something clicked.

"I went back on my little old steel bunk and had a dream that I was over the heavenly pasture, laying up on the air, looking down on the flower trees," he said. "It was a beautiful picture, and I wanted to go back and tell my friends what a beautiful picture that was. I went as far as I could go, and then a voice said to me, 'You can't go no further because between you and them is a great gulf.' At first I didn't know what that gulf was, but then I learned that when you get on God's side, you have to give up that other world."

Clark joined a ministry and traveled across the country to preach the word of God. He also found an unlikely calling as a servant to movie stars. When he married a woman who was hired as Joan Crawford's cook, Otis was part of the package and worked as a butler, serving the likes of Clark Gable and Charlie Chaplin. He said he once overheard Chaplin plotting his escape to England to avoid paying taxes, and he realized that even with his fame and money, the star wasn't happy. "That helped me understand that God's side is the best side," he said.

He stayed in California for most of his life, primarily working with his ministry. But in 1998 he returned to Tulsa after his younger sister, his last living sibling, went into a nursing home. Clark, by then on his own, moved into a shabby public housing project on Sunset Hill, and when he looked out of his third-story window he could see his old neighborhood. "The highway runs right over my grandmother's vegetable garden," he said.

Born in 1903, Clark was among not only the oldest but also the most vigorous of the survivors. He didn't wear glasses or use a cane or wear a hearing aid, and he still made cross-country trips for prayer meetings and other church work. In 2000 he drove his red Subaru by himself to and from Seattle, staying in cheap motels and enjoying the countryside. One stormy night that November, he drove from his apartment to the Greenwood Christian Center on First Street for its weekly service. The Subaru, with 137,600 miles on it, inched along as the rain slashed against the windshield, and the ninety-seven-year-old peered into the night. Asked how his eyes were, he said, "Oh, they're coming along."

He had a round face, an easy smile, and a sturdy build, easily filling out his blue three-piece suit. A silver chain with a cross hung across his vest, and his "clergy hat," a black felt number with a brown braid, sat on his head. The church itself was a converted factory that now sat in the shadow of building cranes, and many of the members, black and white, were young, wore blue jeans, and greeted the eldest congregant as "Dad Clark" or "Pops Clark." The choir, accompanied by a band with electric guitars and drums, sang, "Holy, holy is the Lord," and the congregants stood and stretched their arms, palms aimed skyward, and sang, "Hallelujah!" While their hymns filled the darkened room, Clark remained seated, his shining black shoes tapping to the music, his right arm waving back and forth, his eyes closed tightly, his mind deep in meditation.

The riot, he said on his way home, was what the Bible called "a hidden sin," which had to be brought to light. "We're suppose to repent over it, not just bring it up for argument, and we're suppose to do something about it," he said. "I don't think there's been repentance. A lot of folks don't want to realize that it ever happened, but it did set poor little colored folks back a long time." He considered his own wayward travels part of that legacy. "In my own operation, it broke up my schooling, cut off my education, and got me into the wrong life, the sportin' life. I forgot what it means to be right and wrong."

The rain was still falling as Clark turned into his parking lot. He cut the engine and reflected on the question of compensation. "I noticed in California, when the Japanese came back after the war, they gave them their homes back and they gave them reparations," he said. "They never gave us anything, but they laid it on the colored folks for starting it."

Reparations were owed, he said, "but I ain't losing no sleep over it. If they give us something, I'll use it for my church work."

He had made his own peace long before with the white mob. "God tells us what is right and what is wrong, and we're free to do what we want. He's that kind of loving God. He don't boss you around. But here comes the Devil, and he has the power of evil and he tells people on his side to love money, to love pleasure, and it's all right even if you have to kill someone. But by and by, we all have to give an account, and when the end comes, we will all be accountable to God."

Justice will be served, Clark believed, but it will not come by certified mail from the state of Oklahoma or the city of Tulsa. No public agency or private business could give him what he already had. "My proudest possession," he said, "is my memory of God's blessings."

He opened the car door and walked to his building in the rain. He did not need an umbrella.

Mabel Little blamed the riot for killing her husband, Pressley; he had contracted tuberculosis after the incident while working outdoors, clearing debris and building a house. Blaming the riot may have been a stretch, but Little had plenty of reason to be angry. The white invaders destroyed her beauty salon, her husband's café, their home, and their rental properties. All her life she resented that Tulsa had done nothing for Greenwood's rehabilitation, and sometimes her anger spilled over into a grudge against all whites. She rebuffed Scott Ellsworth's request for an interview in the 1970s because of his skin color.

Little was Greenwood's steely matriarch, a deeply religious woman who dedicated much of her life to youngsters. She bore no children herself but adopted twelve, most of whom she already had family ties with, and she brooked no misbehavior. When she discovered one son had snuck out a window in the evening, she locked the window and did not allow him inside until morning. She taught Sunday school classes at Mount Zion Baptist Church and emphasized diction and the memorization of scriptures. She often talked about Greenwood's pioneers as role models for discipline and sacrifice, but she avoided telling youngsters about the riot because she didn't want to anger them. She told black children that they could be what they wanted to be — not a self-evident proposition in Jim Crow Oklahoma — and she feared that knowing about the riot could dash those dreams.

In time she rebuilt and ran the Little Rose Beauty Salon until its demolition by urban renewal in the late 1960s. Little herself was a woman of glamour, with a taste for mink coats, designer suits, pearls, rhinestones, brooches, earrings, and stylish hats. She never smoked or drank, and even as she aged her dark black skin resisted wrinkles. Her refined appearance, however, belied her grit. In 1971, when Tulsa's Board of Education closed the George Washington Carver School, the only historically black junior high school in the city, Little was part of the group that staged a sit-in at the Educational Service Center. At seventy-five, she was the oldest demonstrator, and she took the closing personally because she had attended the school's dedication in 1928, when George Washington Carver himself spoke of his distinguished career in science. She was the group's spiritual leader — which was needed as the nine adults had no food.

"She kept reminding us that God always answers prayers, and not to be afraid of anything because God is with us," said Julius Pegues, the group's leader. After a day and a half, the police arrested the protesters for trespassing, and they left weary and exhausted — except for Little, who had brought her hairbrush and cosmetics with her.

"She was looking good when she went in, and she was looking good when she went out," Pegues said. (Carver was later reopened.)

By the end of the century her perseverance, her community involvement, and her feistiness had made her a revered, even legendary, figure. Even white Tulsans knew about her. The city proclaimed December 5, 1975, as Mabel B. Little Day. In the mid-1980s, she wrote the eulogy for her own funeral, gave it to the Reverend McCutchen of Mount Zion, then took it back to rework it. "Don't you rush through my funeral," she admonished him. "Take your time to eulogize me." But she continued to flourish, speak out ("God gave me this mouth and I'm going to use it"), and receive awards; the state named a day for her, and the Mabel B. Little Heritage House was dedicated outside the Greenwood Cultural Center.

But the awards and recognition had not calmed her anger about the riot. "I can't understand how people mistreat folks," she said in 1997. "What did we do? We never set anyone's house on fire in the south part of town. We never stole their things. We never went out there." She was outraged not only by the arsonists and looters but also by the "good whites" who did not come to the aid of Greenwood, who callously watched the devastation of innocent lives. In her view, the riot commission didn't need to find proof of aerial bombings or mass graves to show government culpability. The photos depicting the storefronts reduced to rubble, the houses reduced to ash, the children reduced to tears — that was her proof that government had failed to protect its own people. She viewed reparations as an obligation Tulsa had not only to victims like herself but to their descendants — indeed, especially to their descendants. "Our children have suffered," she said, "because their parents lost everything they had."

In 1999 Little went into a nursing home. She resented her loss of independence, but her pride did not crack. Each day she put on her lipstick, rouge, powder, and a salt-and-pepper wig, and she absolutely refused to take medicine. Even after she cracked a rib from a fall, she rejected the pain medication, asking for a Bible instead. Several hours later she announced, "I have no pain because God has healed me."

On October 4, 2000, she celebrated her 104th birthday. She wore a red blouse with a plaid jacket and skirt, a matching hat, and pearl earrings. Attending were Mayor Savage, the Reverend McCutchen, a television news crew, and several friends. The reporter, noting her breadth of experience, commented to another guest, "She's like an open library, but when she's gone, the library will be closed." The group sang church songs, the mayor read birthday cards, and the celebration was capped by a yellow cake with white icing, inscribed "Happy 104th Birthday" and decorated with four lighted candles. "I couldn't get all one hundred and four on," quipped her friend Clara Skillens. Little beamed throughout the affair. Asked the secret to a long life, she said, "Love God and love children, and that will keep you alive."

The following January 13, Mabel B. Little died. The Reverend McCutchen did not rush her eulogy.

John Hope Franklin, strictly speaking, was not a riot survivor — he did not join his father in Tulsa until 1925 — but their four years apart made John Hope a legatee of the riot. In the 1960s he had planted the idea of reparations with Don Ross, so in some ways he helped produce the commission that had generated so much hope and dissension. In his own career, Franklin had traveled from academic prodigy to literary personage to elder statesman, that rare crossover historian who succeeded both academically and commercially. "It would be folly for me to think that I can change the world with my words," he once said, "but I've tried." He had written twelve books, received more than a hundred honorary degrees, and was named chairman of President Clinton's advisory board on race. Despite his many honors, he still faced racial insults in unlikely circumstances. In 1995 he gave a dinner party at the elite Cosmos Club in Washington, D.C., and as he stood at the foot of a grand staircase, a white woman approached and ordered him to take her coat check and retrieve the garment.

Franklin said, "Lady, if you take this check and give it to a uniformed attendant — and they are all in uniform — perhaps you'll get your coat." He spun away. It was a pointed slight for a man who later that evening was given the Presidential Medal of Freedom at the White House.

In 2000, on the seventy-ninth anniversary of the riot, Franklin was invited to speak at a commemoration at Mount Zion. It would be the first time most people in the audience had heard him speak on the matter. At eighty-five, Franklin looked lean and elegant, dressed in a dark suit with a maroon tie; his only obvious sign of age was his closely cropped white hair and thin white mustache.

He began by noting that some years earlier, when he had received an honorary degree from the University of Oklahoma, its president described him as a Sooner. "I pointed out to him," Franklin said dryly, "that my people were here long before the Sooners." He recounted his father's move from Rentiesville to Tulsa and the anticipation of his family joining him. "We waited, and we waited, and there was no word. Then we waited some more, and there was no word. Then we learned from a news account that there had been a race riot in Tulsa."

It was, Franklin said, "an eternity" before the family was reunited. "That eternity was four odd years to be exact [and] for those four years I was denied the presence, the mentoring, and indeed the discipline my father could have given me during those pivotal and important years between six and ten."

When John Hope finally arrived in Tulsa, he learned about the riot by talking to his friends, who regaled him with stories of narrow escapes from burning houses. "And then there was George Monroe, who vividly recalled how he kept quiet under the bed even when the white hoodlums stepped on his fingers. Whenever I think of George Monroe after he became the first African American in Tulsa to drive a Coca-Cola truck, I wondered if his fingers ever hurt when he would get the Coke from the truck."

The riot's effect on those who experienced it, he said, was impossible to determine. "For me, it was like waiting for the next presidential election when maybe my side would win . . . four more years of being deprived of the separate but unequal education Tulsa would provide when I finally arrived in 1925. But the most profound effect in the long run is what it did to this city. It robbed it of its honesty. And sentenced it to seventy-five years of denial."

His indictment elicited applause. He then praised the riot commission's work while acknowledging its difficult task. "Make no mistake about it: the commission has an awesome responsibility. Given
the American taste for pseudo, salacious gossip, for intrigue, for ex-
ploitation, and even for violence, it comes as no surprise that the be-
lated public interest in the riot outside the city invites notoriety that
the city doubtless feels is both undesired and unwarranted."

Franklin paused. "That is something the city rioters, looters, and
arsonists should have thought about on or about June 1, 1921." That
line brought the loudest cheer of the afternoon. "Posterity has not
been charitable, for it has sealed the lips of those who should have
spoken and blinded the eyes of those who witnessed the tragic
events. Indeed a veritable conspiracy of silence enveloped a considerable portion of the city for some seventy-five years." Franklin
urged restraint among the conspiracy theorists, noting that they
were spending resources on a matter whose facts were self-evident:
"namely, that racial hatred and bigotry are so powerful, so full of
evil, so venomous, that they need no conspiracy or period of deter-
mination to do their destructive work. The Sarah Page–Dick Roland
false incident was sufficient in itself to produce the events that some
of us have had to live with for the past eighty years."

Now the time had come to act. "I hope with all my heart that the
commission and the people of Tulsa will arise to their responsibilities to determine what is best for the long-term health and well-being of the city. If it is reparations of some sort, whatever the amount
of dollars you settle on is a mere pittance compared to the three
quarters of a century of suffering on the part of the victims of looting, bombing, burning, and murder that so many endured.

"If it is reparations of some sort, then do it. If a memorial will
serve as a substantial and effective healing force that will contribute
to the future health and well-being of our city, if that's what you
want, then do it. If it is an annual day of remembrance and commemoration to pay tribute to those who were lost in the conflict . . .
if that's what you want, then do it.

"If it is all of the above or some portion of the above that will
bring peaceful closure to more than three quarters of a century of
suffering and agony and soul-searching and penance, then do it. But

whatever you do, it must be done in the spirit of goodwill and mutual respect, and even love. How else can we overcome the past and be worthy of our forebears and face the future with confidence and hope."

The remarks were eloquent and well received, but Franklin did not indicate what he himself would do. His reticence seemed an act of deference. Tulsa's favorite son had not lived in the city for almost seventy years. It was up to Oklahomans to determine the fate of the survivors.

Riot and Remembrance

Scott ellsworth spent two years commuting between Portland and Tulsa, attending commission meetings, interviewing sources,
scouring archives, searching for mass graves, giving media interviews, and constructing an elaborate series of maps that choreo-
graphed the riot. He had assembled a team of scholars who would
draft reports on different aspects of the riot, such as the use of airplanes, legal claims for reparations, and an analysis of property loss.
That research, in turn, would be used by the commission to draft its
own report, with its findings and recommendations, to be submitted
to the state legislature. On February 21, 2000, Ellsworth wrote a letter
to the commission's new chairman, T. D. "Pete" Churchwell, the
president of the Public Service Company of Oklahoma, who had
been on the commission since its inception, describing how the consultants' reports would be structured. He also wrote that the scholars
had amassed a great deal of "historical and scientific" evidence and
that "we now know more about the riot than ever before."

Five weeks later, however, Churchwell informed Ellsworth that he
would no longer coordinate the research. Instead, the commission
was bringing in its own scholars, and individual members — not the
scholars — would have editorial control of their reports. Ellsworth
would have to co-author his riot analysis with two other writers. He
was being squeezed out.

Unknown to Ellsworth, he had antagonized many of the eleven commissioners as well as Don Ross. Some were unhappy that after more than two years of work, Ellsworth had not yet written a single word, forcing the commission to seek an extension from the state legislature. But the commission had only itself to blame: it had never given him a contract outlining a timetable or dictating the specifications of his report. It had given him free rein, and he had taken it.

Tensions also arose over personality and style. An academic lone wolf, Ellsworth could be dismissive of the commissioners' ideas and suggestions, ignoring their requests for information. He believed he was working for the taxpayers of Oklahoma — he would ultimately receive about $122,500, including expenses, for work spanning three years — and he thought he should be allowed to pursue the facts as he saw them. The commissioners resented this attitude.

"Scott suffered from a lack of political skills," said Bob Blackburn, who remained on the commission after stepping down as chairman. "I would say, 'Scott, this is what we need to do.' He would listen to me like you're listening to me, and then say, 'Okay, Bob, let me tell you what we need to do.' I just wanted to go over and wring his neck."

But Ellsworth had also been victimized by a deeply divided commission that could not have been appeased by any historian. On one side, Eddie Faye Gates and Vivian Clark-Adams believed the riot was a planned conspiracy incriminating the local, state, and federal governments as well as businesses ranging from insurers to telephone companies (for allegedly cutting off service). All of them, in their view, owed reparations. On the other side, the Oklahoma legislators Robert Milacek and Abe Deutschendorf believed the state was not liable and did not owe reparations. The other commissioners fell in various places in between — and Ellsworth had displeased virtually everyone.

For example, he rejected the central claims of Clark-Adams and Gates — that the African Blood Brotherhood had played a significant role in the riot, that the violence had been a conspiracy to grab land, and that the Klan had been a meaningful participant. To

Clark-Adams, Ellsworth was no different than all the other white historians who wanted to ignore black voices. "They don't want to talk about conspiracy," she said. "That's not what Oklahoma wants to hear. That's not what Tulsa wants to hear . . . I don't know what Scott's motivation is, but if you are worth your weight as a historian, you will review and summarize all evidence available."

In fact, Ellsworth had researched these claims — he mentioned the ABB in *Death in a Promised Land* — but concluded that the evidence did not support them. That did not appease Clark-Adams, who was also incensed that Ellsworth had not completed his research by February 2000 — the deadline for the commission to submit its final report to the legislature. She urged the commission's chairman, Pete Churchwell, not to rehire Ellsworth. "He left us high and dry," she said. "If a black historian had done that, he would not have been rehired."

At the same time, Ellsworth believed that the National Guard had not only failed to protect black lives and property but also, in some cases, joined the white mob in attacking blacks. The Guard's role, he believed, warranted state reparations to survivors, a position that alienated the two legislators and a state bureaucrat on the commission, Milacek, Deutschendorf, and Blackburn. "There was a real movement to blame the state and the Guard, and [Ellsworth] was willing to jump on that conclusion without having a trail of evidence," Blackburn said. "Where did all that information come from? For him, it was, 'Trust me, I know where all the information comes from.' I'm not comfortable with that."

While Ellsworth might have been faulted for not crediting those guardsmen who protected both black and white lives, the Guard's reports indicated that protection was not always offered. Captain John McCuen described how guardsmen joined "civilians" in Greenwood firefights. "Little opposition was met with until about halfway through the settlement when some negroes who had barricaded themselves in houses refused to stop firing and had to be killed." If the Guard's job was to protect black lives, in some cases it failed.

The defenders of white Tulsa — Beryl Ford, Robert Norris, and Bill O'Brien — also ridiculed Ellsworth, believing he had been duped by the blacks. (Norris said the Negro settlement that came under assault by the Guard had been notorious for its "criminal element." His source? Beryl Ford.)

In the past, Ellsworth had been able to straddle the city's racial divide, but now the stakes were higher — a search for justice that could produce cash benefits to victims. The racial divide widened, and he was caught in the middle. To blacks, he was too white. To whites, he wasn't white enough. The bitterest conflict arose between him and Don Ross — the two men, ironically, who had done the most to rescue the riot from obscurity. They shared similar views on the riot, but they resented each other nonetheless. They both had professional and personal stakes in the matter, they both saw themselves as the true custodians of that story, and they both viewed the other as an opportunist exploiting a tragedy for personal gain. Their clash of egos raised the question — Whose riot was this anyway?

To Ellsworth, who dug out the story in the 1970s and delivered food to survivors in 2000, Ross had cared more about his political career than the riot victims. He begrudged Ross for putting his own name on the Black Wall Street memorial — Ellsworth would have put Mary Parrish or one of the Greenwood pioneers — and bristled when Ross, not he, received the lion's share of credit for bringing the riot story to life in a lengthy *New York Times Magazine* article, which mentioned him only once. He also chafed at Ross's frequent comment that "my anger is the riot's legacy", which struck Ellsworth as arrogant. "The legacy," Ellsworth said, "is about the town, the city, the country. It's much larger than his anger."

Similarly, Ross believed Ellsworth used the riot to raise his own media profile. The reporters who covered the story, most of whom were white, recognized Ellsworth as the riot's authoritative voice. For Ross, who grew up listening to firsthand accounts of the riot and often bragged that he had spoken to more survivors than anyone alive, that was unacceptable.

"Had Scott been hired as a PR and press relations person, I would give him an A plus," he said. "But as a historian, he flunks." He complained that Ellsworth was slow in completing the report — "We could have hired David McCullough for what we paid Scott" — and that he did not take orders from the commission. "I don't talk to Scott and I don't trust him," he said in October 2000. "I would have fired him."

Ellsworth was devastated by the commission's move to diminish his role. The commission had stopped funding his trips to Tulsa, and neither Blackburn nor Ross would return his calls. What hurt him the most was the attack by his fellow Tulsans, the very people he thought he was helping. "I think it's been one of the most painful things in his life," said his wife, Betsy. "He didn't think it would be as polarizing as it became." Betsy, who is white, learned something about the riot's awkward racial dynamics when she visited Tulsa and was approached by an acquaintance of her husband's. "You're not black?" he asked, as if an African American spouse would explain Ellsworth's interest in the riot.

At the time of his de facto dismissal, Ellsworth was reading Correlli Barnett's *Desert Generals*, in which an exhausted British general in World War II realized if he were tired, so too must the German general Rommel — so he attacked. Ellsworth, depressed and demoralized, decided to do the same to win his job back, and he had a general to help him prevail — John Hope Franklin. While Franklin had not done any research, he was cited as the report's lead scholar, and he gave the project obvious credibility. Franklin supported Ellsworth and his interpretation of the riot, as he told Churchwell in a withering conversation. "The light dawned on me," Churchwell recalled, "that there is a much closer relationship [between Franklin and Ellsworth] than I thought." Ellsworth was reinstated as the commission's lead scholar, responsible for writing the paper and coordinating the reports of the other consultants.

In November 2000 the report was completed and submitted to the commission, a 284-page document containing scientific, historical, and legal analysis, maps, charts, footnotes, and tangerine-colored images of "magnetometer anomalies" found beneath Oaklawn Cemetery. Though mass graves had never been found, Clyde Snow sup-

plied the riot's best new information.* He found the death certificates in the Oklahoma State Department of Health for thirty-eight
victims, all male — two higher than the "official" total of thirty-six.
Thirty-eight represented only the confirmed dead. Snow believed
that the actual count was much higher. Using the death certificates
and information from press reports and other documents, Snow
constructed a chart of confirmed riot deaths showing, among other
things, the names, race, cause of death, and wounds of the victims.

The data revealed the unequal treatment of blacks even in death.
Twenty-five of the thirty-eight victims were black. Of the thirteen
white victims, ten (77 percent) had been taken to hospitals, where
their death certificates had been signed by a physician. (It was unclear if they were dead on arrival or if they died after receiving treatment.) But only six of the twenty-five black victims (24 percent) had
been taken to hospitals. Four were taken to Morningside Hospital,
where the basement had been hastily converted to accommodate
blacks. (Greenwood's lone hospital had been destroyed.) The other
nineteen blacks (76 percent of the confirmed killed) died "on scene."
Their death certificates had been signed by the county attorney, suggesting that if blacks could not get medical help on their own, they
were left to die. "Doctors didn't come to Greenwood," Snow said. Indeed, none of the black victims was listed as having died on the evening of May 31, even though several newspaper and firsthand accounts described them lying dead or wounded in the downtown
area. By contrast, four whites were listed as dying on May 31, under-
scoring the swift attention that they had received.

Snow found the death certificate of an infant diagnosed as a stillborn. According to information from the Stanley-McCune mortuary, on June 1 the police brought in the body of a newborn infant
found in Greenwood earlier in the day by two white men. The body
was that of a black male measuring "less than twelve inches long." It
apparently bore no signs of trauma and was identified as stillborn.
The discovery not only captured the horror of the riot but also supported a story from Rosa Davis Skinner. More than seventy years

* Snow called his report "preliminary."

later, she told Eddie Faye Gates how a woman had placed her still-born baby in a shoebox for burial but then lost it during the riot. While black oral history was often criticized by white Tulsans as unreliable or sensational, at least one poignant story had been strongly documented.

Snow's analysis also showed that death certificates for whites had been filled out with far more care than those for blacks. For whites the age, wounds, address, marital status, and next of kin were usually complete, while for blacks that information was left out or filled with a hastily scrawled "don't know." As the always mordant Snow wrote: "Perhaps the [best] that can be said of the physicians, undertakers, police and prosecutors of Tulsa of the time was that they were not hypocritical: they treated their black fellow citizens no better when they were dead than they did when they were alive."

But Snow's report also gave ammunition to the white Tulsans who wanted to protect the city's image. Of the thirteen whites killed in the riot, only two were born in Oklahoma, and all but four bodies had been shipped to other states for burial. Only three burials were in Tulsa. At least four and possibly six were employed in oil-related jobs, while two were cooks and one a "laborer." All appeared to be of a low socioeconomic class except one oil company junior executive. However limited the sample size, the information supported the position that the violence against blacks was perpetrated by ruffians and transients, not the community's leading citizens. What's more, the data showed that whites died on May 31 at 8 and 10 P.M. — before the 10:30 P.M. courthouse confrontation.

Given the neglect of black victims, it was possible that blacks had been shot and killed before the whites but their deaths were simply not reported until the following day. It was also possible that the dead whites, James Paris and Cleo Shumate, fired first and were killed by superior black marksmen. But to Beryl Ford and Bill O'Brien, these white deaths proved that blacks started the riot by speeding into South Tulsa, firing their guns, and killing whites. "What about Cleo Shumate's descendants?" O'Brien asked. "Who's going to pay them reparations?"

Regardless of who "started" the riot, Snow's discovery suggested that by the time the first shot was fired at the courthouse, the preliminary skirmishes had already been fought, and blacks had spilled their enemies' blood.

In response to the consultants' work, Bill O'Brien submitted his own history of the riot to the commission, "Who Speaks for Us? The Responsible Citizens of Tulsa in 1921." The commission was free to use whatever sources it wanted to draft its final report; according to O'Brien, the riot was a "Negro insurrection" caused by "armed blacks" — a phrase repeated thirteen times on one page — and the National Guard engaged in skirmishes with "militant blacks." The "militant blacks" engaged in a lot of skirmishes, while the Negro district that burned down was hardly worth saving. "Most of the area was without sanitation or modern conveniences except gas and water. Streets were dirt roads without pavement or sidewalks. Many of the streets were un-named and houses un-numbered and general confusion was the predominant characteristic of the district before it was reduced to charred ruins by flames." O'Brien had reprised the white history of the riot on a word processor with computer-generated maps. Robert Norris, disputing Ellsworth's indictment of the National Guard, wrote a defense of the Guard, almost 300 pages long, relying on army riot manuals, old court decisions, and analyses on mob violence. Eighty years later, the riot's competing histories continued to flourish.

Some facts will always be in dispute. Who owned Greenwood? Property records are incomplete, but estimates vary from blacks owning 75 percent to whites owning 75 percent. A research analyst at the Oklahoma Historical Society, working for the commission, estimated ownership was about evenly split. But even accepted facts inspire different interpretations. Everyone agreed that a ten-foot fence surrounded McNulty Park — but was it to incarcerate blacks or protect them? Bags of lime were brought into the city after the riot — to whites many years later, they were to disinfect latrines; to blacks, to disinfect bodies in a mass grave. A merchant donated suitcases to the black refugees — were they a gift to blacks who had lost their luggage or a cruel joke encouraging them to leave? The donor's motive is unknown. The same was true of a merchant who gave black women washing tubs — a generous gift to help restore normalcy or a callous reminder of African Americans' roles in society? The arsonists, before torching houses, had pulled out items and stacked them on the street — to protect them for returning residents or to expose the inner lives of their owners? The act has been interpreted both ways.

Bob Blackburn hoped to create a "shared memory" of the riot by discrediting the false claims about the event. But when accepted claims can be used to construct different memories, finding a common narrative is almost impossible.

To examine all of the evidence and write its own report, the commission sought out Danney Goble, a middle-aged, motorcycle-riding white history professor with a penchant for irreverent comments. He once told a newspaper reporter: "The people in southeast Oklahoma don't think their day's complete until they've had an RC Cola or a Nehi orange and a Moon Pie." Some enraged state legislators demanded an apology, while others called for his dismissal from the University of Oklahoma. He said he meant no harm, noting that his own grandmother was from southeast Oklahoma.

Goble was an academic hired gun who had written half a dozen books, including *Tulsa! Biography of the American City*, commemorating the city's centennial in 1997. Though the book was financed by various corporate and government sponsors, it is probably the single best volume on the city. While he celebrated Tulsa's achievements, Goble also wrote about the often-sordid history of the city's race relations, including the riot. He had previously written about the blacks who had been expelled from cities in Oklahoma at the turn of the century. By Oklahoma's standards he was liberal — his first book was on the state's progressives — and was inclined to be sympathetic to minority viewpoints. His wife, Jane, a former student, was half Filipino.

When he joined the commission in the fall of 2000, he had more than 1,000 pages of records to review — lawsuits, transcribed interviews, newspaper articles, property records. At commission meetings, he was puzzled at how fixated some members were on seemingly tangential issues: Eddie Faye Gates on the airplanes, Vivian Clark-Adams on the ABB and the Klan. Goble was also concerned about the research Gates had conducted in searching for black riot survivors, which was one of the mandates of the law. Gates had contacted black newspapers and magazines, posted a registration form on the Internet, and relied on an informal network of sources to spread the word.

Goble noticed that the number of survivors increased from 29 in June 1998 to 61 in August 1999. Then, following the media coverage of the February 2000 vote for reparations, the number surged to 119, with additions surfacing from California to Florida to France. While the increase could have reflected the commission's increased publicity, Gates got little documented proof that they lived in Greenwood in 1921. (She asked for birth certificates.) Were they actually survivors or people looking for a payout? Goble wasn't sure. He was also concerned that while the commission had made an exhaustive study of black property losses, it had not done the same for white property losses, as the law required. White-owned buildings were also damaged — why weren't they accounted for?

His frustration peaked when he read the "preliminary" report for reparations drafted by Gates, Clark-Adams, and Jim Lloyd. "The Tulsa 'riot' was not a riot," they wrote. "It was a well-planned ouster of the Tulsa Natives from their stomping ground by grafters who saw the advantage of making the lands owned by the Tulsa Blacks in the Greenwood area into a commercial district." But the report cited no direct evidence (save the refugees who surfaced in New York) to support their claim. The report found culpability across all levels of government. City officials conspired to deprive blacks of their property and assisted aviators in their planned attack on Greenwood. The county sheriff "secreted Dick Rowland from the county jail on the afternoon of May 31, 1921," according to a 1972 interview with a woman who called herself Dick Rowland's mother (and contrary to the sheriff's court testimony and contemporary news accounts). The federal government was liable because the Thirteenth, Fourteenth, and Fifteenth Amendment rights of blacks had been violated. Also responsible were the Boy Scouts, as several news articles said that whites dressed in Boy Scout uniforms were part of the mob (why the entire organization would be culpable was unclear). And in its most far-reaching accusation, the report linked the U.S. Corps of Engineers with the Ku Klux Klan, whose Tulsa rolls of 1928–1931 showed many truck drivers, cement workers, and city officials. There was, however, no evidence that any Corps workers were Klansmen, but much of the report was based on inference and supposition.

"The truth may never be known about the 1921 Tulsa Race Riot," the report concluded. "Much evidence has been destroyed and/or hidden. The very act and extent of the cover-up in itself speaks of conspiracy."

Goble was livid. "It was a matter of professional respectability," he said. "How can you advance an argument by saying that no one ever talked about it, therefore it must be true?" He was specifically angry with the black commissioners, Gates and Clark-Adams, and he fumed at his wife: "This is crazy! Where do these people get off?" One day Jane stopped him cold.

"They believe it because it's the truth to them," she said. "Maybe you should ask why it's the truth to them."

Goble had thought about the riot as a trained historian using accepted standards of evidence. Race, to him, was an intellectual thing, a historical thing — he understood slavery and Jim Crow — but what did it mean to be black? "It occurred to me that race was not something I could understand if I were not black," he said, "but race for some people is the single most defining quality of their lives. Being black has something to do always with where they are and what they are doing."

Goble considered how his life would have been different if he weren't white. He would not have a tenured university teaching job in Norman, and he would not own a $140,000 condominium in a landscaped subdivision or a $32,000 car or a motorcycle or most anything else in his life. Few blacks in Oklahoma lived as comfortably as he, and he knew that being white gave him unearned privileges. That, he believed, was why many blacks accepted the conspiracy theory of the riot and why most whites didn't. Whites failed to see the evidence, but blacks lived the evidence every day.

This recognition allowed Goble to overcome his irritation with the black commissioners and draft the report. Moreover, it helped persuade him that reparations were indeed warranted. When hired for the job, he had privately opposed them for the same reasons most Oklahomans did — taxpayers today are not responsible for the misdeeds of history. But now he felt he could marshal a case for compensating victims.

January 5, 2001, was a cool, sunny day in Tulsa, and the commission convened at the Greenwood Cultural Center to confer with Goble about his report, which would be submitted to the legislature in February. The commission's work had spanned almost four years; now the end was in sight. It should have been a time of relief. Instead, the meeting represented the most polarizing and at times hostile gathering yet.

The racial divide had been growing in recent months. At Don Ross's behest, the commission changed its stationery from the Oklahoma seal to the African national colors of green, black, and red. Gates and Clark-Adams wore REPARATIONS NOW buttons. At the meeting itself, an audience of about a dozen people showed up, and for the first time whites sat on one side and blacks on the other. The commissioners were also seated along racial lines.

The audience included the diligent troika of Beryl Ford, Robert Norris, and Bill O'Brien, carrying pens and notepads and making sure that no slander against Tulsa would go without rebuttal. Ford, wearing a tan blazer and red and gold tie, had attended numerous meetings but had never addressed the group. That day he was recognized, and he took a chair in front of the horseshoe table. He gave a lengthy overview of his credentials as an explosives and aviation expert, then explained why he did not believe Greenwood suffered an aerial assault, noting that the pictures showed no signs of explosions. He continued to talk as Clark-Adams rose from her seat and circled around the room, ignoring him. Gates appeared similarly distracted at the table. Ford explained why homemade incendiaries would have been impractical in open-cockpit, wood and fabric aircraft.

Clark-Adams, sitting down again, reminded Ford of the black survivors who said they were shot at and firebombed from the sky. "How could you discount all those eyewitnesses?" she asked. "Because they are black, their stories are discounted? I find it hard to believe all those people were wrong."

"I don't know," Ford said. "Talk to a physics teacher."

"Who do you believe?"

"I don't know, but talk to a physics teacher," he repeated. "I'm not disrespecting their stories, but you have to look at the facts."

Rising from the "black side" of the audience was a woman named Karen Simpson, who wore a large Angela Davis Afro wig as an expression of black solidarity. She was angry and loud. "I resent that!" she said. "You're saying that my mother and grandmother are both liars." She said that her mother's white employer had picked up her family before the riot — implying it had been planned — and they watched the fight, including an aerial bombing, from the employer's house overlooking Greenwood. She made it clear she did not want another memorial, which was then being discussed in the legislature. "Instead of you people dedicating five million dollars for a memorial to collect mold, mildew, dust, and whatever else collects on ozone-alert days, just to have something for people to hang their names on, that money should be dedicated to survivors."

When Simpson finished, Ford continued his presentation, theorizing that "coloreds" confused the FIRE IN THE SKY Klan headline from 1922 with a headline about an airplane assault. He mentioned "mass hysteria" among blacks.

"Oh, is it mass hysteria because they're black!" Clark-Adams snapped.

Ford said no, but the more he talked, the more intense were the exchanges. At one point he described the comfortable accommodations of the fairgrounds.

"I don't care if it was the Waldorf-Astoria," Clark-Adams said. "They were taken there against their will."

"What did you expect the community to do?" he asked. "You had 4,000 people homeless. The only place they could house and shelter a person was the ball park and fairgrounds."

Bill O'Brien soon stood up and said that the riot was triggered by "black militants" coming to the courthouse and driving through white neighborhoods. He also referred to the white victims of the riot.

"Every time you bring this up, you talk about the whites who got hurt," Clark-Adams said.

"That's because you people started it," O'Brien said. "You initiated the action, you started the shooting, and only after the whites got organized could they contain the blacks."

"They were freedom fighters," Clark-Adams said.

O'Brien agreed that if he had been black then, he would have been in the street with a rifle too, but added, "It was still an act of militancy."

By the time the meeting stopped for lunch, each side was calling the other "you people."

The commissioners and members of the audience walked across the street to a tiny eatery called Jordan's Fish Market, where the blacks and whites again sat at different tables (except for Jim Lloyd, who ate with the blacks). When Clark-Adams entered the restaurant late and saw the "black booth" filled, Randy Krehbiel, a white reporter with the *World*, offered her a seat at his table. She gave him a quizzical look; then Robert Littlejohn, who sat at the black table, laughed and said, "I think we better take the chair or there may be another riot." There were a few awkward chuckles.

O'Brien wasn't pleased with the day's events, telling Krehbiel that the story was harming Tulsa's reputation around the world. "I think you're way too worried," Krehbiel said, "about what they're going to think of this in France."

After lunch, tempers had calmed, and Ford answered more questions about the possibility of an air raid. Jim Lloyd had overheard Ford say at lunch that if he had to make an explosive devise quickly in 1921, he would have gone to a store and bought phosphorus. Now Lloyd, interrogating Ford as if he were on a witness stand, asked a series of questions to determine if the volatile compound could have been used for such purposes on Greenwood.

"You'd be a damn fool to do it," Ford said.

Goble, who would have to assess whether an air raid took place, thought that was a telling answer: he didn't say no.

When his testimony was over, Ford headed for the door as a black man called out to him, "You're a bigot and you're biased." Ford fired back, "So are you." Thus ended his day in Greenwood.

Though Danney Goble now understood the point of view of the black commissioners, he still didn't agree with them. But if his report didn't satisfy them, they threatened to write a dissenting opinion. A commission that could not determine the facts of the riot would seem ill qualified to make recommendations for justice.

Goble wrote for two weeks, seeking the right blend of historical accuracy, political accommodation, and eloquent prose. One Sunday he spent thirteen hours at his computer, wrote two paragraphs, then threw them out the next morning. In one passage, he used the cadences of Oklahoma cities (a device borrowed from a documentary film that made poetic use of rivers) to give the riot a historical context. The perpetrators' motive, Goble wrote, "was not to injure hundreds of people, nearly all unseen, almost all unknown. The intent was to intimidate one community . . . These are the qualities that place what happened in Tulsa in a territory outside the realm of law. And there waited company. It came from Lexington, Sapulpa, Norman, and Shawnee; from Lawton and Claremore; from Perry; from Waurika, Dewey, and Marshall. In each of these, entire black communities — every child, woman, and man — already had been driven out, its people expelled, in effect, rubbed out."

The commissioners, however, were less focused on Goble's literary style than his conclusions, and his first draft of some twenty-five pages drew fire. He made no reference to planned conspiracies, the Ku Klux Klan, the African Blood Brotherhood, or the federal government's responsibility in the matter. Gates and Clark-Adams wanted all of them included as well as a more incriminating description of how planes were used against Greenwood. Page by page, line by line, the other commissioners also weighed in with criticisms. Goble knew the stakes were high — the commission was writing the state-sponsored history of the riot — but he was still miffed. He had previously told the commission that the report should stick with what was *proven*, not what was *possible*, but some commissioners did not agree with that standard. "I was told Ellsworth was the problem, but that ain't true," he said.

This history of the riot included negotiated settlements on its most contentious points. In his final version, Goble wrote that many people, including some commissioners, believed the riot was a conspiracy. "This is a serious position and a provable position — if one looks at evidence a certain way. Others . . . see no proof of a conspiracy." He wrote that "another nagging question" was the Klan's role, noting that Klansmen were in Tulsa at the time of the riot. But did that presence mean "the institution may have been an instigator or the agent of a plot? . . . Not everyone agrees on that." In his first draft, Goble wrote that the consultant's report on planes "balances" competing evidence on their use in the riot.* Clark-Adams thought that "balances" suggested that the claims had equal merit, so Goble changed the word to "weighs." He then rewrote the sentence to say that the report "demonstrates" that the whole question had no easy answer. He also concluded that it was "possible" that shots and incendiary devices came from planes. Clark-Adams thought "possible" was too weak. Goble relented and replaced it with "probable." Responding to Gates's demands that the federal government be held accountable, Goble wrote: "Fifty years or so after the Civil War, Uncle Sam was too complacent to crusade for black rights and too callous to care."

The changes, while pleasing no one, went far enough to deter any commissioner from writing a dissenting opinion. More important, Goble's summary of the commission's findings repudiated the grand jury's conclusions from 1921, which had been promulgated by the city's pioneers and retained by certain white Tulsans ever since. According to the findings, black Tulsans had every reason to believe that Dick Rowland's safety was at risk; that the civil authorities deputized white men whose illegal actions added to the violence; and that the restoration of Greenwood after its systematic destruction was left principally to the victims. On the critical question of casualties, Goble deleted the confirmed death toll of thirty-eight after

---

* The consultant concluded: "It is within reason that there was some shooting from planes and even the dropping of incendiaries, but the evidence would seem to indicate that it was of a minor nature." Clark-Adams responded: "It's not 'minor' if someone is dropping it on your head."

Jimmie White, a black commissioner, noted that readers would focus on that number instead of the higher, if unknown, actual death toll. So Goble wrote, "Many people, likely numbering between one and three hundred, were killed."

In crafting his appeal for reparations, Goble adopted some of the arguments of the black commissioners, saying that the riot should be viewed against a historical pattern of discrimination in Oklahoma. He rejected the legal arguments for compensation, saying that proving culpability was the court's responsibility, not the commission's. The claim for reparations, he wrote,

> is not a legal argument but another one altogether. It is a moral argument. It holds that there are moral responsibilities here and that those moral responsibilities require moral responses now. It gets down to this.
>
> The 1921 riot is, at once, a representative historical example and a unique historical event. It has many parallels in the pattern of past events, but it has no equal for its violence and its completeness. It symbolizes so much endured by so many for so long. It does it, however, in one way that no other can: in the living flesh and blood of some who did endure it.

Goble argued that reparations could fuse the competing demands of justice and reconciliation. The event, properly understood, was not about "individuals," whose heirs still lived in Tulsa. But it was about Oklahoma — or rather, "two Oklahomas." The riot, he wrote,

> has lingered not as a past event but lived as a present entity [because] it kept on saying that there remained two Oklahomas; that one claimed the right to be dismissive of, ignorant of, and oblivious to the other; and that it had the power to do that.
>
> That is why the Tulsa race riot can be about something else. It can be about making two Oklahomas one — but only if we understand that this is what reparations are all about. Because the riot is both symbolic and singular, reparations become both singular and symbolic, too. Compelled not legally by courts but extended freely by choice, they say that individual acts of reparation will stand as symbols that fully acknowledge and finally discharge a collective responsibility.

Because we must face it: There is no way but by government to represent the collective, and there is no way except by reparations to
make real the responsibility.

When Goble finished his report, he gave it to his wife, who opposed reparations. She read it, then looked up at him with tears in
her eyes. "This is so pretty," she said, "I'm afraid they're going to get
what they want."

Gates and Clark-Adams still were not happy with it (the ABB had
not been mentioned) and were disinclined to sign it, but Churchwell
made personal appeals, visiting Gates at her house, talking to Clark-
Adams on the phone, and stressing to each that "it would be much
more powerful if the group spoke as one." They agreed — but
Churchwell still didn't get his unanimous vote. Robert Milacek, the
Republican state senator, refused to sign because he opposed reparations.

To most Oklahoma lawmakers, the riot was Tulsa's problem, and
they believed they had little reason to help the city.

In one of the nation's poorest and most backward states, Tulsa had
repositioned itself in the 1990s as a new-economy hotbed. During
the previous decade, the city had been hit hard by the energy industry's downturn, but its boomtown legacy — from impressive Art
Deco buildings to excellent art museums to lovely urban neighborhoods — helped lure new business, and the area was transformed
into a technology center for telecommunications, information sys-
tems, and Internet companies. This did little to ease the historical tensions between Tulsa (cosmopolitan, progressive, affluent) and
much of Oklahoma (rural, conservative, poor). By 2000 the Tulsa
area had about a quarter of Oklahoma's population but accounted
for between 60 and 70 percent of high-tech employees and revenues.
The state itself remained one of the nation's poorest. In 1997 its me-
dian income was ranked forty-sixth in the country — $7,000 be-
low the national average — and it was ranked tenth highest in child
poverty.

Tulsa had always been the privileged rich kid in a blue-collar family, and the state legislature would not be eager to send Tulsa money, for reparations or anything else. Oklahomans were also clearly opposed. According to a poll of seven hundred fifty people taken in December 1999, only 12 percent favored tax dollars to be used for reparations. A more remarkable result was that only 26 percent supported reparations *if no tax dollars were used*. Almost three out of four opposed private individuals using their own money to compensate black riot survivors.

Tulsa itself remained racially divided, with black neighborhoods extending several miles north of the old Greenwood district. But the racial boundaries that had been inviolable thirty-five years earlier had eroded. Integrated neighborhoods existed in northwest Tulsa, and African American families were now sprinkled through historically white South Tulsa — in some cases because bankrupt apartment complexes had been converted to public housing projects. These demographic changes, coupled with a voluntary school desegregation program that began in the early 1970s, increased the interaction between black and white youths. Other developments, such as annual Juneteenth jazz festivals in Greenwood and a nascent downtown entertainment district, also brought racially mixed crowds together.*

But in a city of plush country clubs, fine dining, and swank shopping, North Tulsa continued to be defined by hardship and neglect, which contributed to a longing for the Black Wall Street, fictional or otherwise. The community had no large supermarkets, no shopping centers, no hospitals, no theaters, no playhouses, no market-rate apartments, and no family restaurants, save one heavily populated McDonald's. The scars of the riot were still visible in abandoned concrete driveways and ghostly sidewalks, the exposed foundations of long-gone houses and large expanses of empty space. Some economic development had occurred — a campus for Oklahoma State University, the Greenwood Cultural Center, some rehabilitated storefronts on Greenwood Avenue — but most of it was either financed

---

* Juneteenth refers to the day — June 19, 1865 — that slaves in the Indian Territory and several states learned of their freedom.

or subsidized by the government. Private investment was virtually nonexistent. A number of years earlier, the Chamber of Commerce tried to persuade Wal-Mart to open a store in the black community, but the company refused, believing the income levels could not support even a discount retailer.

Other problems in North Tulsa, from infrastructure needs to crumbling houses to the underperformance of black students, deepened its despair, leading some African American leaders to advocate reparations as defined by Randall Robinson: public investment in educational and economic opportunities for black Tulsans. "If they're really serious about reparations, they should put the money in a bank and allow entrepreneurs in the community to get low-cost loans," said County Commissioner Wilbert Collins, an African American who is a former banker. "That to me makes sense, but doling out fifty thousand dollars or whatever it is to each family, that doesn't make sense."

An ice storm that swept across Oklahoma on February 28, 2001, signaled the chill that the commission was about to receive from the legislature. Its report would be presented at a press conference that day at the capitol in Oklahoma City, and three survivors, including George Monroe and Otis Clark, were driven the ninety miles south to attend. Monroe had never been to the capitol and, while walking up its steps, admired its white colonnades and gabled roof. "Damn!" he said. "Oklahoma sure does rate."

The press conference, in the Blue Room on the second floor, was covered by the *New York Times,* the *Washington Post,* the *Dallas Morning News,* and CNN, as well as state and Tulsa media. While Churchwell formally presented the report to Governor Keating, Mayor Savage, and other legislative leaders, the reporters had convened for one reason — to find out what the politicians thought about reparations. The report did not specify a dollar amount but let stand the commission's original vote for reparations, which included money for the victims' descendants.

With the survivors seated in the second row, Keating repeated his position that he favored reparations "if you can show liability on behalf of the state," which adroitly evaded the issue. Liability per se could only be proven in court — the commission didn't even try to show it — so the governor could appear sympathetic to the survivors without antagonizing the white Oklahomans who overwhelmingly opposed payments. Keating did say that he favored the noncompensation part of the reparations proposal: scholarships, tax incentives for Greenwood, and a memorial. Savage offered a similar endorsement. In the past, she had said she supported reparations to victims — but would not say that the city of Tulsa should pay them. Today, she said she supported measures that would "eradicate racism," such as those supported by Keating. Also attending were Larry Adair, speaker of the house of representatives, and Stratton Taylor, the president pro tem of the senate. Asked about reparations, Taylor said, "I don't know. I have not had a chance to read the report or meet with the senators. One thing is clear: what happened was wrong." When another reporter noted that the commission had made its recommendations for reparations more than a year earlier, Adair stepped forward. "I suggest we get some recommendations from the people involved," he said. "I think we need to be very cautious with how we spend the state's money, but the survivors who are here were wronged and probably deserve something."

At that point a black woman from Tulsa stood in the back of the room and yelled out: "I was born in 1955 and I consider myself a survivor because of the damage done in 1921. If you drive through North Tulsa today, you'll see we are still being affected." She went on for well over a minute, unnerving the two legislators, who left the room in the middle of her outburst. Savage and Keating then looked at each other and returned to the microphone. The mayor said she had never heard a survivor "ask for money," that the primary goal was to set the record straight. That prompted a rebuke from Eddie Faye Gates, who stood up to declare that she had interviewed all one hundred twenty survivors, and indeed, most of them wanted reparations.

By the end the politicians felt ambushed, the press felt their questions hadn't been answered, and the survivors felt depressed. George Monroe was disappointed that Keating did not shake his hand.

Asked by a reporter what he thought of the day, he said, "I wish I stayed at home."

Those who believed that Don Ross would push for government reparations were shocked to discover that he himself had abandoned the crusade.

"I've never said the city should pay reparations or the state should pay," he said after the report was submitted. "I don't care where they come from." He agreed with Savage's comment that survivors hadn't asked for money. "I've spoken to more survivors than anyone alive, and most don't even know what reparations mean and don't expect them."

Ross's sudden wavering seemed to confirm his critics' view that he had used the issue for self-promotion — reparations undeniably played well with his constituents. (He was handily reelected in 2000.) But Ross had good reason to change his tactics. Once the commission's work was completed, he had to deal with the legislature, whose conservative politics had few equals.

Virtually anything that required new state funds met resistance. In the same session that lawmakers would consider a riot bill, they revoked the state's vehicle inspection law because Oklahomans, they believed, didn't want to pay five dollars a year to ensure that their cars met the minimum safety requirements. It is unlikely that any discovery — short of a mass grave — would have led legislators to approve reparations. One Republican congressman, Kevin Calvey, said it would be "morally wrong" to ask his constituents in Del City, near Oklahoma City, to fund payments. He noted in a radio interview that blacks commit a disproportionate number of crimes in America. "Why don't we hold black Americans liable to white Americans for reparations for that?" he asked. Like riot reparations, he said, it would be wrong.

Dick Warner, who had done research on the riot for the commission, had his own reason for opposing payments to survivors. He had become friendly with Elwood Lett, the elderly black man who met Warner and Ellsworth at the Rolling Oaks Cemetery. When Lett died the following year at eighty-five — he was buried wearing his white gloves and usher's uniform from church — Warner thought it

unfair that reparations would be denied Lett and the other riot victims who had already died. Reparations, in his view, rewarded perseverance more than suffering. When Lett died, "they just crossed him
off the list," Warner said.

Other white Oklahomans who sympathized with the black survivors opposed reparations because they feared compensation would
generate a backlash against African Americans in general. In this
view, justice was indeed incompatible with reconciliation. Reparations, state Senator Milacek said, "would set back race relations ten
years."

Faced with that kind of opposition, Ross never pushed for compensation. "I'm belligerent in the art of stagecraft," he said, "but I
deal in the art of compromise."

He did sponsor a riot bill, but it offered little consolation to the
survivors or their allies. It called for up to three hundred scholarships for low-income students in Tulsa (not necessarily descendants
of riot victims), an economic development authority for Greenwood, and a memorial. But it allocated no money for any of them.
(Another bill had allocated $750,000 to design a memorial.) In the-
ory, the legislature could fund them in some future year, but there
was no guarantee. Ross called the bill "at best, an opportunity; at
worst, smoke and mirrors."

It was still controversial, however, because of a brief narrative at
the beginning.

"The root causes of the Tulsa Race Riot," it said, "reside deep in
the history of race relations in Oklahoma and Tulsa which included
the enactment of Jim Crow laws, acts of racial violence (not the least
of which was the 23 lynchings of African-Americans versus only 1
white from 1911) against African-Americans in Oklahoma, and other
actions that had the effect of 'putting African-Americans in Oklahoma in their place.'" Sometimes using the language of the commission's report, the bill rejected the claim that the riot had been a
"Negro uprising," outlined the financial and human costs of the incident, and said a "conspiracy of silence" had served the dominant interests of the state for seventy-five years.

These words should have been chosen more carefully. Race relations in the state were less the "root causes" of the riot than a con-

tributing factor, and a "culture of silence" would have been more appropriate than a "conspiracy of silence." Nonetheless, the language was generally accurate, but it still angered numerous lawmakers, including Beryl Ford's brother, Charlie. It "tried to accuse every white person for what a bunch of thugs did," he said on the floor of the senate. "There was plenty of blame to go on both sides. Unfortunately, when you're in the minority and don't have the numbers, you're going to lose."

In the last week of May, during the final days of the session, bitter and at times emotional debates broke out in both chambers. Though the bill included no money for reparations, no money for scholarships, no money for economic development, and no money for a memorial, Republican lawmakers were concerned that funds could be spent on any of those in the future if the bill passed. The "inflammatory" language at the beginning of the bill could also leave the state open for lawsuits.

But for Don Ross the language vindicated history: the state of Oklahoma would officially affirm that whites, acting in an environment of racial hostility against blacks, were responsible for the riot. As an author of the bill, he was responsible for carrying it through the house, which held a narrow Democratic majority of 53–48. The chamber itself, which had been renovated several years earlier, featured a stained glass ceiling and a green and gold rug, and the members sat at dark wood desks piled high with papers. As a debater, Ross was known for his booming voice, animated gestures, and quick wit. Now he presented himself as a humble team player. He had dropped his demand for reparations, he said, a month before and instead drafted a bill that in substance reflected the recommendations of the conservative *Daily Oklahoman*. He then drew on his own experiences to respond to a member's comment about the riot's unearthing the "pains of history."

"It pains *me*," Ross bellowed, "to know that in [Oklahoma's] constitutional convention, both parties barred African Americans from participating.

"It pains *me* that the first bill passed by this legislature was Senate Bill One, completely segregating the state.

"It pains *me* that the grandfather clause was introduced in this state, denying me the right to vote.

"It pains *me* that the only place you could get a higher education was at Langston, with no graduate school, but the legislature would pay your full tuition to go to school out of state.

"It pains *me* that I had to sit in the back of the bus by law.

"It pains *me* that I got hand-me-down books in school that were outdated and that had the southern point of view that was contrary to the way I had been taught.

"It pains *me* that I had no white friends until I was eighteen. I knew two. And one person in my neighborhood, he was called 'Mr. Bootlegger.'"

Ross, breathing heavily, used even more theatrics to describe Greenwood of 1921. "We pulled ourselves up by the bootstraps. We segregated ourselves. We left you alone. We shined your shoes. We grinned and we danced. Wasn't that good enough? And" — singing the following words — "we made money [and] we had millionaires, but we kept on dancing, kept on doing what you told us to do. We scratched our head when it didn't itch, and we grinned when it wasn't funny."

Ross then talked about the bill, which allowed him to believe that "down the road, a memorial is going to be built, scholarships are going to happen, reconciliation is going to begin. You see, I have to believe things like that, I have to have full faith." He tried to defuse the most frequent criticism of reparations, defined as any payment made for past misdeeds. "None of us are guilty for the sins of our fathers, but we are responsible for how we react to the evils that were done," he said.

The vote was taken and instantly tabulated. The bill passed, 53–45 — receiving only two votes more than the required 51. After another round of debate, a second vote passed, 56–44. (Lawmakers vote twice for each bill. The first usually reflects their conscience; the second, binding vote is an effort to generate bipartisan support.)

Meanwhile in the senate, Carol Martin, a Republican, offered the most inventive explanation for who started the riot. It wasn't the whites and it wasn't the blacks. It was the . . . Democrats. "What was the majority party that was in office the day the Jim Crow bill was passed?" she asked. "They were all Democrats."

The bill passed on the first vote by a close 24–20 margin; on the second vote, it was approved, 32–13.

On June 1, 2001, exactly eighty years after the riot, Governor Keating signed into law the 1921 Tulsa Race Riot Reconciliation Act.

There was little celebration. "It's scandalous," John Hope Franklin said. "Look at what they did for the Japanese and for Rosewood. [Oklahoma] is just waiting for the survivors to die, which is what they're doing. Not a smidgen." Currie Ballard, who had proposed the $33 million reparations package, said it was "an appalling nightmarish shame that people who lived through that could not even be given $10,000, or whatever token amount." Eddie Faye Gates and Vivian Clark-Adams continued their fight, joining a racially mixed group of liberal activists to form the Tulsa Reparations Coalition. Its goal was clear, if not the means to achieve it.

Scott Ellsworth, disappointed at the hollowness of the law, began making calls to Tulsa in search of private funds for reparations. He also made another trip home: on August 30 he delivered the eulogy at the funeral of George Monroe, who died at the age of eighty-five.

Meanwhile, Beryl Ford was also fuming. "We're the bad guys," he said. "Just all the white guys are devils. Nothing about humanitarianism." And the memorial? "Bullshit! Who wants to see a monument to a race riot?"

He hoped that the rest of the country would finally forget about the riot, but that wasn't going to happen. A few months later Crosby, Stills & Nash recorded a song about the event, "Dirty Little Secret." "A lot of people died," David Crosby said, "but very few people know about it."

Bob Blackburn acknowledged that the goals of justice and reconciliation were harder to realize than he had imagined, but he felt that the commission's work should be seen as part of a continuing dialogue about race relations in Tulsa. Clyde Snow wondered if annual reenactments of the riot, just like the reenactments of civil war battles, could raise money for the survivors.

Don Ross and the four other black state lawmakers donated

$15,000 toward a private reparations fund for the survivors, and the Chamber of Commerce began discussing the possibility of seeking contributions for such an effort. All the city leaders, black and white, hoped that a memorial would be built. Never mind that one memorial had already been constructed. A second one could be part of a Greenwood tourist site, which would include a museum dedicated to African American history and an entertainment district. But that would take money, public and private, and the new memorial itself — which would try to capture the meaning of the riot — would no doubt inspire the same disputes as the commission's report.

For its part, the state of Oklahoma gave each survivor a gold-plated medal with the state seal.

The night of May 31, 2001, was a balmy late spring evening not unlike the one in 1921. But instead of gunfire in the streets, there was *A Song of Greenwood*, a musical premiere about the riot. The show's creators, Tim Long (white) and Jerome Johnson (black), developed the idea while conducting integrated dance workshops with Tulsa's youth. The pair also worked with church groups, schools, and camps, and they recognized the power of music and dance to bridge the city's racial divide. While black youths went to swing dances and whites found the underground hip-hop clubs, their clothes, language, and attitudes blended together.

"The younger generation doesn't have a problem with that," Long said. "If we've encountered obstacles, it's mostly from older generations."

These incremental changes represent Tulsa's best hope for finding common racial ground. Legal segregation ended more than thirty years ago, but the segregation of history and memory persisted. That divide may never be bridged among the "older generations," but the youngsters who now play on the same football teams, attend the same workshops, and frequent the same clubs may find a narrative of history that brings them together, not apart.

A Song of Greenwood was performed at the Greenwood Cultural Center and featured actors from Tulsa exclusively. The characters of Dick Rowland ("Chance") and Sarah Page ("Jezzie") were lovers, and blacks and whites sang and danced together. But the production did not ignore the riot's tragic history, creating more emotion than the performers anticipated. In one scene, a group of "councilmen" representing the Ku Klux Klan sings a tribute to "Judge Lynch," and one character holds a noose around a black doll. During the song the actor, Bryan Blackwell, saw an elderly black woman in the audience and realized she may have been in the riot. He also saw a young black girl with pigtails, weeping. "I had to go offstage," Blackwell recalled. "The Grand Dragon [a character in the story] and I just went back and cried."

In the second act, a riot erupts after Chance rejects Jezzie, who cries rape. In the chaos that follows, a white man shows the newspaper headlined NAB NEGRO FOR ATTACKING ELEVATOR GIRL and TO LYNCH NEGRO TONIGHT. After the first shots are fired, Jezzie races onstage and admits that she fabricated the charge. But it's too late. The riot of 1921 leaves the stage covered with bodies. The lights go down, and when they come back on, the performers link arms and sing, "Tulsa, you'll survive. You made it through the night." Chance and Jezzie waltz onto the stage with their bags packed and their hands clasped, then disappear behind the set.

The story ends where the city's future begins.

Sources
Acknowledgments
Index

Sources

THE VERY THEME of this book — the dual narratives of history — presents obvious challenges. In writing about the riot, I had to sort through conflicting accounts and offer what I believe is the most accurate version of events. I placed the greatest value on eyewitness accounts, and several documents were indispensable in recreating the riot's general atmosphere and specific scenes of mayhem and in providing the dialogue at the courthouse and elsewhere on the streets of Tulsa.

W. C. "Choc" Phillips witnessed the riot when he was nineteen years old and wrote about it years later in a lengthy unpublished memoir. Phillips was part Native American — "Choc" referred to his Choctaw ancestry — but he identified with white Tulsans and, in fact, adopted the view of most white Tulsans that blacks began the riot. But he was deeply troubled by what he had seen. The title of his memoir, "Murder on the Streets," conveyed that blacks were not simply victims of random violence but they were murdered. His account provides some of the riot's most vivid scenes of mob frenzy and captures the attitudes of the white rioters. Originally I thought the rationale for invading Greenwood — to subdue a Negro uprising — was an excuse by white authorities to justify destroying the black district. But Phillips's memoir underscored that on the night of the riot, many whites honestly (but wrongly) believed that the blacks were trying to take over Tulsa, and from that miscalculation flowed the tragic escalation of violence. Phillips, who became a vaudeville show manager and a member of the Tulsa police force, died in 1991.

Court records also helped me recreate the riot. William Redfearn, a white entrepreneur who owned the Red Wing Hotel and Dixie Theatre, sued the American Central Insurance Company and the City of Tulsa for $85,618.85. He lost the suit, but the trial included testimony from nineteen witnesses, black and white, who collectively described how the riot unfolded from both sides of the railroad tracks. The witnesses included Barney Cleaver, O. W. Gurley, and C. F. Gabe, all of whom I quote.

Further details of the riot emerged in the trial of John Gustafson, including the testimony of John Oliphant, a white judge, and Laurel Buck, a white bricklayer; the transcripts are available in the Oklahoma Department of Libraries, State Archives Division, in Oklahoma City. The archives also include Governor James A. Robertson's correspondence regarding the riot and the "Federal Report on Vice Conditions in Tulsa, 1921."

The *Tulsa World* and the *Tulsa Tribune* were the source of many quotes, vignettes, and other details of the riot.

I relied on numerous recorded interviews of the riot. In the 1970s, the Oklahoma Historical Society sponsored an oral history project, recording the stories of the state's pioneers. Those tapes, about thirty that touch on the riot as well as Tulsa's early days, provided details for my story and confirmed broader themes in the narrative. In the 1990s, Eddie Faye Gates began videotaping interviews with black riot survivors; those tapes, like the audiocassettes, are available at the Oklahoma Historical Society in Oklahoma City. Scott Ellsworth's taped interviews, conducted in the late 1970s for *Death in a Promised Land*, were also helpful and are available in the McFarlin Library's Special Collections Division at the University of Tulsa. In 1983 KOCO-TV (Channel 5) in Oklahoma City produced a fine documentary on the riot, *The Greenwood Blues*, which also included valuable interviews with black and white Tulsans.

Two master's theses were critical to my understanding of the riot. Loren Gill's "Tulsa Race Riot" (1946), for the University of Tulsa, presented a clear framework for the incident and its immediate aftermath. Frances Dominic Burke's "Survey of the Negro Community of Tulsa, Oklahoma" (1936), for the University of Oklahoma, offered the most convincing response to the charges that the riot was a planned conspiracy among whites, and her thesis was also the single best document on the history of Greenwood. It must be said that Burke, who was white, displayed not only excellent scholarship but also courage to do what most white Oklahomans of that era would have never done: go into a segregated black district, ask questions, research, probe, and write a compelling academic report.

While Scott Ellsworth's *Death in a Promised Land* has been eclipsed by the report that he helped assemble for the Oklahoma race riot commission, his book still stands as a model of careful scholarship.

I also benefited from the consultants' reports for the commission, specifically those written by Ellsworth on the riot, Clyde Snow on the dead bodies, Dick Warner on the airplanes, Alfred Brophy on legal claims for reparations, and Larry O'Dell on the property losses.

The Oklahoma National Guard's reports provided important details on the authorities' response to the riot.

While the "white" narrative of the riot was easily discovered through Tulsa's white newspapers, the grand jury report, and Mayor Evans's public statements, the "black" version was more difficult to assemble. Tulsa's two black newspapers were destroyed in the riot, but many other black publications, including the *Chicago Defender,* the *St. Louis Argus,* and the *Wilmington Advocate,* wrote about the incident, and hundreds of riot articles from black or socialist newspapers can be found in the library archives at Tuskegee University in Alabama. The NAACP papers at the Library of Congress also include riot material, specifically on A. J. Smitherman. Mary E. Jones Parrish's *Events of the Tulsa Disaster* provided excellent firsthand accounts as well.

Two key figures in the book, J. B. Stradford and Mabel B. Little, both left behind a substantial record of their lives. Stradford was a frequent contributor to the *Tulsa Star,* and his business philosophy and his aspirations, for himself and his race, are eloquently expressed in many articles in the years leading up to the riot. His lawsuit against the Midland Valley Railroad Company for its segregated cars provided the dialogue for that incident, and his descendants have released excerpts of his memoir, which also provided important first-person accounts of his life. Perhaps the richest trove of information on Stradford can be found in the Oberlin College Archives in Ohio, which hold the Jewel Lafontant-Mankarious Papers (Jewel was a granddaughter) and from the alumni files of Stradford himself. The archives include letters from Stradford and articles about him, as well as interviews with his descendants and stories about their efforts to clear their patriarch's name. Finally, I had several discussions with Laurel Stradford, a great-granddaughter, who supplied additional information about J.B.'s escape from Tulsa.

Mabel B. Little's memoir, *Fire on Mount Zion: My Life and History as a Black Woman in America*, provided many details about her life as well as the early days of Greenwood. Little was also interviewed for *The Greenwood Blues* in the 1980s, and Scott Ellsworth made available a typescript of an interview she gave in the 1970s. In 1997 she gave a lengthy interview for the documentary *The Tulsa Lynching of 1921: A Hidden Story*, which ran on HBO Cinemax in 2000, and Mike Wilkerson, the show's producer, gave me the raw footage of the entire conversation. Finally, Clara Skillens spoke to me at length about Little's final days.

In addition to Burke's thesis, several documents helped me trace the history of Greenwood: Karl Thiele's "Racially Changed Community" (1962), a master's thesis for the University of Oklahoma; George Edward Gawf's "Negro Influence in Public Policy in Tulsa, Oklahoma" (1966), a master's thesis for Oklahoma State University; "A Study of the Social and Economic Condition of the Negro Population of Tulsa, Oklahoma" (1945) by the National Urban League; and "A Concise Review of Housing Problems Affecting Negroes in Tulsa" (1958) by the Tulsa Urban League. James Mitchell's "Politics in a Boom Town: Tulsa from 1906 to 1930" (1950), a master's thesis for the University of Tulsa, nicely detailed the city's rowdy early years, as did the unpublished memoirs of Jenkin Lloyd Jones.

Carter Blue Clark's superb "History of the Ku Klux Klan in Oklahoma" (1976), his dissertation for the University of Oklahoma, provided a road map for the Secret Order's activities before, during, and after the riot. John Higham's *Strangers in the Land: Patterns of American Nativism 1860–1925* provides a national perspective on the Klan.

In addition to the *Tulsa Tribune,* the *Tulsa World,* and the black newspapers already cited, I used the *Oklahoma Eagle,* the *Oklahoma Black Dispatch,* the *New York Times,* the *Washington Post,* the Associated Press, the *Kansas City Post,* the *Boston Herald,* the *Nation* magazine, the *New York City Call,* and the *New York Evening Post.* A number of specific articles deserve mention: *The Crusader,* "Tulsa Race Riot" (July 1921); *Crisis Magazine,* "Tulsa" (October 21, 1921); *Survey,* "In Full Bloom" (October 1, 1923); *Pittsburgh Courier,* "Tulsa — Little Chicago" (March 13, 1926); *Travel,* "Oil Capital of America" (January 1945); *Saturday Evening Post,* "Tulsa" (July 5, 1947); *Holiday Magazine,* "Talk About Tulsa" (October 1954); *Reader's Digest,* "Where Beauty Is Everybody's Business" (June 1957); *Tulsa Magazine,* "Say Goodbye to Greenwood Avenue" (November 25, 1971); *Journal of Black Studies,* "The Tulsa Race War of 1921" (March 1972); and *Civilization Magazine,* "Tulsa Burning" (February–March 1997).

Anyone who is researching a piece of Tulsa history would do well to start with the Settle collection at the McFarlin Library's Special Collections Division at the University of Tulsa. William Settle, a history professor, joined the university's staff in 1945 and spent years amassing government documents, records, reports, news articles, transcribed interviews, and other information about Tulsa. He did this, apparently, with the hope of writing a book about the city. He never did (he died in 1988), but he left behind about thirty large boxes of Tulsa history. They include the *Tulsa Tribune's* 1924 history of the city, *Tulsa: A Story of Achievement,* which provides an exhaustive account of the town's early years (excluding, of course, Greenwood).

Angels of Mercy: 1921 Tulsa Race Riot and the American Red Cross includes Maurice Willows's official Red Cross report and his personal memoir; the book was edited by his grandson, Bob Hower.

The best history of Tulsa is Danney Goble's *Tulsa! Biography of the American City* (1997). The first half of the century is chronicled in Angie Debo's *Tulsa: From Creek Town to Oil Capital.* The best book in untangling the land disputes in the Indian and Oklahoma territories is Murray R. Wickett's *Contested Territory: Whites, Native Americans and African Americans in Oklahoma, 1865–1907.* Other useful books about Oklahoma, Tulsa, and Greenwood include Courtney Ann and Glen Vaughn-Roberson's *City in the Osage Hills: Tulsa, Oklahoma;* Nina Lane Dunn's *Tulsa's Magic Roots* (which includes Loyal J. Martin's personal account of his role in the aftermath of the riot); John Gunther's *Inside U.S.A.;* James Scales and Danney Goble's *Oklahoma Politics: A History;* William Butler's *Tulsa 75;* John Woodard's *In Re TULSA;* C. B. Glasscock's *Then Came Oil: The Story of the Last Frontier;* Robert Gregory's *Oil in Oklahoma;* Ronald Trekell's *History of the Tulsa Police Department, 1882–1990;* Charles Barrett's *Oklahoma After Fifty Years;* the University of Oklahoma Press compilation *Oklahoma: A Guide to the Sooner State;* Eddie Faye Gates's *They Came Searching,* transcribed interviews with Tulsa's black pioneers; John Brooks Walton's *One Hundred Historic Tulsa Homes;* Hannibal Johnson's *Black Wall Street: From Riot to Renaissance in Tulsa's Historic Greenwood District;* Charles James Bates's *It's Been a Long Time;* Jonathan Greenberg's *Staking a Claim: Jake Simmons and the Making of an African-American Oil Dynasty;* B. C. Franklin's *My Life and an Era;* and Beryl Ford's *Tulsa Times,* a three-volume pictorial history.

Two classics about the Jim Crow South are John Egerton's *Speak Now Against the Day* and Leon F. Litwack's *Trouble in Mind.* David Levering Lewis's two-volume biography of W.E.B. Du Bois provided information about not only Du Bois himself but also the historical context of America's first quarter of the twentieth century, and John Hope Franklin's *From Slavery to Freedom: A History of African Americans* should guide any author tackling the African American experience. Books about other black communities include James Grossman's *Land of Hope: Chicago, Black Southerners, and the Great Migration;* Gilbert Osofsky's *Harlem: The Making of a Ghetto;* Kenneth Kusmer's *Ghetto Takes Shape: Black Cleveland, 1870–1930;* Alan Spear's *Black Chicago: The Making of a Negro Ghetto, 1890–1920; The New African American Urban History,* edited by Kenneth Goings and Raymond Mohl; and Joe William Trotter Jr.'s *River Jordan: African American Urban Life in the Ohio Valley.*

Riot books include Paul A. Gilje's *Rioting in America; Democracy*

Betrayed: The Wilmington Race Riot of 1898 and Its Legacy, edited by David Cecelski and Timothy Tyson; Iver Bernstein's *New York City Draft Riots;* and William M. Tuttle Jr.'s *Race Riot: Chicago in the Red Summer of 1919.* A book that stands alone is *Without Sanctuary: Lynching Photography in America,* which captures the horror of lynching and provides brief narratives about individual incidents.

Urban Policy in Twentieth Century America, edited by Arnold Hirsch and Raymond Mohl, provided an excellent context for the displacement of blacks through the construction of interstate highways and urban renewal programs.

The issue of reparations is discussed most rigorously in Randall Robinson's *The Debt: What America Owes to Blacks.* Other helpful books are Elazar Barkan's *The Guilt of Nations* and *When Sorry Isn't Enough,* edited by Roy L. Brooks.

A good biography of Clyde Snow was written by Christopher Joyce and Eric Stover, *Witnesses from the Grave: The Stories Bones Tell.*

Acknowledgments

THIS WAS AN ambitious book: a story that spans a hundred years, integrates numerous characters, and weaves together the themes of memory, reconciliation, and justice. If I succeeded, I owe considerable thanks to my editor at Houghton Mifflin Company, Eamon Dolan, who spotted my temporal disconnects, logical gaps, false starts, and weak kickers. Eamon is a throwback, an editor who edits rigorously for the sheer joy of helping his author tell a compelling story. In this case, he shared my belief that this book was not simply about a riot in 1921 but about one community's search for justice, and he ensured that every subplot, anecdote, and character contributed to that story. Eamon's assistant, Emily Little, handled countless demands with care and grace, and while her contributions will never make the headlines, they were warmly appreciated. My manuscript editor, Luise Erdmann, is a literary hardliner, demanding precision and clarity in every sentence and caring about the text, the typeface, and the design of the book as much as any author.

My agent, Todd Shuster, helped shape my proposal, alerted me to potential pitfalls in the narrative, and encouraged me throughout my research and writing. His ear for a good story, plus his own interest in social justice, made his advice invaluable.

When I began this book, I was told that Oklahomans were open and honest, and with rare exceptions I found that to be true. I traveled to Tulsa each month over a nine-month period, stayed there for seven to ten days, and walked into many strangers' homes and offices. I am grateful for their hospitality, and I should say that both blacks and whites treated me equally well. I interviewed more than a hundred people and cannot thank everyone individually, but I do want to mention a number of people.

John Hope Franklin receives many requests for interviews, and I suspect he is weary of talking about the riot. But he welcomed me into his home in Durham, North Carolina, and spent several hours discussing Tulsa and his youth. I confess I also asked him about his career and his life — questions that had nothing to do with the riot. He kindly responded to all my queries, though it meant interrupting his work on his autobiography, *The Vintage Years*.

Scott Ellsworth and Danney Goble not only gave me a great deal of their time but also shared research documents on Tulsa and the riot. Early on, Ellsworth encouraged me to examine the legacy of the riot, and Goble's candid discussion of how his work on the commission forced him to reexamine his own views on race was much appreciated.

Whenever I needed to know something about Tulsa, past or present, I called Dick Warner, and he either knew or somehow found the answer.

Don Ross kindly cooperated with my requests for interviews, and I didn't even mind paying for his dinner. Love him or hate him, he is never dull company. His assistant in Oklahoma City, Roxanne Blystone, promptly and graciously returned all my calls. Don's son, Kavin, provided me with videotapes of several events described in the book, and his early tour of Greenwood helped me get my bearings. The staff at the Greenwood Cultural Center also helped me with photographs, directions, and other details.

Special thanks are due to Veneice Sims, Otis Clark, and George Monroe, each of whom I visited several times. People may disagree on reparations, but no one would dispute the integrity and strength of these three. My thanks also to Scott Ellsworth and Eddie Faye Gates for introducing me to these and other survivors.

I am in debt to the Tulsans, white and black, whose conflicting views of the riot provide an important thread in the last third of the book. I spoke at length to Beryl Ford, Robert Norris, Bill O'Brien, Vivian Clark-Adams, and Eddie Faye Gates. While I may disagree with them about the riot, I believe, with rare exception, that their views reflect their own experiences, and they were generous in sharing them with me.

Pete Churchwell ensured that I understood what was happening with the riot commission. Alfred Brophy shared his research and his ideas with me. Bob Blackburn, Jim Lloyd, and Currie Ballard also helped shape my understanding of the reparations debate. Ed Wheeler taught me how to fire a gun, Clyde Snow gave me a primer on mass graves, and Coni Williams and Michelle Powell, both formerly with the Tulsa Historical Society, cared about this story as much as I did. Paul Lee supplied research documents that he had accumulated on Greenwood. I owe special thanks to Michael Wilkerson for sharing his research tapes and other documents he accumulated while producing his HBO documentary on the riot, *The Tulsa Lynching of 1921: A Hidden Story*.

My thanks also to the following people, some of whom appear in the book, but all of whom helped me: Keith Bailey, Florence "Bisser" Barnett, Dewey F. Bartlett, Leland Bement, David Breed, Robert Brooks, Louis Bullock, Carter Blue Clark, Clyde Cole, Wilbert Collins, Patrick Connelly, Abe Deutschendorf, Drew Diamond, Jim East, John Ehrling, Nancy Feldman, Carmen Fields, John Gaberino, Reuben Gant, Tom Gilbert, James Goodwin, Bruce Hartnitt, Juanita Hopkins, Jerome Johnson, David Jones, Jenkin Lloyd Jones, Nancy and Ted Kachel, Stephen Kerr, Bill LaFortune, Ed Lawson, Ken Levit, Nancy Little, Robert Littlejohn, Guy Logsdon, Tim Long, the Reverend G. Calvin McCutchen, Robert Milacek, Ken Neal, Julius Pegues, Bob Pendergrass, Susan Savage, Sister Sylvia Schmidt, Larry Silvey, Karen Simpson, Laurel Stradford, Paul Sund, Oliver Thompson, Maynard and Judy Ungerman, Clayton Vaughn, and the Reverend John Wolfe.

Lori Curtis and Gina Minks at the McFarlin Library's Special Collections Division at the University of Tulsa were unfailingly helpful.

I am indebted to "Choc" Phillips's widow, Elaine, his daughter, Susan Ward, and his son-in-law, George Ward, who shared with me Phillips's memoir.

Many reporters helped me along the way. Randy Krehbiel of the *Tulsa World* kept me abreast of what was happening in his city. My thanks also to Jeff Huston of the *Oklahoma Eagle*, Claudia Kolker of the *Los Angeles Times*, Kelly Kurt of the Associated Press, Lois Romano of the *Washington Post*, Brent Staples of the *New York Times*, and Frosty Troy of the *Oklahoma Observer.*

Thanks also to my friends at the Best Western Inn in Sand Springs, which serves the best free breakfast in Oklahoma.

As always, I am indebted to my parents, Gloria and Ed Hirsch, to whom this book is dedicated; my brother, Irl Hirsch, his wife, Ruth, and their daughter, Barbara; my sister, Lynn Friedman, her husband, Howard, and their sons, Sam and Max; and my mother-in-law, Aileen Phillips.

I owe particular thanks to my three-year-old daughter, Amanda, who didn't understand why I kept going to "OK-a-homa" but always welcomed me home with a hug and a kiss. While I was writing the book, our son, Garrett, was born, which I guess makes him our "riot baby," and his toothless smile was another source of inspiration.

Every book takes a toll on the author's spouse, but my long research trips made this book particularly grueling for my wife, Sheryl. Her support, encouragement, and love kept me going and made the book possible. When she joined me on one of my trips to Oklahoma, we had a memorable time. It just goes to show you: too few men can say to their wives, "Honey, we'll always have Sand Springs."

Index